God's Secret

Books by the same author

The Fruit of the Spirit

Think on These Things

A Positive Faith

God's Secret

Colin Attridge

Acknowledgements

All Scripture quotations unless otherwise indicated are taken from The Authorized (King James) Version. Rights in the Authorized Version in the United Kingdom are vested in the Crown. Reproduced by permission of the Crown's patentee, Cambridge University Press.

Scripture quotations marked (NIV) are taken from the Holy Bible, New International Version®, NIV®. Copyright © 1973, 1978, 1984, 2011 by Biblica, Inc.™ Used by permission of Zondervan. All rights reserved worldwide. www.zondervan.com The "NIV" and "New International Version" are trademarks registered in the United States Patent and Trademark Office by Biblica, Inc.™

Scripture quotations marked (KJV) are taken from the New King James Version®. Copyright © 1982 by Thomas Nelson. Used by permission. All rights reserved.

First published 2022

ISBN: 978-1-874508-07-6

(also available as an e-book ISBN: 978-1-874508-08-3)

Published by:

Dawn Christadelphian Publications
5 Station Road, Carlton, Nottingham, NG4 3AT, U.K.
Printed and bound in Great Britain

Contents

	Preface	vii
	Foreword	xii
1	Life can be confusing	1
2	Ancient wisdom	9
3	Secrets	16
4	Not what you might think	26
5	Fear is key	39
6	God is extremely likely	47
7	Communication	56
8	What's wrong with everyone?	63
9	The solution	77
	Psalm 34	92
10	An A–Z of God's Secret	94
11	Forgotten something?	102
12	The humble who boast	112
13	Making God bigger	124
14	No fear	134
15	Happiness	147
16	No trouble	159
17	Angels	168
18	Taste and see	178
19	Everything you want	187
20	Has everybody got that?	195
21	Righteousness is the way	202

Preface

22	Watch your tongue	213
23	You're a bit of a devil	224
24	Depart and pursue	233
25	Surveillance	241
26	The good, the bad, and… no-one else.	251
27	The grace escape (Part 1)	265
28	The grace escape (Part 2)	276
29	God is near	284
30	Keeping bones	292
31	Outcomes	301
32	Redeeming features	313
	Appendix 1: The last days	325
	Appendix 2: Acrostic	332
	Afterword	337
	More books available from DCP	338

Preface

The 'Wow Factor'

I was at a business conference a while ago. After the company's MD and FD had outlined the company's position, goals and values, we the audience were treated to the wit and wisdom of a motivational speaker. He was rather good, too: informative, amusing, competent, and even motivational at times.

A buffet lunch was provided after the speakers had finished, and I found myself standing alongside our motivational speaker in the queue. So we got talking. I couldn't help making the following observations which had occurred to me while I was listening to his talk. We'd been told about being 'cutting edge', 'adapting to a changing market place' and providing the 'wow factor' for our clients. It was all very thrusting and up to the moment, as these things inescapably are. But it occurred to me that the values listed by our MD that underpinned all this go-ahead, up-to-the-moment thinking that we were to employ, could best be described as surprisingly traditional. It seemed to me that to get ahead of the game we had to be rather old fashioned.

The values championed were honesty, trust, caring and so on. These concepts have been around for thousands of years and usually march under the banner of religion. So I suggested to our friendly motivational speaker that, maybe, we would achieve the 'wow factor' simply by applying basic Christian ethics to the way we dealt with our customers. He and our MD seemed to be preaching a religious message more than a business one. And after thinking about it he had to agree that, yes, at heart, that was what it was really all about. It was good old-fashioned Christian values. If customers saw that we really cared about them and that we could be trusted, then that was a significant 'wow factor'.

God's Secret

As a national housebuilder, the houses our company built were not dissimilar to those of our competitors, and due to market forces would be priced around the same. But if customers knew us as a company with **integrity,** who delivered on promises and went the extra mile to show we cared about them, then that would put us ahead. That was the message. Integrity was the 'wow factor'.

The emphasis was on being genuine. The idea was that we should not only **appear** to be caring, but actually **be** it. Not like the cynic who says: 'It's all down to sincerity; and if you can fake that you're home and dry.' Our business leaders wanted us to have a biblical approach to our work. And although they avoided using overtly religious language, a spiritual approach was what it really amounted to.

There is something tremendously appealing and reassuring about people with integrity. They stand out in a crowd. We warm to them. We want to do business with them. We want them for our colleagues and our friends. We want them for our husbands or wives, our sons or our daughters, our boyfriends or girlfriends. And we want the people we most admire in the arts, sports and politics to have integrity. And it appears that we want our building contractors to have it too.

In essence this book is about a particular kind of integrity. It's about a way of thinking and acting that is better for us than any other. Which sounds like my ego talking, I know, but the way of life I'm going to describe is not of my own invention. I'm not suggesting that you think and do things this way because I have personally worked out what life is all about and I know best. I'm not that clever, and neither is anyone else if they're honest. No, I simply want to share with you the answers that I have learned from a very special and ancient source. In this book's second chapter, which is headed *Ancient Wisdom*, I'll disclose that source. The 'wow' in 'wow factor', it turns out, is an acronym for **w**ords **o**f **w**isdom.

Preface

You might think that all integrity is the same. But it's not that straightforward. Integrity means being true to ourselves; integrating who we are with how we act, which is laudable and fine if we're right in the first place. If we're being true to a set of principles that are beyond question, that's wonderful. Most likely, though, that's not the case. And if we're being true to principles that are mistaken, then we'll have integrity, no question, but we'll be thinking and acting in the wrong way. Honour among thieves is a form of integrity. Thieves can be true to who they are but it doesn't make them right or good. The standard model of integrity can be relative in much the same way that morality can be. It can move with the times, change with circumstances, or be tailored to suit what we see as our own best interests.

But there is a special kind of integrity that not only keeps us on the right track and brings an unparalleled level of contentment and security into our lives, it also links us with something absolute and eternal. It has always been right and always will be, so it has no need to change with fashions of thinking. It holds good at all times and in all circumstances.

As we'll see in the pages ahead, *'There is a way that appears to be right, but in the end it leads to death.'* (Proverbs 16:25 NIV) You and I need something a whole lot better than what merely **appears** to be right but which actually isn't and leads us nowhere! We need God's Secret. I sincerely hope you will be blessed with the 'wow factor' of learning and living it.

Colin Attridge, Surrey, 2022

PS. I've known and lived by the Secret described in this book for some decades now, so I know it works. I also know from long experience the pitfalls of failing to live by it. Which doesn't mean I've suffered supernatural payback from stepping out of line, only that I've given myself unnecessary problems or worried

God's Secret

needlessly. True religion is not a stick-and-carrot affair. It's bigger and better than that. It's not about continually striving to do good and be better than we were yesterday, last week, last month or last year. Our focus must shift away from ourselves. It's about finding out who God wants us to be and trying to be that. And 'be' is the key word here. God's Secret is essentially about who we **are**, not what we do. You won't find a list of do's and don'ts. Just plenty to think on. Get your thinking aligned with a truly right set of precepts and principles and doing the right thing will take care of itself in a remarkable way. You'll have integrity of the rarest and best kind.

Acknowledgements and Dedication

My sincere thanks to all those who've helped knowingly or otherwise in the production of this book. Those who probably do know they've helped are as follows:

Firstly, thanks to my wife, without whose unflagging support and occasional input as a 'sounding board' such a work would not be possible.

Grateful thanks to my good friend Colin Dryland who read the initial draft and whose comments and suggestions were so helpful in shaping this final version.

Many thanks to Dan Giles for his feedback on and contribution to the Grace chapters, and thanks to Simon Perfitt and Laurie Broughton for their helpful comments on the Evolution chapter.

Thanks to everyone on the editorial panel at the Dawn Publishing Office for their work and feedback.

Thanks to Emma Perfitt for her excellent art and design work. I'll be very happy for people to judge this book by its cover.

Among those who probably don't know they've helped are all those over the past four or five years who have asked, "How's the book going?" Their mostly unwitting encouragement helped to keep it going.

Dedication

This book is for everyone who needs to know or be reminded of God's Secret: probably you; certainly me.

FOREWORD

This book is primarily written for those who are still looking for answers to the big questions. Perhaps, in reality, that includes everyone to some degree. But the intention behind the book is to reach those who think of themselves as unbelievers, don't-knows and not-sures when it comes to the spiritual side of life. Which includes those who are dissatisfied with the version of religion they are currently with. Maybe this is where you are right now. It's for those who have a hankering after something more in life, something spiritual, but at the same time something which makes good, sound sense, something which holds together, and is practical and positive.

Religion and spirituality can so often appear to be anything but sensible and practical. They can either be rigid and rule-bound at one end of the scale, or 'believe what you want because love is all that matters' at the other end. And in between these extremes there are many shades of rigid to relaxed religion. It can be quite an off-putting selection. So, hopefully *God's Secret* will come as a breath of fresh air to all of you who are looking for something away from all that. This book takes a bit of a step back. Though it might feel like more of a flying leap right into the middle of it sometimes.

A reminder and a remedy

Yes, *God's Secret* is essentially a spiritual or religious book. The title rather gives it away. And, if I'm honest, the book is not saying anything radically new and different from what true religion and spirituality have always been saying. But the reality is that true religion and spirituality have been lost sight of over the years by so many of us, and we desperately need a reminder of what they really are. It's as if we've been misdirected, and while we were looking away, true religion and spirituality were replaced by something else, similar but different, and we didn't notice the switch. The purpose of this book is to try to help remedy the situation.

A book of two parts
Although this book is for those who are looking for God's Secret, it is hoped that it will also prove useful to those who are believers and who are already trying to live by their beliefs. I suggest that if this describes you, then you might want to go directly to Part Two of the book. This is where God's Secret is reviewed in a step-by-step process with the aid of a particularly helpful short section of the Bible. But, of course, you may want to re-encourage yourself in your beliefs by first reading the ground-laying chapters of Part One. In these early chapters we address the likelihood of there being a God, and the way in which He is likely to have communicated His existence and purpose to us. And I use the word 'likely' not to convey doubt but to move the **possibility** of these things onto surer ground.

As this book is for the general reader, I've been sparing with references, not including them unless really necessary. Pages strewn with references to Bible verses, or suffering from serious attacks of the footnotes, can be distracting and can clog the flow of reading. Sometimes I've just given a general pointer where to find something: just the book of the Bible without chapter and verse. Apologies to those who think I've been too sparing.

Self-plagiarism
Most of this book is newly written material. But a few of the points made have appeared in previous books and magazine articles. Anyone familiar with the *A Positive Faith* series in the *Dawn Magazine* might recognise a paragraph here and there.

Not letting you down
We expect writers who tell us how to live our lives to 'walk their talk'. And when they fail, as some prominent writers have in the past, we feel let down. Rightly so, too, because these people are

presenting us with their best advice, and they themselves are either not taking it or it doesn't work.

Happily (and not at all smugly) I can honestly say I won't be letting you down like that. Not because I never fail to follow the counsel in this book (or in previous books, for that matter). Not because I'm so skilled at applying all these things that I never put a foot wrong. (I wish.) It's because this book is about God's Secret not mine. So I'm as likely to fall short of living it as anyone else. Any failure by me to live up to it doesn't detract in the slightest from the validity of the book – and certainly not the validity of the Secret itself. When it comes to knowing and living God's Secret, we're all in this together. You, me, and everyone else – we're all trying and failing to ascend to the giddy heights of the wisdom of God.

We're all aspiring and not attaining.
But failure in this great endeavour is nothing to be dispirited about. Only God can be perfect, after all. We are all going to be considerably further down the mountain than He is. But however close we get to understanding and living His Secret it will make an enormous difference in our lives. So we don't let the fact that we won't make it to the very top put us off climbing. The view's pretty good however high we go; and even in the foothills, come to that. The truth is we don't have to be perfect to be successful in the endeavour this book outlines. You'll find that whatever distance you go in your understanding and living of God's Secret it will benefit you immensely. And you **will** be successful if you truly aspire to be, however far short you fall. That's a bit of a paradox, I know, but it happens to be true. It's a part of the way the Secret works. So read on and somewhere up ahead you'll find out how that can be so.

PART 1

GOD's SECRET

HOW WE KNOW OF IT

1 LIFE CAN BE CONFUSING

It's not you.

It's life.

That's the problem.

Life can be confusing. There are so many things vying for our attention. The average corkboard or magnetic notice board in most kitchens (or the digital equivalent, whatever that might currently be) is a microcosm of most people's lives: scraps of information and reminders, postcards and post-its – the important things jostling alongside the not so important and the fun things. That's life for most of us – a haphazard kind of existence through which a vague sense of direction occasionally surfaces – all too briefly. Superheroes of organisation, the sort who know exactly where everything is and when everything is, and who are working methodically towards exactly where they want to be in one, five and ten years, are rare and probably very tiresome individuals. And even they will probably find life ultimately confusing. Because it just is.

Not only confusing it's a struggle, too. In a 2020 interview, when asked what was the best piece of advice he wished he could have given to his twenty-year-old self, Canadian Astronaut Chris Hadfield said: 'to recognise that every single person you meet is struggling'. He said that no matter who they are, or what they are, or what they do – deep down, and sometimes not so deep down, everyone is struggling. To realise that, is to get a truer picture of what's going on inside everyone you are sharing this world with. As he looked back, Hadfield had picked up on something that the wise man Solomon also commented on in his old age. He looked back and said of life that it was all *'vanity and vexation of spirit'*. But, and here's a pointer to what lies ahead in this book: Solomon sometimes assumed the role of someone speaking the accepted wisdom of the day, in order to comment on it and show that it wasn't the whole story. Knowing God's Secret, as he did, he knew there was a better way, and that the struggle, or the vexation, was optional.

Added to all the confusion and struggle, however organised or disorganised our lives may be down here amid the clutter of everyday life, whenever we look up and try to comprehend the grand scheme of things, we're flummoxed. The big questions generally remain big and unanswered questions. What's the point of it all? Why are we here? What on earth is really going on? Surely somebody must have a clue, even if we don't.

Plan B
Most people assessing their lives will probably concede they are living Plan B at best. Quite a few would be happy to graduate to Plan B.

Maybe there's a secret to life that you don't know? Do you ever have the feeling that you might be missing something vital? From what I gather, many people have that feeling from time to time, so it's pretty safe to assume that you do. There's a half-formed thought at the back of many people's minds that says, if only they could live life in a certain way, do certain things differently, or learn particular skills, then life would somehow make a lot more sense and be more satisfying. Everything would click into place.

But the longer people go on thinking like this without arriving at satisfactory answers, the more they are likely to conclude that the answers probably don't exist. Or if they do, that they will never find them. And perhaps nobody ever does, or ever will find them. So they carry on regardless, living an okay kind of life, trying to divert themselves from the likely pointlessness of it all. But all the while they can't shake off the need they feel for something that will pull everything into focus. So they might take up some mystical pursuit, or follow a religion in which they only partially believe, but which gives a crumb of hope and comfort, telling themselves, 'Well, you have to believe in **something**.' They might even throw themselves heart and soul into that something – not so much because it's right but because they desperately need a something. They need also to divert themselves from the uneasy thought that there might after all be nothing.

Maybe this describes you. Probably not in every way, but perhaps in part. It would be surprising if it doesn't. Uncertainty about what's really going on, and the notion that we're missing something vital that would explain it all, seems to be fairly widespread. Leo Tolstoy put his finger on a sad truth when he said, 'most men live lives of quiet desperation.' And I'm sure most women do, too. This is a pretty awful state of affairs, isn't it? But the good news is that life doesn't have to be like this. No-one has to be like this. There most definitely is a secret to life. And it's well within our capacity to comprehend it, take hold of it, live by it, and enjoy the considerable difference it will make to us.

Not a self-help book
I know this all sounds like the introduction to one of those fix-your-life-in-ten-days, pop-psychology, self-help books. That's intentional, because I've consciously borrowed a little from the style of those kinds of books. They are upbeat and direct, easy to assimilate, and they are tailored to meet the requirements of people who are dissatisfied with life and who are eagerly searching for solutions. So there are some similarities. But this book differs radically from those books, which offer only limited concepts and temporary solutions at best. Yes I know the self-help and popular psychology books often say something along the same lines – that they offer something different from and better than all the others. But stay with me for a few more pages and I hope you'll see why this time it could actually be true.

How many people, after all, will simply buy **one** self-help book, read it, apply it, and skip merrily on their way with their life forever fixed? Very few, if any, will do that. No, they'll usually buy another, and then another – and perhaps all the books by a particular author with a particular system or a particular angle that seems to provide what they need. Then they'll probably move on to another author with another angle. And they'll probably keep pace with the ever-changing fads: from the *Power of Positive Thinking* to *The Secret*, to *NLP*, to *The Power of Now*, to *Mindfulness*, and so on.

This may sound cynical, but the multibillion-pound self-help industry depends on people going back for more. The path to self-actualisation, dubbed *The Road Less Traveled* by M. Scott Peck in his ground-breaking 1978 book of that title, seems more like a packed eight-lane superhighway these days. So many people are being prodded along a supposedly spiritual path by the continual outflow of books and magazines, articles and videos on the subject. The industry has been styled the Self-Help and Actualisation Movement, which, as one critic noted, supplies the unfortunate acronym SHAM.

But we should be rather more kindly disposed than that critic. Even he had to admit that there was some good in self-help material. And it's only fair to assume that many of the writers of such books genuinely believe in what they do and sincerely want to help people. Also, in its defence, it has to be said that self-help is necessarily an ongoing process. There are few if any magical epiphanies that lead instantly to permanently redirected lives. Life-change is almost always an ongoing, incremental process – with some of the increments being in a reverse direction sometimes.

I've heard it argued that positive thinking doesn't work because you have to keep doing it. You get all enthusiastic and hyped up about something, or life in general, and the next day you have to do it all over again – or maybe later the same day. So it doesn't work, they say. But realistically self-help requires an ongoing commitment because the problems that people are trying to overcome are often deep-seated and won't be banished overnight just by reading some well-meaning gems of popular psychology, some of which may work, some of which may not.

Life changing?
The claim of self-help books is often that they will change your life. That's neither the claim nor the intention of this book. Not initially, anyway. The intention here is not to change your life, but to change you. There is a difference. And a lot of people miss it. It was Ghandi who famously said, 'If you want to change the world, start with yourself.' That's also true of changing your personal world: you should start with yourself. That means you give priority to what's going on inside you not what's going on outside. Most people opt for trying to change what's around them because that seems like the right place to start. It also has the appeal of being easier than working on yourself. But unless you do something about who you are, as opposed to what's going on around you, you won't achieve any worthwhile and lasting change.

'Wherever you go, there you are' is an adage that sounds like an obvious and even trite thing to say, but so many people overlook what's simple and obvious when they try to improve things for themselves. Changing your environment by, say, moving house, getting a new job, going on a cruise, or whatever else you can come up with to get yourself away from things and make a fresh start, won't significantly change you, because you'll still be pretty much the same person when you get there. You may achieve a better setting for your life, but you'll still carry the same internal dissatisfaction, and a thirst for change which hasn't been sated, because what you actually need is change in yourself not in your environment.

So, this book is not aimed at changing your life, it's aimed at changing you. Changing your life, though, will follow hot on the heels of changing yourself. Because the one can't happen without the other. When we become different, our experience of the world becomes different.

Tapping into something bigger
But, as I said, this is not a self-help book. Though it is intended to **help**, and you will have to apply **yourself** to what it says to get

results. So what's the difference? The difference is this: this book does not put forward the author's personal theories on how life works and how it should best be lived. I don't want to be anybody's guru (I have difficulty bending my legs in a guru sitting position). But there is something that I fervently want to share with others. I have noticed that popular psychology (the self-help industry), and psychology generally, get it truly right only when they tap into something bigger; and usually without being aware of it. Over the years, I've read fairly widely in these fields and it occurs to me that when something really works for people – when it really makes good and practicable sense and brings results – then it can usually be found in some form or other in a rather special book that I've also been reading for some years – the Bible.

It certainly looks like the great thinkers and writers on the human psyche, from the ancient Greeks, through Freud, Jung, Adler and others down to the present day, have been reinventing the wheel for centuries now; and coming up with observations and solutions that have already existed for millennia. For example, Carl Jung's concept of The Shadow Self, that dark side of ourselves that we can never wholly conquer, is what the Apostle Paul referred to as a law of human nature, when he said, *'I find then a law, that, when I would do good, evil is present with me.'* (See Romans 7:18–23) Not that every single thing they gave us was an inadvertent rehash of an older idea, but generally the stuff that worked best was. The bulk of what they wrote is now of academic interest only and some of it very quaint and of its time. But generally whenever they gave us something of real and lasting worth, whether they knew it or not, what they gave us had most likely been real and lasting for quite some time already. They merely systemised and repackaged it in their own way.

Go direct
The same can be said about what works and doesn't work in the self-help and popular psychology books. Everything they've got wrong will prove of no value, and everything they've got right will most likely be so because they've tapped, knowingly or not, into

something higher. It will save you a lot of time and trouble if you go directly to the original ancient source of wisdom.

If you're looking for a quick, and therefore temporary fix for your life, from a book that doesn't ask too much of you and insists that you are inherently wonderful and can achieve miracles if you follow a few simple rules, then this is probably not the book for you. Believe me, you are probably destined for chronic disappointment if you go down that road. But if you're looking for sound wisdom that will make your life work, and you're prepared to invest some time and effort into understanding and applying it then please read on. You're in for a rewarding journey.

The truth under the heap

A major problem when it comes to getting to grips with finding the real answers to life's biggest questions is that we have a built-in rebellious streak. That's why so few of us find the real answers. We actually resist them. Can you believe that? We are inclined to shy away from them even when we have a good idea where and what they might be. As Winston Churchill said, people 'occasionally stumble over the truth, but most of them pick themselves up and hurry off as if nothing had happened.' We have a perverse natural resistance to going where the right answers are to be found. And then we wonder why we can't find them and why we have to survive on guesswork and ignorance.

It's as if we've been offered a mouth-watering feast of good things and we choose to dine on a few paltry scraps, and then complain about how hungry we are. Because going to the feast doesn't appeal. Maybe it's located across town. Maybe we're not too sure of the host. Maybe it means sprucing ourselves up a little. Maybe we don't want to find the cab fare. In a similar way, we come up with excuses for ourselves for not looking where life's answers are to be found.

We'll talk more about this self-defeating resistance and what to do about it later. For the most part, we resist the real solutions that are available to us because they lie buried within religion. Not a place where people generally want to dig. But that's where the answers are buried. Smothered, I should say. So much unhelpful, misleading and unnecessary stuff has been heaped upon the original simple, refreshing and inspiring truths at the foundation of the Christian faith, that the truth of it is almost unrecognisable now. I'm sure that if a group of believers from Jesus' day could transport themselves down to our day, they would not recognise their own religion. Sometimes I hear criticisms of Christianity from prominent atheists and humanists, and I know that what they are finding fault with is the heap that's accumulated on top of the religion rather than the real thing buried underneath. The aim of the chapters ahead in this book is to take a big shovel to the heap, move the heap aside, and look at the truth that's still sitting there mint fresh and unchanged by the passage of time.

I know you have no problem with this being a religious book, because you already know that from the book's title and the introduction. Even so, I feel I should reassure you this is probably not like any religious book you will have come across before. That's not a boast about my great prowess as an author and researcher (because on both counts I'll fail to do this sublime subject justice). I say this because the source material is rather special. The source material for this book is, in general, the Bible. But in Part Two, the source is an inspired ancient poem found within the Bible that you may not be aware of. Or if you do know of it, you may not be aware of the extraordinary store of wisdom that it holds.

So read on.

2 ANCIENT WISDOM

Have you noticed how the best wisdom tends to be ancient? Any wisdom worth its salt has usually been found on scrolls of flaking papyrus the colour of super-strong tea in the darkest recesses of an ancient cave, having lain undiscovered for thousands of years. In the storybooks there's usually an intrepid character who will overcome countless obstacles in order to reach it, and bring it back to an astonished and grateful civilisation.

In real life, too, the claim is often made by this or that self-styled enlightened group of souls that they have rediscovered the wisdom of the ancients. We might be forgiven for believing that the ancients have cornered the market on wisdom. They are regularly called upon to provide credibility for any number of groups claiming to have accessed the secret of 'life, the universe, and everything'.

Heretics and madmen

Somehow the wisdom of more recent men and women doesn't have the same appeal. Though why our distant forebears should have been considerably smarter than us is not easy to fathom. Have we become progressively less smart down the centuries? That doesn't seem likely. And if the ancients were so clever, why was it beyond them to get their wisdom across to us in a clear and permanent fashion, long ago?

A common explanation is that the world was not ready for them. They were forced into hiding and their teachings were circulated only in secret. They were so far ahead of their time, so revolutionary in their ideas, and so potentially powerful, that their contemporaries who were in power, especially the religious leaders, branded them as a threat – saw them as heretics and madmen rather than visionaries. Hence their writings were secreted in caves. And their truths had to be couched in allegories or written in codes, so that only the initiated would understand them. And every now and then the cry has gone up from some group or other, that at last the long-lost secret wisdom of the ancients has been discovered and can now be revealed! The key to understanding it will of course rest with some group who will explain it all to us and tell us how to join them.

That scenario isn't about any religious group in particular; it's a composite of the kind of thing that has happened periodically down the centuries. I've strung it together to illustrate the point that age is sometimes pressed into service to add credibility where wisdom is concerned.

Age and credibility

I don't mean to sound dismissive of ancient wisdom. The best wisdom **was** manifested thousands of years ago. We can be sure of that, as you'll see. But I just want to draw attention to the fact that for wisdom to carry any weight we seem to prefer it to be old. Ancient wisdom can have a more authentic feel about it. Someone claiming to have rediscovered the lost wisdom of the Victorians is not going to enjoy a very large following.

Even wisdom in the 21st century is more likely to be credited to the aged ones among us. After all, age and experience ought to count for something. White hair and a beard can lend respectability to a person's pronouncements, probably because that's how renaissance painters depicted prophets and saints, and God Himself. Though realistically it's unlikely that an immortal God will show signs of ageing. With the ability that He must have to look however He wants, it's extremely doubtful that He would choose the appearance of an ageing man.

I suggest that if it were possible for us to see God, He would appear ageless, completely beyond our ability to define Him in such a narrow way. We assess someone's age from where they appear to be on their journey from the cradle to the grave. God is outside such a frame of reference. But to be fair to renaissance artists, they most likely used an aged appearance as artistic shorthand to convey wisdom. Which brings us back to the original point. We generally prefer our wisdom to have been around for a while because age adds credibility.

Could it be true, after all?

But what if there's a nugget of truth at the heart of this belief that some ancient peoples came into possession of truly great wisdom and preserved it for posterity? What if there is a way of thinking and living that has been on record for thousands of years that is far superior to anything that anyone has since come up with? What if there really is an ancient manuscript that describes a way of life from which we could all benefit tremendously? What if this manuscript describes a way of life that corresponds perfectly with how we are designed to function as human beings? And what if this wisdom were of supernatural, superhuman origin? What if it were eternal wisdom? That's a big collection of 'what ifs', I know, but if it were all indeed the case you'd be interested, wouldn't you? I certainly was when I found it – in a biblical place called the Book of Psalms.

Such supernatural ancient wisdom is spread throughout the entire Bible, but in some places it seems more highly concentrated. There are some very stand-out passages. And one of those passages homes in particularly on something called God's Secret. Others might, too, but this is the one that caught my eye.

Locating God's Secret

If there is a secret to life, as many of us suspect, then something going by the name of God's Secret sounds like it could be the very thing we're looking for. You probably didn't realise there was such a thing. And even though it is mentioned in the Bible, I'm guessing that even many of those who are familiar with the Bible haven't heard of it either. The Bible is a big book, and two words used together like this can easily go unnoticed, or unremembered – even two majorly important words. But God's Secret is definitely there, and, as I hope to show in this book, it **is** the very thing we're all looking for.

God's Secret is referred to by name in only a few places in the Bible but it's found throughout the whole book. We'd find aspects of it on every page if we had the level of insight and understanding to recognise them. It has many facets or components, and we'll be looking at a good number of them in the pages ahead, particularly in Part Two. But although there are many facets to it, the Secret is made simpler for us because it's characterised by two things in particular. All the many aspects slot beneath one or other of two main headings.

We know this because we are only explicitly told two things about God's Secret in the Bible. These are the essential requirements for knowing it. They are **fear** and **righteousness**. We'll have more to say about them in the coming chapters. One thing I will say here, though, is don't let your first impression of those two words influence your thoughts unduly as to what God's Secret might be about. You're almost certain to be wrong.

As the many different facets of the Secret are to be found scattered everywhere we look in the Bible, I was wondering how best to draw them out and build up a coherent picture. I didn't want to be roving all over the Bible, backwards and forwards, while presenting them to you, because that would produce a rather unfocused narrative. What I needed was a relatively small portion of the Bible where most of the elements of the Secret are brought together in one place. Somewhere they are clustered. But I wasn't sure whether such a place existed.

Found it

Then I found exactly what I was looking for in Psalm 34. This is the perfect vehicle for explaining God's Secret. It's a short Psalm, or song, of only twenty-two verses, written by a man who was thoroughly acquainted with the Secret, and who wrote the Psalm

Ancient wisdom

with the specific purpose of teaching us about it. So, as I say, it's perfect for our purpose here. It couldn't be better.

An intrepid explorer searching for an ancient manuscript that reveals the best possible wisdom by which to live this life – and which at the same time connects us with something eternal – should they stumble across an ancient Hebrew scroll containing Psalm 34, they would find exactly what they were looking for. It contains the essence of God's Secret. This Psalm leads us to the answers to all the big questions. It tells us how to get a hold of the most precious things that it's possible to have. I can truthfully say that the Psalm's content is more precious than life itself, because what it contains is the key to much more than this life.

Below is the Psalm in full. I've kept it in the language of Shakespeare's day because that helps to remind us that it is ancient wisdom – though it is in fact a lot older than the 17th century. It's a good idea to read it through now to get the feel of it, even though we won't be going through it systematically until Part Two of the book. In fact, that's the whole purpose of the second part: to reveal God's Secret by going through this remarkable Psalm verse by verse. Every one of its 22 verses leads us to an aspect of the Secret. It's printed again at the beginning of Part Two for handy reference.

Bear in mind that everything that the Psalm is saying will not be immediately obvious on first reading. Some of it reads a little cryptically, but don't let that concern you now, because the purpose of Part Two is to sort that out. It's a Psalm composed by David, the famous giant-slayer, king, warrior, musician and poet of ancient Israel. That's quite a CV isn't it?

Psalm 34

1. I will bless the LORD at all times: his praises shall continually be in my mouth.
2. My soul shall make her boast in the LORD: the humble shall hear thereof, and be glad.

God's Secret

3 O magnify the LORD with me, and let us exalt his name together.
4 I sought the LORD, and he heard me, and delivered me from all my fears.
5 They looked unto him, and were lightened: and their faces were not ashamed.
6 This poor man cried, and the LORD heard him, and saved him out of all his troubles.
7 The angel of the LORD encampeth round about them that fear him, and delivereth them.
8 O taste and see that the LORD is good: blessed is the man that trusteth in him.
9 O fear the LORD, ye his saints: for there is no want to them that fear him.
10 The young lions do lack, and suffer hunger: but they that seek the LORD shall not want any good thing.
11 Come, ye children, hearken unto me: I will teach you the fear of the LORD.
12 What man is he that desireth life, and loveth many days, that he may see good?
13 Keep thy tongue from evil, and thy lips from speaking guile.
14 Depart from evil, and do good; seek peace, and pursue it.
15 The eyes of the LORD are upon the righteous, and his ears are open unto their cry.
16 The face of the LORD is against them that do evil, to cut off the remembrance of them from the earth.
17 The righteous cry, and the LORD heareth, and delivereth them out of all their troubles.
18 The LORD is nigh unto them that are of a broken heart; and saveth such as be of a contrite spirit.
19 Many are the afflictions of the righteous: but the LORD delivereth him out of them all.
20 He keepeth all his bones: not one of them is broken.
21 Evil shall slay the wicked: and they that hate the righteous shall be desolate.
22 The LORD redeemeth the soul of his servants: and none of them that trust in him shall be desolate.

Ancient wisdom

Later in the book, we're going to show you how this is a Psalm to build your life on. There is a treasure chest of matchless wisdom to be found here by anyone smart enough and eager enough to hunt for it with the same eagerness they would hunt for hidden treasure of incalculable value. This treasure, as you'll learn, is what's referred to elsewhere in the Bible as God's Secret. It's no exaggeration to say that it is the most rewarding thing that you or anyone could ever possess. So let's press on before I run out of superlatives.

3 SECRETS

Do you have any secrets? Surely we all know things about ourselves and other people that we think are best kept away from the public domain. Not that we're hiding anything shadowy or sinister, it's just that we all have things we'd prefer to keep private. No harm in that. Sometimes things just aren't anybody else's business but our own. As children we shared secrets with our best friends. Our secrets were exchanged in furtive whispers behind cupped hands in school corridors and playground corners with those we knew we could trust. And woe betide anyone who broke such a confidence! Exclusion from the circle of friends was usually the outcome. As we grew up, our school days secrets evolved into office gossip: information passed around the workplace about this and that. Added to this, we have the gossip superhighway of social media.

We might also have begun to learn family secrets as we grew up. Things that had been kept from us as children might have been brought to light when the time was considered right for us to know them. Or we may have stumbled across them to our delight or dismay! Secrets are things that only a select group of people know or should know. But that's not all they are.

Secrets meant to be shared
Another familiar use of the word 'secret' is to describe the knack of doing something right or very well. Somebody living in the era before tea bags might have said that the secret to making a good cup of tea is to warm the pot first, then pour the water on the leaves the moment the kettle boils and then let it stand for three minutes before pouring. That would be their secret to a good cup of tea (it might not be yours, though, but please don't write to me about it!). Or it might be said that the secret of a good marriage is to keep the romance alive. These things are not secrets in the sense that people feel obliged to keep them under wraps − the very opposite.

Secrets

People are only too pleased to share these kinds of secrets. This is where secret means a way of doing something well that is not commonly known or used.

God's Secret has something of both the above elements in it. It's something that only a particular set of people know about. It's also the key to doing something extremely well. In this case the Secret holds the skills that will enable us to enjoy a much more meaningful and purposeful life than people usually experience. It's the Secret to life.

It's both remarkable and sad that God's Secret is discovered by so few. In chapter one we mentioned that the route of popular psychology, *The Road Less Traveled* as M. Scott Peck described it, has become rather crowded these days with seekers after enlightenment. And it's tempting to assume that because so many people are trying it, that the road must be leading in the right direction. But the road to true wisdom is regrettably a comparatively lonesome road. In fact it's this road more than any other that deserves to be called the road less travelled.

Resistance

There's resistance to taking this road, as we mentioned before, and the world is the poorer for that. But don't let the lack of fellow travellers deter you from travelling the road yourself. It was the American poet Robert Frost who first wrote of the road less travelled in his poem *The Road Not Taken.* He wrote, 'I took the one less traveled by, and that has made all the difference.' He was writing about the wisdom of following your own path through life and not going with the herd. There's a lot to be said for that when it comes to charting a career path or following your plans or dreams. You don't want the regrets that come from letting other people smother your enthusiasms. So striking out in your own direction is a commendable thing to do, and a rare thing, according to Frost.

God's Secret

But assertively going your own way like this is not such a good idea when it comes to settling on the spiritual and ethical path that you need to take. Because, when it comes to this hugely important decision, your own path can easily be a wrong one. Following your gut feeling, or what you'd prefer to be true, or what seems to work for you – this is not the most sensible way to decide what's really true about life, and what would **really** work for you.

Far better than following your own path is finding and following the right one. Your own path is as likely to lead you astray as the path of every other person who has ever tried to work things out for themselves. M. Scott Peck, by his own admission, went wildly astray somewhere along his own path after writing his book. He either didn't follow his own advice, or he did and it wasn't good advice. Either way, his version looks best avoided, as is every other self-determined path.

The chances of anyone working life out for themselves, completely unaided, or of getting it right by accident, are so phenomenally slim, as to be near non-existent. Not the sort of odds to pin your hopes of a meaningful life on. The answers don't lie within us, as the self-help writers are fond of telling us. The truth, more correctly, is out there. So don't invent your own path; find the right path if you can. And be assured, you can. Because that's where God's Secret comes in.

Comparatively few find this path, but don't let that concern you. As we said, it might truly be called the new road less travelled. Numbers are no sure guide to where truth is located. Huge numbers of people follow ideologies that are mutually exclusive, and so huge numbers of people must therefore be wrong. The comparative fewness of those who know and live by God's Secret should not put us off wanting to do so ourselves. Those on this path have found the Maker's instructions for how to live. What could be better than that? And you won't by any means be alone when you travel this road. In every generation there have been people who have known God's Secret. Just as there are such people today. And as the subject has come up of those who've found it in the past, let's see how some of those enlightened individuals of old can help us learn about it now.

In excellent company

Whatever your thoughts about Jesus, you must credit him with being a hugely significant figure in the moral and religious landscape of the world. And when we go to the Book of Psalms, as we'll be doing later, to learn about God's Secret, we'll be going to one of the places Jesus himself went to learn about it.

It's worth giving a thought to how Jesus knew all that he did. The big truths about life weren't already inside his head as he lay in the manger, nor were they divinely placed there later. Even for Jesus the truth was out there. Joseph and Mary were good people who would have set him on the right path from the outset. They knew who he was, how special he was, and they would have encouraged him in the reading of his real Father's writings in the Old Testament.

From an early age Jesus would have become increasingly more acquainted with that part of the Bible we know as the Old Testament. Jesus learned about his Father's will and ways from the very books of the Bible that we have today. It's extraordinary, isn't it, to think that we have access to the identical counsel or Secret of God, that played such a huge part in making Jesus who he was. We can learn the things he did from the very place he learned them. No doubt he was a better pupil than anyone before or since, but we can still go a long way in our understanding by taking notice of what he did. And we now have even more to look at than Jesus had when he was learning about the Secret, because since then he and some of his followers have explained it further in the New Testament.

It's remarkable to think that when we delve into a book like the Book of Psalms, as we will later, we are doing exactly what Jesus himself did, seeing what he saw, and finding the very Secret of life that he found.

But let's move on now and think about another man who discovered these things.

Have you heard the secret of God?

Let me to introduce you to a man called Job. You may have heard of this biblical character. You will at least have heard the phrase *'the patience of Job'*, because this man was famous for his patient endurance. He suffered a great deal and he bore it well. A 'Job's comforter' has become the term for someone who isn't very sympathetic towards you when you're in trouble. The real Job had three such characters in his life. At one point, one of them, a man named Eliphaz, asked Job mockingly, *'Hast thou heard the secret of God?'* (Job 15:8) And Job could have answered with a resounding 'yes' to that. Because he certainly had heard it.

Job was a truly righteous, God-fearing man. He was wealthy and healthy, too. But one day his prosperity vanished, and then he lost his health. This in no way diminished his love of God, but understandably it did make him wonder why such bad things had happened to him when he had always tried to do the right thing. What he didn't at first know was that God was showing Job's critics that Job didn't do the right thing solely because of what he gained materially from pleasing God.

Those who were jealous of Job's success in life were convinced that he wouldn't be so righteous and God-fearing if God wasn't so generous to him. They thought that if he were stripped of his great prosperity and good health it would expose the real Job: someone who was only religious for what he gained from it. But God knew Job better. Job's love for God was not dependant on his prosperity or fitness. To prove it, God removed Job's prosperity and good health from him.

When Job confessed he didn't know why things had suddenly gone so wrong for him, because he'd always done his best, Eliphaz accused him of being self-righteous. He said that Job couldn't have been a truly righteous person after all for God to have done this to him. And when Job protested his bewilderment at what had happened, his so-called friend mocked him and said in effect, 'You think you know more than other people about the way God works. Isn't it clear that God is displeased with you because of how you've been?'

Because Job felt he knew better about his situation than his three friends did, they were affronted. 'So you think you have direct advice from God Himself, do you?' they said effectively. And, it must be said, Job certainly gave the impression that he did. The reason being, as I said, he really did know from God how life works. And although he was a little perplexed, he was prepared to trust God and patiently await the outcome. He knew the Secret of God. Why am I so certain of that? Well, it's because of what we're told about the character of Job in the opening paragraphs of the Bible book that bears his name. This is how Job is described:

> *'There was a man in the land of Uz, whose name was Job; and that man was perfect and upright, and one that feared God, and eschewed evil.'* (Job 1:1)

A later verse says there was no one else quite like Job in the whole land, and from that opening description who can doubt it. Later verses also tell us how very wealthy, kind and generous he was, too. He was quite a character. But how can we tell that he had the Secret of God that this book is about? There's nowhere in the Bible that directly says Job had it. But it's simple to work it out from the description we have of him.

Two statements about God's Secret taken from elsewhere in the Bible will settle the matter. One is from the Book of Proverbs, the other from the Book of Psalms. And these two statements provide us with the two foundation facts about God's Secret. Here they are:

> *'His secret is with the righteous.'* (Proverbs 3:32)
>
> *'The secret of the LORD is with them that fear him.'* (Psalm 25:14)

These are the two main elements of God's Secret we mentioned in the previous chapter. Everything about it relates to one of these two elements, sometimes both.

Those who know His Secret will be **righteous** and they will **fear** God.

They will qualify on both counts. And Job did exactly that. He was called **upright**, and that's the same word as **righteous** in the original manuscript. We'll say more about this matter of words in translation as we progress. Sometimes words in the Bible could be better or more consistently translated. It's not a great problem, and it doesn't detract from the truth and reliability of the original writings.

Job was also described as one who feared God. He was both God-fearing and righteous. So, when Eliphaz taunted him, saying, *'Hast thou heard the secret of God?'* Job could have said, well, yes, he had. He probably didn't, though, because he knew it would only lead to more accusations of being a know-all.

Counselling

As the subject of word meanings has arisen, the word for 'secret' in the original Hebrew also carries the idea of 'counsel' and has occasionally been translated that way. The counsel of God means the opinion or the advice of God. God's Secret covers the same things really. So you can think of it as God's **advice**, or God's **counsel** if that works better for you. That's what it comes down to.

We go to someone for counselling when we need their considered opinion and advice. We go to someone who has the appropriate knowledge of our problem, and who is someone we can trust. We want their counsel. That's a good way of thinking about God's Secret: it is His considered opinion and advice for us. We can't get better opinions or better advice about life than from God Himself. There is none better. He is the ultimate Counsellor with the ultimate counsel.

But, just as it is with going to a counsellor in the normal way, if we need to, so it is with going to the divine Counsellor. There are certain steps we need to take. First we must be aware of our need for a counsellor, and then we have to go to them. They don't turn up on our doorstep out of the blue and ask if we need advice about the particular problem that is their speciality, and neither does God come to us unsolicited with His counselling, with His Secret. He has made Himself available, though, by freely offering us access to His counsel. It's up to us to take advantage of it whenever we need it. He's always there. And once we're aware of how helpful it is, and how life-enhancing it is, we'll be spending a lot of time in counselling.

This is not looking good

The news that the righteous and the God-fearing are the ones who know God's Secret may not have been exactly what you were hoping to hear.

The thought of becoming righteous and God-fearing in order to learn the Secret may not have the greatest appeal for you. But trust me on this, the reason why you might be feeling your mental brakes coming on here, is because you have the wrong idea about what being God-fearing and righteous mean. The probability is high that you need to revise your ideas about these things. So stay with me. They are not what you might think. And we'll look at what they really are in the following chapters.

Where did they get it?

We've settled it that God's Secret is with the righteous and the God-fearing. And these are not two different sets of people; they are the same people who have both characteristics. But where exactly do the God-fearing, righteous people get these characteristics from? We need to know that, if we want to be like them – and so that we, too, can know God's Secret.

Though I should make it clear that becoming God-fearing and righteous are not stepping-stones **towards** knowing God's Secret, they themselves are the essence of it. We don't become God-fearing and righteous and then turn our attention to knowing the Secret, because we will have already gained it by accomplishing those things.

Returning to the question: where do God-fearing righteous people get these characteristics from? – The obvious answer is from God. It's His Secret, after all. But in almost every case this didn't happen in a direct one-to-one fashion. And it's almost one hundred percent certain that it's not going to happen in that way for you either. It certainly didn't happen for me that way. God works in more subtle ways. And, more to the point, He'd rather we did something towards learning His Secret than have it handed to us on a plate. How do I know this? because God tells us He wants us to search for His wisdom, for His Secret, as we would hunt for hidden treasure. In the Book of Proverbs He tells us:

> *'Yea, if thou criest after knowledge, and liftest up thy voice for understanding; if thou seekest her as silver, and searchest for her as for hid treasures; then shalt thou understand the fear of the* LORD, *and find the knowledge of God.'* (Proverbs 2:3–5)

God wants us to find the knowledge of His Secret for ourselves in His communication to us that we call the Bible. He wants us to put some effort in. We do tend to value those things more that we've put some time and energy into getting. That said, it's not meant to be an off-putting chore. God wants us to enjoy the process or He wouldn't have likened it to a hunt for hidden treasure.

And it's always good to have someone along to help out and share the excitement when you're treasure hunting, which is where I come in.

This is how the righteous and God-fearing get to know God's Secret: they search for it with the sort of enthusiasm they'd summon if they were hunting for treasure. Think of the effort you'd put into locating a multi-billion-pound hoard of gold or a priceless artefact if you had a pretty good idea where it was buried, and you knew that it would be perfectly legal to keep it. It's safe to say you'd be hugely enthusiastic.

So, what would you do, and what would you **not** do, to find something worth more than all that gold? Because all that gold and the priceless artefact put together couldn't buy what God's Secret offers. Priceless security and peace of mind, which will continue for ever. Peace *'like a river'*, as it's referred to in the Bible (Isaiah 66:12) – peace which just keeps on flowing.

As you'll discover, God's Secret isn't only about how to live this life well and meaningfully; it contains the Secret of eternal life.

There's nothing more rewarding than finding out what it means to be righteous and God-fearing, (in case I haven't quite got that across yet), so let's start doing that in the next chapters.

4   NOT WHAT YOU MIGHT THINK

Words are wonderful things. It would certainly have been difficult to produce this book without them. Words enable us humans to do far more than other creatures. They enable us to grasp and convey all sorts of ideas and delicate shades of meaning. But sometimes they get in the way of our understanding. Especially when their meanings evolve and we start using them in different ways. Unlike rolling stones, words do tend to gather some moss as they roll down the centuries.

Take this word 'righteous'.

It's more usual to think of the word 'righteous' in a negative way because we rarely use it now except at the back end of 'self-righteous'. We might refer to someone with a smug, superior attitude as self-righteous, but we'd never think of calling a person with the opposite attitude righteous, because in our heads that conjures up someone pious, dull and humourless. We'd probably say they were decent or friendly or something like that. The word 'righteous' sounds archaic and churchy, so we have some resistance to it. That wouldn't normally be a problem, except that now, as a result, when we hear that God's Secret is associated with righteous people, we might draw back thinking that maybe it's not for us.

We probably have no great interest in becoming righteous. Because that's not how we'd like people to think of us. 'He's so righteous' or 'she's really righteous', is not what we want to hear about ourselves. But the reaction to the word 'righteous' hasn't always been negative. When it was used by the early translators of the Bible the word had very positive associations. People were pleased and flattered to be thought of as righteous. Not so much nowadays, though.

No substitutes
In view of this, how should we proceed? We could go for a more modern translation, of course, but most of the more recent ones opt for 'upright', which is probably as unwelcome to modern ears as righteous. Having thought about it, in the end I decided that it's better to stick with righteous, but to rewind the meaning back to its original positive one. So whenever you come across the word in the pages ahead, please switch off any negative associations that come to mind. And at the same time, switch on all the positive associations that you'll find in this book as we pick up on the word's original meaning in the Bible. Look at the word in a new light – or rather an old light.

What if I told you that God's Secret is with people who are genuine, straightforward and decent – people with integrity? If you look in a good thesaurus, those are the kinds of synonyms for righteous that you'll find; along with ethical, fair, good, honest, honourable, just and moral. These aren't outmoded words that describe fusty old attributes we want to distance ourselves from. They represent some of the finest qualities we can aspire to, characteristics that appeal to most of us. These are the qualities we most admire in the people we most admire. They are traits of character we most want to encourage in ourselves. And they are all qualities that are found in true righteousness.

When the Bible speaks of righteous people, it means those who have or who aspire to all these fine qualities, and more – very much more, as we'll see. This is how we are meant to understand the words righteous and righteousness when we read them in the Bible. And this is the way we want them to be understood in this book. We don't need to use substitutes. We can use the original words but view them in the same way that the early translators intended them.

Being right about what's right
The original Hebrew word for 'righteous' is quite often translated simply as 'right' – and it follows that the righteous are people who

are right. It's a happy coincidence that in English there's a linguistic connection between right and righteous, which helps us to spot the link. The righteous are people who have got something right. Which is what we might expect, because the people with whom God shares His Secret are going to be right about a lot of things.

What exactly are the righteous right about? What has God's Secret let them in on? Because it must be something big to come from God Himself. It must be on a level high above the secrets we ordinarily hear of, like having the inside track on what's happening among the people we know, or, to give 'secret' it's other meaning, more than just a better way of doing something fairly mundane.

In short, the righteous are in on the Secret of what is right about life generally. They have inside knowledge concerning what's really going on in the world and how things really work. We'll explain this further shortly. Before we do that, let's think a little more about the righteous themselves.

That certain something

'His secret is with the righteous.' I've mentioned before that the righteous have integrity; that they can be trusted; they are reliable, honest and decent people. And you'll appreciate why I'm making all these complimentary remarks about them when we take a proper look at what makes them tick in Part Two. And perhaps surprisingly, what we'll also learn about them is that they are far from being staid and sombre characters, as some of the qualities they have might suggest. David, who wrote the Psalm we'll be looking at, was considered righteous and he was far from dull. The righteous know how to engage enthusiastically with life. We'll also learn that they have a calmness and assurance about them that springs from a deep well of security. God's Secret hands us the keys to **perfect** peace. Which is no exaggeration, as you'll discover.

Not what you might think

The righteous themselves aren't perfect by any means. They have their flaws and failings. Becoming righteous through knowing God's Secret doesn't rid us of every one of our faults. It does help us, though, to eliminate many of them, and to lessen the influence over us that the remainder might otherwise have. One of the advantages the righteous gain from living God's Secret is how to handle their imperfections in a positive way, and not allow them to drag them down. Even though they have low times, as David did, they know how to get up again. And it must be said, the low times occur, more often than not, because they lose sight of the Secret and start living according to it less and less. Waking up to it again is the way up. And that option is always available.

Speaking of perfection...

In case you were wondering, when we read earlier that Job was *'perfect'*, that's a Hebrew word better translated as blameless. Job was **counted** blameless because he feared God and followed the way of righteousness as best he could. God tends to overlook the faults of those who are making an effort, and He is even happy to view such people as blameless. There's more on this important subject later in the chapters on grace. Job wasn't perfect or blameless in the sense that he never failed. As you'll see if you read the Book of Job, for all his famed patience, he needed to learn a few things. And he could be tetchy at times.

The righteous are not perfect (we must leave 'perfection' to the self-righteous). The righteous aim high in life and, with God's help, they achieve many good things, but they know their limitations and acknowledge their weaknesses. The Bible tells us that there is great strength in being able to acknowledge our weaknesses. It keeps us in touch with the truth about ourselves.

Hopefully, the above outline sketch of the character of the righteous has made them more appealing and less off-putting. We'll be filling in the details in Part Two. But basically they are kindly people with integrity and purpose. Which is hugely underselling them, I realise, but I want to get across that being righteous does not make us odd and aloof, all wrapped up in little cocoons of righteousness. In many ways the righteous are just like anyone else you might think of as a 'kindly person with integrity and purpose'. But they are more than this because being righteous in the way that God intends defines them further and makes them extraordinary. It sets them apart as the kind of people with whom God is willing to share His Secret.

The righteous are the sort of good, decent people that many of us might already consider ourselves to be. But they are a lot more than that because they have God-given insights into what life is really all about. They have found the answers to the big questions that elude most people, and their lives are different because of that. It couldn't be otherwise. They live on another level because of what they know.

What is right?

Now let's get back to the subject of what the righteous are right about. They are right about many things, not because they are remarkably clever, but because they have the good sense to listen to the One who is right about everything – God. Let's start with morality. Knowing God's Secret, the righteous know what is morally correct. They know what is right and wrong. You might think that most people know something as basic as that, but that's not the case. We do have a kind of moral compass, an instinct for what is generally right, but it's by no means foolproof. And people with the same general set of instincts about what is right can reach different conclusions.

Philosophers have been struggling with the problem of how to define what is right for centuries. And agreement on it is a major problem when we acknowledge no absolute standard of right and wrong. Unless we have agreement on it, we can't pin it down. Absolute and unchallengeable rightness on moral issues can only come from someone who is all-knowing and infallible. There are no such people among us. So if we remove God from the picture then how can anyone say what is right? If we are no more than intelligent animals, who have emerged through a chain of biological accidents, then where does our morality come from? Or, more to the point, where **should** it come from? Who should decide? You? Me? The government? The UN? The philosophers? The scientists? Who is qualified to say what is truly right when we discount God? Without Him there can be no certainty about right or wrong.

There is no right and wrong in the animal kingdom. Quite a few creatures would be facing murder charges if there were. If we are just another species of mammal on an adjacent branch of the evolutionary tree, then why should we have right and wrong? If this is all we are, then we don't have morality. Not in any absolute and unchallengeable sense. We have only what we decide is right and wrong. So, to ask the question again: who should decide?

Consensus morality

Perhaps there should be a vote on it, a world-wide referendum, to decide exactly what good, moral human behaviour should be. In this hypothetical situation, every individual above an agreed age of moral responsibility makes a list and submits it. The top twenty items become our moral standard, fixed for all time. Though it wouldn't be fixed for all time because people change, societies change, and amendments would become necessary.

It occurs to me that if we had a global referendum every twenty or thirty years, then we'd probably produce a slightly different list each time. We would have a fluctuating morality, and any righteous people, in order to remain righteous, would have to be rather adaptable. Or, if they maintained their integrity and stuck resolutely to what they believed, then righteousness would shift around to different groups within the population as the years went on and people moved in and out of the agreed consensus of righteousness.

Imagine if we had taken our census of morals every fifty years for only the last thousand years, what differing moral standards would have emerged with each top twenty. Especially if we were careful to include all peoples, however remote from Western ideas of civilisation, in our poll. We'd probably look back in horror at the results of some of those polls. Though I fear that we'd be conceited enough now, armed with the latest morality poll, to believe that our present generation is the most likely to have it right – something which a generation living fifty years hence would find more than mildly amusing, I'm sure.

Morality and people farms

Yes, it's hypothetical and we are playing with the idea, but there is some serious intent behind this. Because in a world without a fixed and authoritative standard of right and wrong there can be no righteous people. We have nothing concrete to build our morality on. Even the idea that it's morally wrong to kill another human being can be challenged in wartime. Without absolutes we might even reach the horrific situation described by the time traveller in H.G. Wells's novel *The Time Machine*. His time traveller visited an England of the far distant future where the dominant race, the Morlocks, farmed the weaker race, the Eloi, for food. Not a likely scenario, we might think, but who's to say how the moral climate of the world might shift in desperate times? If all we have is a consensus on what is right and wrong, then anything might be acceptable at any given time.

No fixed standard – no righteousness

Without God true righteousness is not possible. Without a God-given standard we have only **the prevailing version** – a morality of thought and action that is dependent on the current worldview, where and when we happen to live. And a righteousness that tacks back and forth with the prevailing moral winds has no integrity, and therefore logically it isn't righteousness.

Morality without God

I'm well aware that leading atheists argue that we can be moral without God. And since Darwin published *The Descent of Man* in 1871 it has been argued that our moral sense evolved from social instincts that we share with the animal kingdom. Though, noticeably, many species in the animal kingdom have more sharply honed instincts than we do and yet haven't evolved morally as far as we have, nor do they show any signs of doing so. According to evolutionary theory, our moral sense developed with the realisation that our communal good and the survival of the species are best served by us being kind to one other. It's better for us if we don't all kill one another. So morality is a survival tactic. That's the theory. And it depends on us believing that our presumed early ancestors were smart enough to have notions about the survival of their species beyond their own personal survival.

In recent times a branch of science has emerged known as the neuroscience of morality. It's a science that involves monitoring what happens in the brain while we're making moral decisions. It has become possible because of the advent of CAT and MRI brain scanning technology. What the scans reveal is that morality appears to be hardwired into our brains. We might think that we learn our morality from our parents or society, but the scans point to something different.

There appears to be a kind of moral grammar already in place in our brains governing what we subsequently take on board. What our parents, teachers, and society in general teach us, seems as if it has to conform to a template already in place. The normal human mind has a feel for what is right that is inborn. This is what the research seems to show. There is an intuitive emotional response to a moral question.

I realise that it slots in well with evolutionary theory that our brains can be shown to have this hardwiring. The assertion might be made that our morality has evolved to become a part of our nature. Though there is no evidence to show that it was ever **not** a part of our nature. Evolutionary biologists simply assert that everything about us has evolved, because that's their job, and that will include our moral faculty.

A place without a path to it

We appreciate that science has by its very nature a speculative side to it, and that to advance our understanding of the world scientists often have to take leaps of the imagination. After they have leapt they try and fill in the gaps between here and where they've landed. Often they do this very well, and we all benefit from where they take us. But sometimes they take leaps that land them in places to which they never successfully build the bridge from here to there. When this happens, they can either abandon the idea, or if it still seems to have merit they can put it on the back burner, in the hope that new information will one day take us there.

What happened regarding the leap of the imagination that took them to evolution, however, is that although they have never successfully built a path of proof to reach where they landed, they act as if they have. They haven't put it on hold waiting for proof. They have allowed their assumptions to harden into facts. Why would scientists be so unscientific? I would suggest that believing evolution to be true has become an imperative, because the only alternative is special creation, which is unthinkable to them. There are no other options on the table. It's more a matter of avoiding what they don't want than substantiating what they do want.

Some years ago, when I first began looking into evolutionary theory I had the reverse reaction: I began to believe more and more strongly in special creation because the only alternative is evolution. I found evolutionary theory untenable. I'll say more about why later. Though what I recall most from reading *The Origin of Species* in my twenties was how wrong-footed Darwin seemed to be by what he called 'the extreme imperfection of the geological record'. It struck me as a euphemism for the lack of any real proof from the fossils in the rocks for what he was saying. He blamed the problem on the palaeontologists for not having found a complete enough fossil record, and on their annoying habit of classifying the fossils they had found as distinct species, when he felt that some of them ought to be partially evolved intermediate varieties. Over 160 years later we have a more perfect geological

Not what you might think

record, but it's still not teeming with proof for Darwin's theory as he thought it would be.

That evolutionary theory has assumed the intellectual high ground is both amazing and alarming. Amazing because there are many legitimate objections to it. Alarming because it leaves us with no real moral obligations towards one another. Which is fine if it's true. There's no point in us running away from truth. If it's true then let's live with that and work out what to do with it, while not pretending that there is any absolute right and wrong, or that anyone has any more right than anyone else to decide what is right and wrong.

What's more likely true, though, is that we're not advanced animals who have a set of rules that we've fashioned from the instincts we acquired in the long struggle for existence. No, what's more likely is that we are the result of intelligent creation.

Assumptions as facts

Allowing assumptions to harden into facts is an easy error to fall into, and more common than you might think. I notice it sometimes when I'm reading: a suggestion is made, and then a sentence or two further on the suggestion reappears stated like an established fact. It happens in conversations, too, and can even be used deliberately as a sleight-of-hand debating tactic. But scientists do well to avoid it. As indeed do religionists.

I watch myself to try and make sure I don't fall into this error, which is easy when writing a book like this. But I know that once the two key premises of this book are established – that God is extremely likely, and that the Bible is His most likely communication to us – then everything else I have to say, barring the odd asides, is predicated on those two things and is therefore also extremely likely to be true. Chapters six, seven and eight are devoted to some of the evidence for these key premises.

Personal feedback
In addition to the evidence offered in these chapters, in Part Two we'll be looking at the way in which God's Secret can be verified through personal experience. By the results, that is, of putting it into practice. I realise that this kind of evidence may be thought of as entirely subjective, and therefore open to dispute. But if the feedback we get from the world around us matches what we would expect if God's Secret is working in our lives, then that's more than subjective, it is empirical, and convincing.

The *'perfect peace'* that can be accessed through God's Secret, as you'll find later, is very real, even though it's the result of entertaining certain truths in our minds. Subjective? I suppose so. Very real? Most definitely. Some things are 'all in the mind', in the sense that they are completely imaginary. There's no disputing that, because we can worry about things that never happen. But that shouldn't put a question mark over everything that goes on in our heads. Our reality exists in our heads, too.

The time before the beginning
Getting back to our thoughts on the supposed evolution of our moral faculty, where it leads the atheist is to a comfortable place where we have evolved an innate moral sense, and we don't need God for our morality. We can work it out for ourselves and make it whatever we want it to be. A believer in God, however, can go to the even more comfortable place of Proverbs chapter eight.

This is a remarkable chapter that is often overlooked. It takes us on a journey back in time beyond the Creation to when our world was just an idea in the mind of God. Our world didn't begin with the dramatic opening words of Genesis chapter one: *'In the beginning, God created...'* The beginning of our world was as a **thought** in the mind of its Creator as described in the Book of Proverbs. The physicist and astronomer, Sir James Jeans, once observed with insight that 'the universe looks more like a great thought rather than a great machine.'

Not what you might think

Proverbs 8:22-31 says that God's wisdom was in both the planning and execution of our world. His wisdom is built into the very fabric of what He made. There is a logic, an order, a set of discernible laws, observable within all matter, and in how it acts and reacts. It's what microbiologists see when they stare into microscopes. It's what astronomers see when they look through telescopes. It's built into all Creation, underpinning it, holding it all together. We might refer to it as the Laws of Nature. But it's not a Mother Nature at work; it's a Father in Heaven. It's what the neuroscientists are seeing on the MRI and CAT scans when they find evidence for an inborn moral sense in human beings. Specific areas of the brain are activated by moral decisions.

There is something about us that we call a conscience. There's also common sense. We do have an instinct for what is right hardwired into us. Our moral compass was installed a long way back. But it's not perfect, because we are not perfect. We're human. We're a downgraded version of what we were created to be, and will one day be again, only better. The best thing we can do with our imperfect moral faculty is to align it insofar as we are able with the perfect wisdom that installed it in the first place.

To return to it, for righteousness to exist there has to be an unchanging set of principles. And such a thing can only come about if there is an infallible source for our morality. Righteousness only makes sense in the context of a fixed, God-given morality. So there is an inherent logic to the sentence that says: *'His secret is with the righteous.'* Because there has to be a God, or a *'His'*, for there to be any *'righteous'*.

Incidentally, I'm aware that some people these days object to the pronouns He, Him, His, being used for God, so we will be looking at this gender issue later. I use the male pronouns throughout this book and I will explain why.

God's Secret, His counsel, His advice, provides us with the fixed morality that makes righteousness possible. Knowing and applying His Secret is what makes righteous people righteous. The moral precepts that His Secret contain are what the righteous are right about. And we will be delving into them in Part Two. But God's Secret provides us with far more than a perfect set of principles to guide us. As if that wasn't enough! It also contains truths about life's meaning and purpose. **How** to live and **why** we live are inseparably bound together in the information that God offers us in His Secret.

'His secret is with the righteous.' That's the first of the two main facts we are given about God's Secret. The second of them, you'll recall, is that *'The secret of the* LORD *is with them that fear him.'* (Psalm 25:14) We'll explore what that means in the next chapter.

5 Fear is key

Probably the briefest and most repeated piece of reassurance in the entire Bible is *'fear not.'* It was often said by an angel whose sudden appearance had just startled or terrified someone. So quite a good thing for them to say. Injunctions to *'fear not'*, along with similar ones like *'don't be afraid'* appear over 200 times in the Bible. But for all this encouragement not to fear, at the same time we are told in the Book of Proverbs that *'the fear of the LORD is the beginning of knowledge'* and in the Book of Psalms that *'The secret of the LORD is with them that fear him.'* So on the one hand we are repeatedly told **not** to fear and on the other hand we are told that fear is good and important. It looks confusing but it's fairly easy to put straight.

What's happening here is that we are looking at two entirely different kinds of fear. In the original Hebrew text, two different words are used. It's the translators who have caused the confusion by translating both words as *'fear'*. Incidentally, you don't have to take my word for it when I talk about the meanings of words in the Bible. There's a book called a Bible Concordance, which is available in bookshops or online, where you can verify what I say if you feel the need. Of those available I generally use the *Analytical Concordance To The Holy Bible* by Robert Young.

When we're told to *'fear not'*, that means exactly what it says. Don't be afraid. But when we're told that *'The fear of the LORD is the beginning of knowledge'* we are being told that a **reverential awe,** or a **great respect** for the Lord is the starting place for knowledge. That's what it means. And I still don't understand why in so many of the modern translations the opportunity hasn't been taken to make the distinction clear. Maybe new ones eventually will.

So we have a fear that is negative, and which we should avoid, and we have a reverential awe that is positive, and which we should embrace. But why does God need us to fear Him in this way? Why should the Secret of the Lord be with them that greatly revere and admire Him?

Getting real

It's not that God **needs** us to be in awe of Him. It's so often a mistake to try and apply human psychology to God. It cannot fulfil any need of His to have comparatively insignificant creatures regarding Him with awe. God is not like us in that He has an ego that needs to be pandered to.

But we're told that God can be pleased with us and even take delight in us, and that He created all things, including us, for His pleasure (Revelation 4:11). A significant part of the pleasure He takes from His Creation is having a positive response from us. He is a God of love, so when we respond positively He is happy with that, and when we respond negatively He is saddened. This is what we would expect; it's what we're told in the Bible, and it seems very like the workings of the human psyche. But when God is disappointed with us His sadness is more for us than for Himself, because we are the losers.

The reason He wants us to be respectful and in awe of Him is because of what that does for **us**. It opens our eyes to reality. It's our acknowledgement of a fundamental truth about the way things are. And appreciating the reality of who and what God is, gives us the motivation to become spiritual beings, instead of remaining what the Bible calls merely natural beings.

If we pay no attention to God and think of ourselves as the masters of our own destinies, the lords all we survey, then we're missing out on reality. Keeping God out of the picture is limiting not liberating. It puts us in a far smaller world. Bringing God into the picture expands our worldview and brings much-needed perspective. It's no exaggeration to say that the acknowledgement of a higher power opens our minds to a higher dimension, a spiritual dimension, where we discover and appreciate that life is far more than our common lot.

What we generally think of as reality is more of a virtual reality, not the real thing. It's the product of an agreed consensus of how things are, to which we've all subscribed. It closes off the spiritual dimension where reality is located. God's Secret is the way back to reality for us. The effect of learning His Secret is rather like taking off a VR headset and coming out of an artificial world.

We'll have more to say about this in Part Two, but, in essence, the reality of our situation is that we are disappointingly small and insignificant, while the One who created and sustains the universe is unimaginably large and significant. So if we are not in awe of such a Being, then we have not properly grasped the situation.

Take another look
This puts me in mind of my first visit to Niagara Falls. I recall that I was not in the least impressed by what I saw. The Falls were a huge disappointment. The reason for this was that it was late April and the early spring sunshine warming the ice in the Niagara River below the Falls had created a thick mist. My family and I stood beside the Horseshoe Falls, on the Canadian side, and all we could see was about a metre's width of water plunging down about a metre's drop. The view was not at all impressive.

Thankfully, we were staying with friends nearby, and were able to revisit a couple of days later and see how impressive the Falls truly are. But if we'd only ever seen what we saw on the first visit we'd have remained underwhelmed. It seems to me that many people are similarly unimpressed with, and dismissive of God because they've had only a limited view of Him. They really need to go back and take another look. They would do themselves a great favour by discovering the reality.

What things usually create awe in us? Probably things from the natural world. Something like the Grand Canyon, maybe? For me, as mentioned, it's Niagara Falls. Or, still in Canada, the stillness and beauty of canoeing on a lake in Ontario. Or flying low over Lake Huron in a seaplane, picking out some of the 'thirty thousand islands' below. You doubtless have your own exquisite moments of being awed by your situation and surroundings.

Ordinary heroes

Probably there are certain people you are in awe of because of their talents and accomplishments: writers, musicians, artists, architects, scientists, statesmen, adventurers and sportsmen. We all have our heroes, don't we? But there's a lot of truth in the saying that we shouldn't get too close to our heroes. I've discovered, as maybe you have, that generally our heroes turn out to be quite ordinary people, and sometimes disappointingly so.

I recall when I was in my twenties I was a great admirer of a particular author. His books showed a soaring imagination, and his ability to weave a complicated tale with an impressive vocabulary was, for me, second to none. When I met him in London a few years later, quite unintentionally, I was taken aback by how ordinary he was. We chatted about his newest book and I didn't feel in the least starstruck. My fault really for expecting someone larger than life – like a character from the vivid landscapes of his books.

On another occasion I recall standing at an event chatting to somebody whose acquaintance I'd just made. He was an affable, regular kind of guy (a bit like me really). We talked for a while about this and that, and then suddenly some girls approached us asking for his autograph. And when they'd gone I found myself saying clumsily, 'So you're famous, then.' He explained that he'd been a professional football player with Chelsea Football Club. He'd played in a cup-winning side. He still wore his cup-winners' medal on a chain around his neck and proudly pulled it out of his shirt neck. He said his name and it registered only vaguely with me. But then, he was someone else's hero, not mine. But a quite ordinary character, really. About a year later I spotted his obituary in a newspaper. He had died comparatively young. There was a sadness about this hero; the way he clung to his glory days and seemed to be all too disappointed by his own ordinariness.

Our heroes really are just ordinary people when we get right down to it, hardly any different from ourselves, with surprisingly similar flaws and foibles. Even so-called superstars can be super normal. If ever I'm with my daughter and a song by a particular singer is playing somewhere, she'll poke a little fun by saying, 'Do you know who this is, Dad?' It harks back to the time I spent with a group of people, one of whom was an internationally famous recording artist. I spent some time trying to work out who he was, and even when I knew his name I couldn't think what he did for a living. These so-called superstars are confusingly just like you and me when we encounter them. We really have no need to be in awe of them. And the best way to keep our heroes intact is not to stand too close to them.

Deep space

Perhaps you're in awe of the real super stars when you look up at the night sky. It is awesome to ponder how many there are. Incredible, too, to think we see just a small portion of the countless stars that make up the Milky Way, in which our entire solar system is a mere speck.

There was a night back in 1997, perhaps you remember it, when all the planets in our solar system were lined up and strung out like pearls on a string. Five of them were visible with the naked eye, even in places where the city lights dulled the view. I recall standing in our garden with my then young son and excitedly finding and naming each planet in turn. Usually we don't appreciate the depth of space when we look at the star-field above us. The whole sky looks flat, every star looks the same distance away, just some brighter than others. But that night with the planets strung out in line like that, we could see the perspective, and grasp something of the true depth and immensity of the heavens. It was truly awe inspiring – no other words for it.

God's Secret

The only sane response

Whatever it is that evokes awe in you when you experience it or contemplate it, whoever your greatest heroes might be, these things and people all shrink to near nothing when placed beside God. Even in our wildest imaginations, I doubt that we come anywhere near to comprehending the power and immensity of a Being who inhabits infinity and eternity. If there are other dimensions, as some suggest, then doubtless He inhabits those too. We have neither the vocabulary nor the imagination to fully appreciate who and what God is. Even the meagre amount that our minds can cope with is enough to take our breath away. It doesn't take much to work out that we should be in wonder of such a Being. It's the only sane response to who and what He is.

This is why the Bible says that *'the fear of the LORD is the beginning of knowledge'* and *'the beginning of wisdom'*. This is where we must begin. An appropriate awe of God is the essential starting place for understanding our world and our place in it. This is our ticket to reality that will motivate us to get in sync with what is really going on in the world. Without it, we simply won't make any progress understanding how life works. All we'll have is our own guesswork and that of others to go on. We might think of some of it as informed guesswork, but it's still guesswork. And that's not what we should be centring our lives around.

The necessary knowledge and wisdom we need for successful living will elude us until we glimpse something of the awesomeness of our Creator and respond appropriately – which means taking proper notice of Him. Until then we will have neither the motivation nor the tools for advancing in the right direction in life. This is why *'the secret of the LORD is with them that fear him.'*

God and the sea

The fear of God is in fact a form of love for Him. This kind of fear is where **love** begins, as well as being where knowledge and wisdom begin. In the normal way, fear and love are incompatible; they work against one other; but in this case they work together.

And for me, how this happens can best be illustrated by the way in which a sailor thinks about the sea. A sailor loves the sea. It's his life and his livelihood. He's never happier than when he's aboard a ship and surrounded by the ocean. But at the same time he has a huge respect for the sea because it is so vast and powerful. He knows that to lose his respect for the sea's tremendous power would not only take so much joy out of his life but could also cost him dearly. A sailor's fear of the sea is a rich mixture of love and respect.

There are parallels here, and you don't need me to spell them out. The point I'm trying to reinforce is that fear, as a high regard for someone, is a very positive thing. It's not at all the same thing as being terrified of them. Unimaginably powerful though God is, that's not how He wants us to feel about Him. Chiefly because He loves what He has made.

God simply is awesome. He is omniscient, omnipotent, omnipresent and even omnicompetent (and, no, I didn't make that last one up). He is the Mighty Creator and Sustainer of everything. And yet He wants to share His secrets with us. Not all of them, of course, because we'd probably blow a few brain fuses with the overload before we took on board even a fraction of them. As our Creator, He wants us to know vital secrets that will set our lives on the right track. He wants to take us into His confidence about some very important matters.

Before we say anything more about righteousness and fear, which we'll do in Part Two, we really must first address the matter of the existence of God. Because before we can be in awe of God, and before we can commit ourselves to living by His blueprint for our lives, we need to be satisfied beyond reasonable doubt that He exists. There's not a lot of point to this otherwise. Though **hold that last thought** – because, strange as this may sound, even if you're still hanging onto some doubts about the existence of God, I would still recommend that you look into the blueprint for life in Part Two, think about it, even try to live by it, and see what effect

God's Secret

it has on your life. Because that experience is likely to lead you to concede that the wisdom of the Secret is extraordinary, and most likely from a higher power who deserves your utmost respect.

But first, is it reasonable to believe that there is a God?

If you're already thoroughly convinced that there is a God, you might want to move on to chapter nine. Then again, you might want to remind yourself how reasonable it is to believe in God, in which case read on.

6 GOD IS EXTREMELY LIKELY

This is one of the shorter chapters in the book. You might think that strange considering the size of the subject. But the matter of whether there is a God, is not really that complicated. When we touched on the subject earlier, we mentioned that there are only two options when it comes to how everything happened. Either everything evolved or God created it. It's simply a matter of which is more credible. These are mutually exclusive scenarios, and there are no other options on the table. There are some variations on the theme of evolution, but they all have huge time frames and natural selection in common.

Not all of them leave God out. But trying to bring Creation and evolution together, by suggesting, as some have, that God created us using evolution, is a nonstarter, because it brings God into the picture, and He tells us He did it differently. This mixing of the two ideas is known as Theistic Evolution, and is a concession to evolutionary theory that we don't have to make. As we'll consider shortly, the planet may indeed be millions of years old, but not this human phase of it.

Whether an intelligent Being created our world and life upon it, or these things happened on their own, is not complicated because we don't have to know **all** the facts. If we had to make a decision based on knowing everything then **no one** would be able or qualified to decide. It would be impossible. We could come to a decision only if we were fully conversant with the Bible, archaeology, ancient history, evolutionary theory, cosmology and genetics. At least. And whichever side we came down on, we would have to keep track of current developments in all of these fields, in case new finds altered the balance of likelihood in one direction or the other. Nobody is capable of that.

God's Secret

The only person on record to have come anywhere near being capable of it is Solomon. His knowledge was second to none in his day. He was as close to being a professor of everything as anyone has ever come (see 1 Kings 4:30–34). And he concluded that God made everything. One of the lecturers at the London university my son attended had what he called 'a hobby of collecting degrees'. He probably has more letters **after** his name than I have **in** mine. But he's no Solomon. Powerful people from afar don't beat a path to his door to hear his insights as they did Solomon's.

No, we can't know everything before we decide between God and evolution. But we can look at how feasible they each are. We can look at the general assumptions behind the two options and make our minds up from those.

A Big Bang

The likelihood of there **not** being a God is extremely slim. Realistically the odds for life happening by chance are astronomical. Astronomer and mathematician Sir Fred Hoyle calculated the odds at 1 chance in $10^{40,000}$. Such a number would take quite a few pages this size to write out in full. The scientific establishment is still groping and very much in the realm of theory when it comes to explaining how life began on our world.

Science is progressive by nature and has areas that are necessarily fluid and speculative. As we said before, we must be careful not to mistake its speculations for hard facts. The origin of the universe nearly fourteen billion years ago from a Big Bang seems like a credible explanation, especially when packaged in plausible-sounding scientific language. But the concept of a Big Bang wobbles noticeably when we query where, before this universe suddenly expanded into being, did the material that exploded come from. The answer would seem to be that it came from the then non-existent universe. An answer which clearly has a flaw in it. Added to this, where did the force come from that acted upon the materials and made them explode? The answer would

God is extremely likely

seem to be that this also came from the then non-existent universe.

Expanding the idea

Cosmologists are smart people. They can see as well as anyone that there are problems with this. They know that the Big Bang is only a possible scenario, not a fact. And they have added other scenarios. One is that the material that formed this universe came from a pre-existing universe which, having reached the extent of its expansion, slowed, and then collapsed back on itself.

They suggest there could be a multi-billion-year cycle of expansion and collapse. But that doesn't solve the mystery of where the material for the first Big Bang, and the force that acted upon it, came from to start the cycle. This idea of ongoing expansion and collapse also requires us to believe that all the matter in the universe – billions of stars and other material – could collapse back into something no bigger than the full stop at the end of this sentence. Because that's what they speculate would have to occur in order to trigger each Big Bang. Matter of this density crammed inside something this small would become unstable and explode. I guess so!

Plausibility has surely left the room. Even if we concede that our universe began as a tiny dot because all the material for it was **latent** within that dot (rather in the way that a few cubic metres of expanding foam can be pumped from a comparatively small cartridge), it's surely not possible for the entire universe, having once formed and expanded, to collapse back to its original latency. Try putting all that foam back in the cartridge!

When Sir Fred Hoyle coined the term Big Bang he was being derisory about all the pseudo-science surrounding it. Author Terry Pratchett summed up the inherent problems of Big Bang theory when, in his book *Lords And Ladies,* he said with great insight and humour: 'In the beginning was nothing – which exploded!' Okay, it may actually have been nearly nothing, but it still sounds hugely unscientific.

Meeting the eternal

The physical Creation shares something in common with space and time. All three appear infinite. However far in space we travel we cannot comprehend coming to the end of space. If it stops then what lies beyond? If there's a wall, how thick can it be, and what's behind it? It's the same with time. However far back we go, we can always imagine being able to go back another twenty minutes or so. Was there ever a day that didn't have a yesterday? (Though, of course, days and nights are local events and don't exist across the universe.)

But, and here's a poser, if time does go back forever from the point where we are now, then however did we get here, because it would take forever to get here? That one really messes with our minds. A similar problem exists for physical Creation. Whatever cause is put forward for Creation, we can always ask what caused that. And what caused that. And... you get the picture.

Whatever cause anyone puts forward to explain the origin of the universe they will always need a cause for their cause, and then a cause for that, *ad infinitum*. But realistically it must stop somewhere. Even in scientific circles it's believed that there must ultimately be a cause at the root of all things that is **eternal** and doesn't require anything to have caused it. At the root of space, time and matter there must be something eternal. It's extremely unlikely that these things continue to extend forever. In fact, that's the impossible scenario. At some point everything must meet the eternal and stop.

The Eternal is likely to be God

Evolutionary biology cannot account feasibly for the transition from inert chemicals to living organisms. For inert matter to become alive is a staggering leap for it to make, no matter how many billions of years we give it. It's unscientific to say that given enough time impossible things can happen. Two and two won't equal five no matter how many billions of years we wait. Geneticist Michael Denton says the break between the non-living and the living world 'represents the most dramatic and fundamental of all the discontinuities in nature'. The difference between a living cell and even the most highly ordered non-biological matter, such as a crystal, he says, 'is a chasm as vast and absolute as it is possible to conceive'.

The transition from non-living to living matter is inconceivable because of the vast, unbridgeable difference between the two. The implications of this are enormous. If it's far more likely that the transition could never have occurred, that means that it's also far more likely that living matter has **always** existed.

It's a pity that in English grammar there isn't a punctuation mark that means 'pause and think about what you just read', because if there were I'd be using it right now. It's such an important point that whatever cause anybody might put forward for the existence of living matter, realistically it can never be something non-living. Because that transition is so highly improbable. The gap is too large. We need something living to produce life. And however far back we might want to push it, however many billions of years we want to allow it, we still need something living to produce life. It won't come from inert matter.

So if we go back far enough we must ultimately arrive at something living that is eternal. And what might that be? Or rather, who might that be? As it happens, we don't have to go far back, or count backwards many steps in the process, because only one step is necessary: the step from an eternal living Creator to life on Earth.

It's the thought that counts

Our biology is complex and marvellous. But the most amazing thing about us is not our biology but our minds, our consciousness. For us to occur by chance requires that non-living matter would not only have to become alive, it would also have to become self-aware. Another unbridgeable chasm opens before us. The chasm between a living organism, like a tree, and a living, **thinking** organism like you and me is vast. Scientists have identified a low-level sense of awareness in trees and plants. There seems to be a rudimentary system of communication among them, but it's a long way short of our own level of awareness and our ability to interact. As, even at best, is the awareness of animals, birds and insects. Though it's not likely that even their level of awareness could have developed from inorganic and totally unaware materials.

It's hard to conceive of any point at which a collection of non-living elements could become something which is alive and self-aware in the way that we are. However long we wait for it to happen. What's more there is nothing in science that can support such a thing happening.

Who are you if there is no God?
For me, the most convincing proof of God is my own consciousness. I know that nothing can be more subjective than my own personal sense of myself, but I cannot believe that I am no more than an electro-bio-chemical reaction in my head. Do you believe that's all you are? Do you believe that your sense of self is just the product of neurons firing off electrically and chemically in your brain matter? At what point do the chemicals in your brain become you? How do these chemicals make the leap to conscious awareness that is you?

I realise that brain imaging techniques can show particular areas of our brains 'lighting up' when we think particular kinds of thoughts, or have particular emotions, or move a particular finger, but this still doesn't explain who is deciding to move that finger or have that particular thought or emotion. We can find the crew but we can't find the captain. Someone once said that looking for consciousness in the composition of the brain is like doing a chemical analysis of the ink on a page of writing in order to understand what's been written.

A real Big Bang?

It's simply neither reasonable nor scientific to believe that life could develop from non-living matter. And it's extremely doubtful, too, whether human consciousness could evolve from non-thinking matter. The sensible conclusion is that consciousness has always existed, just as living matter must always have existed – and that, if we go back far enough, we will arrive at something conscious that is eternal. The Creation account in Genesis shows God creating the first human from inert material, the dust of the ground, and then 'breathing' life into it, or imbuing that which He had formed with life. That's real science because life has to come from life.

The background radiation that cosmologists interpret as a Big Bang occurring nearly 14 billion years ago, by which everything inexplicably and unscientifically came out of nothing, or nearly nothing, might better be explained as the moment of God's initial creation and distribution of the materials that He required to make the universe. This is pure conjecture, of course, much like the Big Bang theory itself, but it might better explain both the appearance of the materials and the force that acted upon them.

In this scenario, the elements that God employed for the purpose of producing and supporting life would have been among those first materials He created. And should we wonder why He waited nearly 14 billion years to bring humankind into being, then two reasons come to mind. Firstly, He's in no hurry because He has all the time He could possibly need to do whatever He wants to. Secondly, He may not have waited long at all, but have created life in numerous locations across the universe soon after its establishment.

In astronomical terms, planet Earth is in something of a backwater, tucked away in one of the vast arms of the spiral nebula we call the Milky Way. We're cut off from what's happening in deeper space. So a lot could be happening that we are unaware of, even with the aid of our most advanced telescopes and probes. This could be deliberate. It's feasible that we have been given such an obscure cosmological postcode in order to keep cursed humankind from contacting and adversely affecting the peoples of far-off worlds, should they exist.

Perhaps this is the reason for the background radiation that cosmologists have detected. They may conceivably have found evidence for the moment in time when God brought the materials for the universe into existence and dispersed them. It's not an explanation that they will be embracing any time soon, I should think, but more plausible than everything exploding from nothing. Because that would be magic, not science.

This alternative Big Bang theory doesn't mean that God set evolution in progress. God tells us how He created the world and ourselves, and that it took days not millennia. Though the Genesis account does hint at the planet having already existed for aeons and having supported life before Adam. The opening scene of the Book of Genesis describes a world covered by a vast ocean. The Bible account can be read as God customising planet Earth in a few days to make it habitable, rather than creating the planet itself at that point.

What God did then was create fully formed living species, and **not** single-celled organisms along with the right conditions for life in all its forms to develop over millennia. No doubt He could have done that, but it's not the way God tells us He chose to do it. He clearly gave some species the ability to adapt to changing environments, but not to evolve into entirely new species. We don't find that happening.

A pre-used earth would also explain some of the confusing and misleading findings of anthropologists and palaeontologists. They assume that everything they unearth belongs to this Creation when it's likely that some of it could belong to a previous phase. The planet itself may be very old, but not this phase that dates from Adam.

Category error

As I said, God is extremely likely. Something, or rather Someone eternal is required to explain everything. And to ask who **made** God shows a woeful or wilful ignorance of what the word **eternal** means. What kind of a question is – who made a Being who has **always existed**? It's what students of philosophy call a category error. It's a non-sequitur, like asking what colour your opinion on something is, and it doesn't belong in serious discussion.

So, having arrived at a place where God looks more likely than not, the next questions are these: If there is a God, who is He? And has He made Himself known to us? These are questions for the next chapter.

7 COMMUNICATION

It is far more likely that God exists than that He doesn't. But who is He? Has He made Himself known to us in any way? If there is a God who made the world and us, then it's a fair certainty that He did it for some good reason. A superior eternal intelligence is hardly likely to do pointless things. Even you and I are rarely given to that. So, there must be a point to what He has done. And there would also be some point in making that point known to us. If we don't know what life's all about and what's expected of us, then there might as well be no God as far as we're concerned. If He has left us totally in the dark about who He is and what He has in mind for us, then we are quite justified in not believing He exists and going our own way.

We might assume that there is a Creator from seeing the beauty and complexity of nature. But nature tells us nothing about who God is and what His plans for the world might be. Trees and grass are no clue. And without some form of signature the Creation is an anonymous work. The architect is unknown to us. So, the matter of communication is of supreme importance to this issue of who God is. Has there ever been any kind of communication to us from God? Do we have anything that looks like it might be the kind of communication we'd expect from our Creator?

Well, yes, we do. We have a communication that looks every bit like what we'd expect to find. We'll come to that in just a moment.

The culture factor
We look around and see a lot of potential communications from a higher Being. Each culture seems to have its own. And it could be argued that for us to properly understand and appreciate a particular religion, we should grow up in it, or live for some time in the culture that spawned it, and which it now permeates. Only then are we equipped to critique it with anything approaching credibility.

Communication

Which sets off another train of thought. Because from this it might be argued that religion is primarily a cultural phenomenon. We take on the religion of our culture because, in some cases, it's the only religion we come into contact with. Where does that leave the notion that one Creator, God, gave His one communication to the world?

A real communication from our Creator would need to cross cultural boundaries and be accessible to all. But perhaps it once did this. What if it had originally been known to all, but over time some cultures shut it out? Their forebears moved away from the original one religion, both geographically and culturally, and drifted into their own versions of it, and in some cases moved progressively further from it, until it was unrecognisable as the set of beliefs it started out as. Or they moved away and over time completely lost track of the original one-and-only religion and started up new religions born of their fears and superstitions.

There are twenty-three major religions in the world today. It's a bewildering array, especially when we consider that some of these subdivide into numerous sects, each claiming the right interpretation of their particular holy writings. There have been over thirty new religious movements since the start of the 20th century. And if, before we can come to a decision about who is right, we have to comprehend every world religion, with all its divisions and offshoots, together with all the minor religions and ideologies of the world, it would probably take us more than a lifetime. We would spend our entire lives seeking a truth that might always be over the next horizon. And if we ever did make it to the end, by then we'd have probably forgotten where we started. This is the way of befuddlement rather than enlightenment.

Narrowing the field

So, who is right? There must be some sensible criteria that we can apply. For example, we'd rightly be sceptical of a religion that appeared on the scene just a decade ago, with a brand new message, claiming to be the one true faith. We'd expect a communication from our Creator to have been around for a considerable time, so that all generations, right back to the beginning in fact, had the opportunity to learn about it. Also, if this new religion of recent years, subsequently attracted no more than ten adherents, and never influenced anyone beyond a twenty-mile radius, we'd dismiss it as irrelevant. We'd expect our true Creator's message to be widespread.

So, we have two reasonable criteria we can apply in order to narrow the field. A true communication is likely to have been around for as long as humanity. And a true communication is likely to be widespread, global. That means we can narrow the field considerably. Only four of the world's religions come near to meeting these two requirements.

Keeping it positive

What I don't want to do here is take a negative excursion into what I think is wrong with some of the communications that claim to come from God. It's an easy and unprofitable process, knocking down the things we don't believe, instead of explaining the things we do. So I'm going to keep this positive. I'm simply going to home in on the **one** communication among the four world religions that has **all** the right credentials. The collection of communications that we call the Bible is the one most likely to be of supernatural origin. A sweeping statement, but let me explain.

To begin with, it has age on its side and historically has been more widespread than others. It also has a global rather than a more culturally defined message. It speaks with the authoritative voice of a Creator, and stays within the bounds of what is feasible rather than straying into what is fanciful. On these criteria alone it is the front runner. Added to which, the Bible tells us far more than we could know or work out for ourselves. And, much as some scientists, not all of them, denigrate the Bible, real science is not in conflict with what it says.

Also its production evidently has far more than a human hand in it. What makes me say this?

Would you believe me?
If I wrote something down and told you it was the Word of God, then you'd very likely think I was mad or kidding you. You'd probably politely excuse yourself and go looking for some easier company. And I wouldn't blame you. You wouldn't believe me for an instant. So why should anyone believe that the people who wrote the Bible actually wrote the Word of God? They were people like us. It's quite a lot to swallow to say that what they wrote was God's Word, a communication from the Creator of the universe. And yet for centuries, millions of people have accepted the Bible as such. Why would they do that? It seems to go against all reason. Though, of course, weight of numbers alone doesn't guarantee truth.

Let's try another tack. What if I was a respected spiritual teacher in my community, generally level-headed, not given to making wild statements, and I said that something I had written was the Word of God? You might pause briefly, but you'd probably still walk away. You'd guess I wasn't thinking straight. Okay, but what if several people who knew me well accepted that what I'd written was the Word of God? You'd think, maybe, that people can be very gullible, but it might halt you for a minute or two more.

And what if the things I'd written also described a way of life that actually worked, which made good sense as a philosophy for living, and had a timeless quality about it. And when you tried living experimentally in the way it described, in that spirit of open-mindedness for which you pride yourself, you found that it brought some meaning to your existence, and a level of peace of mind you'd never known before. You might begin to think it possible that what I'd written could have been given to me from a higher source. Finally, you also noticed that some of the things I'd foretold in my writing concerning local and global events had turned out exactly as I'd said. Putting all this together you might well concede that my claim, that what I had written was the Word of God, didn't sound so crazy after all.

But there are more of us

Now imagine that there were around forty other people just like me, all of whom could match my profile as a professed writer of God's Word. And now see in your mind's eye a group of dedicated people taking care of the writings that we had all produced and putting them together as one book. Moving me out of the picture, and inserting a succession of inspired spiritual teachers, and that pretty much describes the development of the Bible as a book written by men but which is actually the Word of God. What at first sight seems far-fetched becomes reasonable when you take account of how it came about.

One of the very things you'd think would cast doubt on the authenticity of the Bible, actually gives it more credibility: the fact that it's not the work of one person like most religious texts. It was not the product of a single religious teacher: not of Moses or David or John or Paul. It is the combined output of around forty writers, all claiming to have written under the inspiration of God. That's not normally how books happen. It would almost certainly be fatal to the flow and cohesion of the finished product. Especially when you know that most of these forty or so writers weren't contemporaries. Some of them didn't even occupy the same century as others. Some of them didn't even occupy the same millennium as others! They were spread across sixteen hundred years. As I say, that's not normally how books happen.

Can you imagine a collection across the centuries of pieces by, say, William Shakespeare, Jane Austin, Charles Dickens, J R R Tolkien, J K Rowling and a few others – can you imagine that book ever achieving a unified plotline, let alone having a few characters in common? I can't. But those are writers of fictional tales, and to get the analogy closer we'd have to find writers on religion and the human experience from across the centuries. People far more likely to disagree. And another thing…

Not writers
Something else unusual about the writers of the Bible is that most of them weren't actually writers. Writing wasn't something many of them generally did. They were kings and courtiers, soldiers and shepherds, herdsmen and fishermen, legislators and statesmen, priests and prophets. One was a tax collector, another was a doctor, and another was an ex-scholar and tentmaker. Hardly any were professional scribes.

Put it all together
So, bringing all this together, we have a book, the Bible, that was written over a period of sixteen hundred years by around forty people from over a dozen walks of life, few of whom were actually writers. Oh, and I should mention that these forty-odd people were spread across the continents of Asia and Europe, from Rome to Babylon. These people were separated by time, location, and social status. And yet the Bible they produced is not a collection of disparate works, bound together as an anthology of writings by various authors, it is a single book, narrating a single, epic account.

The claims of its individual contributors, that they were relaying the Word of God, begin to look credible. The epic that they have produced is just the kind of thing we should be looking for in a communication from a Creator who wants to tell us the point of it all. And the unusual and unlikely manner of its production strongly suggests a supernatural hand behind it.

The Bible is the work of a **Creator**, a Being who is **creative**, that is – a Being who knows how to put drama and human interest into His message for us. The Bible is not just a prosaic list of do's and don'ts; it's a message for humankind woven into the vibrant story of our creation, development and destiny. It tells us our story through history and poetry, prophecy and wisdom. It is the work of a supremely creative mind, which tells us, incidentally, why we ourselves are so creative. We are made in His likeness, which is why we produce and love art, music, literature and so many other forms of artistic expression. There is no real place in 'natural selection' and 'the survival of the fittest' for the development of the arts. Our creativity comes, more reasonably, from something that is a part of the nature with which we have been created.

However...

Although we have this creative, expressive side to our nature, there is another, darker side to us as well. We'll have more to say about that later. But this is probably a good place to give some thought to the darker side of this world in general. There is a lot wrong with this world. And all the pain and suffering here is probably one of the chief sources of doubt about the God of the Bible, who portrays Himself as a loving Being. This is something we have to make some kind of sense of and can't ignore.

If it doesn't bother you, if you have somehow reconciled the existence of a God of love with a world of pain, then please skip the next chapter. Probably, though, it's something that tiptoes around the back corridors of your mind even if you're a believer, let alone if you're an agnostic or an atheist. It's certainly something I have struggled with over the years. The big issue here, though, is not whether we can arrive at an absolutely conclusive answer, but whether the lack of one is sufficient to invalidate all that is shouting 'yes' to there being a God. Let's give it some thought.

8 What's wrong with everyone?

If God is so good, why is the world He created so bad? It's a good question, and the lack of a good answer turns a lot of people away from religion. So many horrendous things occur in this world, sometimes even in the name of religion, that the idea of it being presided over by an all-knowing, all-wise, all-loving God, seems out of the question. We hear it said when something like a school shooting happens, how could God allow such a thing? It doesn't add up at all, does it? Not only does this kind of thing turn people away from religion, it can make it seriously hard for those who are already religious to cope with believing in God. At one time I'd have put my own hand up to that one.

C. S. Lewis addressed the issue in *The Problem of Pain*, and it's worth reading his thoughts in that book. The problem with Lewis, however, is that he believed in the devil, and that coloured some of his thinking. For reasons that I'll explain later I don't believe such a supernatural being exists. We're capable enough of generating all the evil in this world without supernatural help. And the Bible confirms that we are. That being the case, we are left wondering why God allows it.

Let's take a walk
But, for the moment, let's take a walk. Join me on a street somewhere on the edge of town. It's a nice day for it. And I need to stretch my legs. As we're walking down the street we notice that the houses aren't in good shape. Some have broken windows. Some have doors hanging off their hinges or tiles missing from their roofs. Some have front drives where the paving bricks are broken up or missing. Here and there, fences are down or damaged. We take all this in as we walk.

Now, on noticing these things, would you turn to me after a while and say, 'Why ever did the architect design houses like this?'

Would I then turn to you and say, 'I was just thinking the same thing myself? And why on earth did the builders put them up like this?'

I'm pretty sure we'd both know that architects don't produce working drawings showing broken windows, doors off hinges and tiles missing from roofs. And much as those in my industry get criticised sometimes, builders don't actually build them like that.

We would know, as we walked past those houses, that they were originally designed and built without those defects. We'd know that they once looked good, and people were happy to live in them. We'd realise that since then the houses have become dilapidated. For some reason, be it neglect, vandalism, or whatever, they have fallen into this poor condition. That's the logical way to think about what we see. And this is how we should be thinking when we look at this world. We shouldn't look at the present state of things and wonder why God made a world like this. He didn't.

Something happened
When God had finished His work of Creation, He, in a sense, stepped back to admire it, and pronounced it *'very good'*. (Genesis 1:32) I don't think He could do that now. In fact, when He looks at this world now, He deplores the evil He sees just as we do, only more so because He can see it all, and we can only see a fraction of it. This isn't the world as He originally designed and built it. It's a world that's fallen into disrepair. And whether you accept the account of Adam and Eve as reality or allegory, either way, it was certainly given to us to tell us that something went wrong. Something happened back then to change everything from its original state of being *'very good'* to its present state of not being so good. So if you have the feeling that things shouldn't be like this, then you're absolutely right.

It doesn't take a misanthrope to notice that there is a bad streak in us all. Some people even take delight in having it. Proverbs 4:16 sums them up like this: *'For they sleep not, except they have done* mischief; and their sleep is taken away, unless they cause some to fall.'* The worst kinds of people lose sleep over it, if they haven't harmed anyone lately, says the Proverb wryly. Most of us, though, aren't so bad. At best we're more like the Apostle Paul, who did all in his power to overcome his bad side. But even he had only partial success. The rest of us are somewhere in between Paul and the sleepless ones who haven't hurt anyone lately.

Many of us will relate to something Paul wrote in a letter to the believers in his day: *'For the good that I would I do not: but the evil which I would not, that I do.'* (Romans 7:19) You might expect someone known as Saint Paul to be perfect, but he clearly wasn't according to this (and we'll have something to say later about why some people are referred to as saints in the Bible). However hard Paul tried to do only what was good, he found it impossible. Equally, however hard he tried to stop doing wrong, he couldn't manage that either. That doesn't mean he was unusually bad. He was better than most people at handling our wayward nature. But by his own admission he fell short, and he wanted to make it clear that, essentially, he was just the same as everyone else, and that he failed sometimes.

But that wasn't the main purpose of Paul's confession. More than that, he wanted to tell us **why** we do wrong things, or why we sin, and what we can do about it. We'll get back to what he said in a moment.

We all know as well as Paul did that life's a bit of a battle. Knowing the areas in our lives that need attention, we're trying to be better fathers or mothers, better husbands or wives, better workers, better citizens, better friends and colleagues, or just better people generally than we've been so far. You name it, you probably feel you could or should be doing it better than you are. You make some progress, but you easily drop back again. Time and again you fail in certain ways, and it frustrates you. There are things you dislike or even hate about yourself, yet you have little or no success in dealing with them. You've tried so often to overcome some weakness, some failure, some habit, some fear, some phobia, some addiction, but it's still with you, and seems like it might always be.

Welcome to the club

On top of all that, you're probably telling yourself that your problems are unique to you. Other people aren't troubled by these things. Or not so badly as you are. They don't have your character flaws, or your doubts, fears, and insecurities. Truth is, though, that you're pretty much the same as most other people. What you feel about yourself is the normal human condition. Some people may be better at dealing with it than you; and others may be worse. Some may be better at hiding it, but we're all pretty much the same deep down. There's a story told by one of the ancient Greek philosophers that someone once rushed into a crowded assembly room shouting frantically 'All is known! All is known!' and everyone fled in panic. The room emptied. A guilty conscience seems like the default setting for us. Because we all have things to feel bad about.

Fundamentally flawed

But why is that? Do you ever wonder why we should all be like this? What is it about us humans? Your dog, if you have one, doesn't get dispirited because its bark isn't quite what it could be, or because it had a row with your neighbour's cat the other day. Your dog never feels it fails at being at dog. Failure is a peculiarly human trait. No doubt it's a result of us having a more sophisticated level of self-awareness. That's why your dog isn't so bothered.

But why doesn't being more aware make us happier? It should do. It certainly gives us the propensity to be far happier. But, annoyingly, at the same time as alerting us to much that is good, our higher level of awareness can easily sabotage our happiness by drawing our attention to all that's wrong with us and with our world. Solomon, who was wiser and more aware than most people, lamented this sad fact of life when he wrote: *'For in much* wisdom is much grief: and he that increaseth knowledge increaseth sorrow.'* (Ecclesiastes 1:18) He was talking about the grief that comes from increasing our knowledge and understanding of this world, of the human condition, which cannot be fixed by human effort and ingenuity. It can be dispiriting to learn that no amount of well-meaning endeavour or scientific advancement can fix the flaws in our nature that are the real problem with our planet.

Solomon thought he could use his great wisdom to fix things, but it only served to show him that it can't be done. He realised that he had to leave it to God. Increasing our knowledge and understanding of God's Secret is the antidote to such despair for us, as it was for Solomon. This is where we learn that God does have the problem in hand, and that He has already set the solution in motion.

There's no getting away from the fact that we are fundamentally flawed, both individually and collectively. Almost everything we do to improve things, to create a better self or a better world, tends to go awry. There's something pulling us in the wrong direction all the while, either from inside ourselves, or from others around us. It has characterised the history of our planet. If someone invents the wheel to benefit us, someone else will put it on a chariot and go to war with us. If someone creates amazingly clean nuclear energy, someone else will build nuclear bombs to threaten us. If someone builds an internet for us to enjoy unprecedented levels of communication, someone else will use it to spread lies or steal from us. Everything is sabotaged by our nature. So much time, money and energy are wasted in our societies, trying to defend ourselves from the general baseness of our own human nature. Why?

Original or evolved?

The Bible puts it down to what some religious people refer to as original sin. This refers to the failure of Adam and Eve in the Garden of Eden. The first humans disobeyed God and it led to a change in their nature. They'd been created and pronounced *'very good'* along with everything else God had made. But after sinning, their very-good-ness was downgraded to the flawed nature that they subsequently passed on to the rest of us. Now we're all subject to sin, disease and death. That's original sin. And whether you view Adam and Eve as history or allegory the concept of original sin is a far more probable explanation of our plight than you might think. It looks even better when parked alongside evolutionary theory on the subject of morality.

From an evolutionary standpoint, our tendency to do wrong has developed over millennia along with everything else about us. We've evolved into a mixture of good and bad: morality and immorality are both products of evolution, and apparently equally valid aspects of us. As T. H. Huxley once said in a lecture: 'The thief and the murderer follow nature just as much as the philanthropist' (cited by John Gray in *Seven Types of Atheism*). If we have evolved, then both the best and the worst in us are legitimate expressions of our evolved humanity. Calling them right and wrong is inappropriate and we shouldn't condemn or punish those who would harm us, steal from us, or abuse us in any way, because they are simply being who they are, just as decent folk are just being who they are. That almost seems like a reasonable conclusion. Except we know it isn't.

Off the rails?
Nowadays evolutionists and humanists would probably say that we've reached a point in our cognitive development where we're in a position to make sound judgements about right and wrong. They will no doubt see the supposed emergence of an awareness of right and wrong as part of the evolutionary process. And that promoting the right will eventually save us from the wrong and keep humanity safe on its path of betterment. But the repercussions are worth considering.

If evolution really has been happening to us all these years without our knowledge, then I would think that all the while we didn't know that it was happening to us, we would have progressed in the right direction. But now that we're able to know what's going on, we can interfere and inadvertently thwart the process or derail it completely. The decision that good and nice is better than aggressive and ruthless seems to fly in the face of how evolution has supposedly worked until now. Should evolutionists really view a more moral species as the way forward? Has humanity evolved sufficiently enough for us to take charge of the evolutionary process? Redirect it, or halt it altogether? Should evolutionists really be taking the helm and steering the ship themselves? Evolutionary theory leads us into these deep and dark waters.

Constants

Science does not have all the answers. And the scientific community is surely aware of that. The last words on subjects like evolutionary biology and cosmology are a long way from being said. Any scientist who believes they already have been said is a stranger to reality. The scientific model of the universe is under constant review, and the current thinking can sometimes change rapidly. If you're pinning your colours to the mast of science, then be prepared to keep moving them. That's not a criticism; it's simply the way it is in the necessarily ongoing process of scientific thinking.

The moral elements of God's Secret outlined in Part Two of this book were first penned by an inspired psalmist around 3,000 years ago. But these elements pre-date the Psalm on which we've based Part Two by a few thousand years more. These principles are constants: they have never required revision, nor will they. They have been the best principles on which people can build their lives from the earliest days of humankind.

What's wrong with us?

Going by what the Bible says, the bad side of our nature will never be eradicated by education or coercion, by suppression or genetic manipulation, or by any other means of our own devising. It will continue to surface however hard we try to push it down. In Bible terminology humankind has been **cursed**, and we can't **un-curse** ourselves. Only God can undo what has been done.

The Apostle Paul referred to this curse as *'sin that dwelleth in me.'* He knew this inclination to sin was a part of his very nature. And he knew that to be true for all of us. Let's go back to what he said in that letter to the church at Rome that we mentioned earlier, where he explained how he felt when he battled with his own waywardness. He not only lamented it, he also told us what causes it, and what can be done about it. *'For I delight in the law of God after the inward man: but I see another law in my members, warring against the law of my mind, and bringing me into captivity to the law of sin which is in my members.'* (Romans 7:22–23)

While we're looking at this, it won't hurt to notice that Paul didn't say he felt the devil was tempting him. He said he felt the pull to do wrong coming from within himself, from his very being, *'in my members'*. This pull towards what's wrong, and failure to stay right is inside us and inescapable. Paul sums up the experience of everyone on the planet who has ever tried to live the righteous life. And in so doing he explains why the world is as it is, why you and I are as we are. We are all wayward by nature. It's simply in us.

But Paul didn't believe we evolved this way. Nor did he give houseroom to any of the theories of his own time about why we are like this. The ancient Greeks weren't so ancient in his day, and their thinking clouded the thinking of his time in much the same way that human philosophy can cloud our thinking today. So Paul didn't tie himself up in knots of doubtful logic over how to deal with what is wrong with us. For him it was straightforward.

Paul firmly believed that Adam was responsible. He believed that Adam and Eve were real people, not allegorical or mythological figures. Earlier in that same letter to the believers at Rome he wrote, *'by one man sin entered into the world, and death by sin; and so death passed upon all men...'* That's where he believed his problem came from. And that's why he believed we all have this problem. One man at the outset of Creation caused a problem that affected everyone. He fouled up the source and the whole river of humanity that flowed from him was polluted. And if it seems disproportionately unfair that the entire human race should suffer for what one man did, then remember that he and Eve **were** the entire human race back then. In Eden it applied to everyone, and it still does apply to everyone. Nothing's changed in that respect.

Down to us

The world is in a mess because of what **we** do, not because of what God **doesn't** do. God has taken a small step back, but at the same time He's told us in His communication to us how to make the best of our situation. Not only make the best of it but ultimately turn our situation around completely.

His Secret, His counsel, is our guide. Collectively we've let it slide and we've created a world of crime, violence, immorality and deceit. A lost world. Collectively we don't want God's solutions, but we are ready to blame Him for the continuation of our problems. And, in addition to this, we refuse to believe in **Him** because of what **we** are doing to this world. Humanity seems to be conflicted, not wanting God to 'meddle' in its affairs, and yet complaining when He doesn't.

I particularly mentioned a school shooting at the beginning of this chapter because of something I'll never forget that was said after one occurred in the US. A reporter, trying to empathise with a Christian woman who'd been personally affected by the tragedy, said to her, 'It must make you wonder why God would let such a thing happen in a school.' The woman looked the reporter in the eye, shook her head, and answered sorrowfully 'They haven't allowed God in schools for years.' Her lament gives voice to what is wrong with our world generally. For the most part, we're not letting God in.

Why does God allow it?

I heard a leading atheist the other day saying God can't be good because He allowed so many children to be swept from their mothers' arms in a great tsunami. Where was God when that happened, he wanted to know indignantly. For him this was reason enough to deny the existence of a loving God. And it sounds like a strong case. It is heartbreaking to think on such things. But I can think of an even stronger case that might be brought, because I believe the flood that occurred in Noah's time is an historical fact. And at that time God was not just **allowing** thousands of men, women and children to be killed through inaction, but causing it. So why did God **cause** that to happen?

The reason given was *'And God saw that the wickedness of man was great in the earth, and that every imagination of the thoughts of his heart was only evil continually.'* (Genesis 6:5) God also saw that *'the earth was filled with violence... and, behold, it was corrupt; for all flesh had corrupted his way upon the earth.'* (Genesis 6:11–12) We might say that for the God of love the world had almost become unlovable. I say almost, because in the righteous man Noah He saw something worth saving. The world had become an appalling place and it was going nowhere so God almost ended it.

Noah and his family were most likely believers before the flood came. Certainly by the time they set foot on dry ground again they would have been a family of believers. What they'd been through together, and what Noah, *'a preacher of righteousness,'* had taught them in the many months they'd spent afloat, would have made them all believers for certain. But when it was over, and as the family grew larger and spread further afield, for many of them their belief in God waned. The truth of God, His Secret, was lost to all but a comparative few of the ever-growing population. The majority went their own way, forgetting God, inventing their own gods and beliefs, or believing in nothing but their own imagined wisdom.

So the majority moved away from God's wisdom, care and protection. As time went on children were born never even knowing of God's existence. Cultures were spawned where He was forgotten. And the world reverted to being an arena of wars, discord, crimes and corruption once again – and to an appalling place where children are torn from their mothers' arms by tsunamis. But God has promised He will not flood the earth again as He did in Noah's day. However bad it gets, out of love, He will see His purpose through with this world despite mankind's obstinate refusal to be a part of it. And He has left His Secret in the world for as many as will discover it.

Are people really so bad?

It's not that we are all irretrievably rotten to the core. When Paul said, as he did in that letter to the Roman believers, *'For I know that in me (that is, in my flesh,)* **dwelleth no good thing***: for to will is present with me; but how to perform that which is good I find not'* (Romans 7:18) – when he said that, he wasn't writing himself off, and all the rest of us in the process, as completely bad, without a trace of goodness in us. Because if there were no goodness whatsoever in Paul, he would not have been lamenting his badness, he would have been embracing it.

He was making a distinction in this verse between his human nature, which he called his *'flesh'*, and his spiritual desire to do good. He was making the point that naturally speaking it is hopeless for us to try and defeat the curse of our human nature. Every scrap of resentment, fear, anger, anxiety and doubt that we feel within ourselves; every bad thought, desire and reaction that we have; these are all generated by our sin-cursed nature. We can't eradicate it all. We must face the truth, as Paul did (and it can come as quite a relief to acknowledge it) that *'no good thing'* dwells in our *'flesh'*. We aspire to overcome the *'flesh'*, but we can't because it's what we are. The only solution is a spiritual one.

A 'God-shaped hole'
There is a spiritual potential in us all. It links with the moral compass we spoke of earlier. It manifests as feelings that things ought to be better than they are, and that there is more to life than we generally experience. It has been called a 'God-shaped hole' in our lives which nothing but God can fill. This is why He has given the world His communication, the Bible. By this means we can learn His Secret, fill that 'hole', and bring our spiritual propensity fully alive. His Word points us in the right direction.

The spiritual way the Bible speaks of is essentially one of love. When we act from love – when we do good, and when we look for the good in others – we act not from our human nature, we *'walk in the spirit',* as Paul described it. We act from that spiritual side of us that is latent in us all. It can lead us to do better things for others and ourselves. The reality, though, is that for so many people this spiritual propensity remains largely untapped; it is underdeveloped, and often misinformed and misdirected. The reason for this is because people are constantly trying to fit other things into that 'God-shaped hole', which don't fit properly. And never will. Instead of opening themselves up fully to the truths about life and love that only God can provide, they develop a narrow form of spirituality based on limited human ideas of what works best.

But aren't there plenty of good people?
People can be very loving. They can do lots of good things prompted by a general feeling that this is how they ought to act. The day-to-day kindness of many people is admirable. The self-sacrifice and dedication of some people can be of a very high order. It seems harsh to say that so many people's spirituality is untapped, underdeveloped and misinformed, but in truth it is. Because what they have falls a long way short of the love revealed in God's Secret. Yes, most people we know are very nice, kindly people, who do many good works, great works sometimes, and we should be thankful and grateful for all that they do. The world

is undoubtedly a better place for it. But what they achieve is of only limited value and duration.

This is what the wise man Solomon lamented when he said that everything done *'under the sun'* is *'vanity and vexation of spirit'*. (Ecclesiastes 1:14) *'Vanity'* here means 'short-lived and of little worth', like a puff of vapour. He meant that whatever we do in our human, earthbound, *'under the sun'* state is of limited value and limited duration. Even our best efforts are futile by this reckoning. We must look elsewhere for something of true worth and endurance. Solomon summed it up like this: *'Let us hear the conclusion of the whole matter: Fear God, and keep his commandments: for this is the whole duty of man.'* (Ecclesiastes 12:13) In essence, he concluded that the only way of escape from a fleeting and futile life is to be God-fearing and righteous. That sounds familiar. He's directing us to God's Secret.

Only by acquainting ourselves with, and living according to God's Secret, will we ever overcome the curse of our nature, in which there is nothing good. Aligning our efforts and aspirations with God's Secret connects us with what is eternally good and right. This is how we put what truly belongs there into that 'God shaped hole' in our lives. And we become related to God's plan and purpose for this world.

An eye-opener

That said, all the while we have human nature we will not achieve perfection, nor does God expect that of us because, as Paul found, however spiritual we become, our human nature will still frustrate our best intentions to be good. As Jesus said once, when remarking on the weakness of his disciples, *'...the spirit indeed is willing, but the flesh is weak.'* (Matthew 26:41) For the time being, we are held back by the weakness of our *'flesh'*. The fact that Paul was more spiritual than most meant that he felt the problem more keenly. As a rule, the harder we try, the more strongly the 'flesh' will resist our efforts. We cannot win. But we don't have to. Once we understand God's Secret, we have the spiritual good sense to seek reassurance in the grace of God, as Paul did.

The knowledge that there is nothing good in our fleshly nature is something of an eye-opener. It makes us realise that striving to be truly good, and expecting to attain moral perfection by an effort of will, or through following another man's or woman's prescribed system of thought, or whatever, is a path of disillusionment at best, and at worst it could lead to depression and mental illness. Our imperfections cannot be dealt with by our own best efforts. However, God's Secret shows us how His grace can deal with them for us. We'll say more about this in Part Two. God didn't bring Creation to a halt when Adam failed, because He foresaw that much good would eventually come of this world. As we said, He's taken only a small step back. He's still very much present, and He has promised that He won't allow us to continue messing up this world indefinitely.

Stay with me for something remarkable

I realise all this talk of Adam and Eve as our true ancestors may be stretching your credulity to breaking point, but stay with me please and you'll see something remarkable. We're going to look at something of the beauty of divine symmetry and of divine logic, and of God's unshakeable love for His Creation. Whether you chose to take this on board is entirely up to you of course. But read on, I encourage you. You can always put this on hold at the back of your mind if you wish, while you enjoy the uncovering of God's Secret which begins in chapter ten.

What follows immediately is some intriguing material that you've most likely never come across before. It's not the kind of thing that usually comes up when religion is discussed.

9 THE SOLUTION

First we need to go back to Paul's letter to the believers at Rome. We've seen the reason he gave for the origin of everyone's waywardness. He blamed Adam. You may recall we said that he not only gave us the reason, but he also gave us the solution. In exasperation Paul said: Who will deliver me from this? What's to be done? Is there any way out? He said it in frustration, because he felt the problem so keenly, but he also said it rhetorically, because he already knew the answer. He went on to thank God for Jesus. Somehow Jesus was his answer. And somehow Jesus is the answer for everyone. To understand why this should be we need to go far, far back in time. We need to go back to a time even before Adam.

There are many remarkable verses in the Book of Revelation, but there are few quite so remarkable as the one we're about to look at. Revelation 13:8 describes Jesus as *'the Lamb slain from the foundation of the world'*. From the context it's clear this is about Jesus. Twenty-eight times in the Book of Revelation the word 'Lamb' is capitalised as a reference to Jesus. Here we're told that he was *'slain from the foundation of the world'*. Which can't be right, surely?

When does history tell us he was crucified? Around 2,000 years ago. So why is this verse saying that it happened at the outset of Creation? Or is it really? Something else is going on here. Because the next verse says, a little cryptically: *'If any man have an ear, let him hear.'* We all have *'an ear'*, two of them usually, but this means that we need to have *'an ear'* for what's really being said. Tune in properly and get on the right wavelength. It's a nudge to tell us that something else is meant.

We know Jesus' death occurred around 2,000 years ago, but this verse from Revelation is saying that **there is a sense** in which it also happened when the world began. Before I came across this verse I used to wonder why a God who knows all things would proceed with a Creation He knew would fail. He knew Adam would fall short, and that the world would be blighted with sin, disease and death, so why would He press on with it? Why not abandon it, start again, or go somewhere else and do something that would work a whole lot better? The reason is that God, even as He went about the creation of the world, already had Jesus in mind as the one who was going to put right what Adam did. That's what the verse in Revelation is getting at. Jesus is *'the Lamb slain from the foundation of the world'* because he was crucified in God's mind from the very beginning. Otherwise God wouldn't have initiated the Creation.

Two Adams

God knew Adam would fail, so He planned for a second Adam who wouldn't fail. Jesus is referred to as the second Adam in the Bible. Both of them are referred to as sons of God, though one of them was created and the other was born. *'The first man Adam was made a living soul; the last Adam was made a quickening spirit.'* (1 Corinthians 15:45) One was made from the dust of the earth and animated with the breath of life; the other was born as a result of the action of the Spirit of God upon Mary his mother.

God had no intention of abandoning His purpose with the world. He knew that by proceeding He would achieve something better. Where we might have seen failure, God saw opportunity. Try to imagine for a moment how it could have turned out for this world had Adam not failed. Within a decade or two the idyllic world established in the Garden of Eden would probably have spread across the globe. The Adamic race would have been healthy, intelligent, industrious and long-lived. They would doubtless have enjoyed lives of peace and prosperity in harmony with God and nature. What could have been better than that? Why not give up on Adam and Eve, carry out the threat to end their lives if they failed, and restart Creation with a new couple who wouldn't go wrong? In a way, that's what God did with His second Adam.

The solution

But let's go back to that question: What could be better than that – than the idyllic world God originally had in mind? How could that be improved? It looks like the best outcome for the world.

Here are some suggestions:
- It could be improved by a world of people who deeply appreciate what they've been given, because they have been rescued from a **bad** world.

- It could be improved by a world of people who have learned to love and trust God in trying circumstances; who have developed their characters through adversity; and who have demonstrated their love in ways that people who have known only an idyllic world could never have done.

- It could be improved by a world of people who have learned about love from experiencing a world where it wasn't the norm.

- It could be improved by a world of people whose love for God and for one another is **real**, because they've had the choice to not love – unlike the population in the original plan who would have been predisposed to love.

- It could be improved by a world populated with people who have chosen it and longed for it rather than having just been given it.

In short, how much more God could love a people who have loved and trusted Him through the experience of human nature in a human world, than He could love those who'd known only the undemanding ease and safety of an idyllic world?

We might also take into account that one of God's supreme attributes is creativity. Consider how much more His creativity can flourish in the lives of humanity in a world where billions of diverse and disparate stories are interwoven! Far more than in an idyllic world where all lives would be safe and similar. The failure of

God's Secret

Adam brought about a situation where God's creativity as well as His love could flourish in the lives of so many people. We'll say more on this when we talk about the work of the angels in Part Two.

It's hardly surprising we're told that these are *'things the angels desire to look into.'* (1 Peter 1:12) It seems certain that what God has done here on earth is unprecedented. Unique. Even the angels look on in fascination at what is happening on our small planet. There is the thought that they themselves may have come from a world where everything went unfailingly right. So they don't have the benefits of having come through the kind of experience we are going through.

Divine symmetry

God introduced a second Adam into the picture in the person of Jesus Christ. And we have some divine symmetry: one Adam the reverse image of the other:

First Adam	made very good	disobeyed	brought death
Second Adam *Jesus*	made mortal	obeyed	brought life

Though it's not so much divine symmetry as divine fairness and justice at work. What the table shows is that:

- Adam, **without** the pull of human nature still did the wrong thing and brought death to humanity.

- Jesus, **with** the pull of human nature still did the right thing and brought life to humanity.

The Apostle Paul summed it up succinctly when he said: *'For as in Adam all die, even so in Christ shall all be made alive.'* (1Corinthians 15:22) If we wanted to sum up the entire message of the Bible in one brief sentence I don't believe we could get closer than that. But a word of caution is needed: we have to be

The solution

careful how we understand that verse. From a casual glance, it looks as if it's telling us that through Adam we were all doomed to die, but now because of Christ nobody dies, and we're all going to live forever. Appealing as that is, it's not what Paul meant.

Being *'in Adam'* and being *'in Christ'* work differently. One is automatic; the other is optional. Being *'in Adam'*, which means being **in** the lineage or family of Adam, is automatic. We don't have a choice about being descended from him. It happens at birth for everyone. But being *'in Christ'*, which means being **in** his family as adopted children of the same Heavenly Father – that is a choice we make for ourselves.

Not complicated

So we have a choice. And, incidentally, I'm not asking anyone reading this book, and who isn't a believer, to make a choice **right now**! That's not possible for you unless you already know a lot more than we've covered so far. I'm simply showing you the way to God's Secret, as revealed in His communication. What you do with what you learn throughout this book is for you to decide in your own good time. I hope, of course, that you'll grasp the truth of it with both hands and reap the full benefit of following through on it someday soon. For the moment, though, all I ask is that you sit back and see what you make of it. Nothing more.

As I was saying, we have a choice. We either line up behind the first Adam or the second Adam. We can stay where we are, or we can escape to a better place. God hasn't left us without a future because of what the first Adam did. He has given us the opportunity to connect with an endless future. And making the change isn't complicated. It doesn't involve any great feats of mental exertion. There are no volumes of theology to struggle through. It could hardly be simpler. In fact, if any of what I'm saying in this book makes God's message sound complicated, then that's my fault, not yours, and certainly not the Bible's. God's message to us is not prefaced with the words 'for theologians only'. He sent it for all of us to read, understand, and enjoy. But if you're new to it, or if you're new to seeing what it's really all about, then some of what follows in Part Two will help you to connect the dots. Though, however you're getting on with this book, once you've finished it I suggest you read it again with the benefit of having more of the overall picture.

The essentials

If we decide to make the change from Adam to Christ, there are certain things we have to do. It doesn't happen by merely deciding to do it. Some sectors of Christianity claim that this is all it takes, but that's not what the Bible says. It's not **that** simple; but it is fairly simple. The requirements are easy, logical, and seriously beneficial. The three essential steps are these: believe, be baptised, and then try to live a God-fearing and righteous life.

That last one will ring a few bells as God's Secret. And although understanding and living by God's Secret is the third step, it's also very much a part of step one. Because our beliefs are developed from learning and living God's Secret. So we're kind of starting where we want to finish. But we can't fully put into practice what we gain from our accumulation of beliefs until we take the step of baptism, which symbolises and confirms our adoption into the family of God, as we'll explain below.

The Apostle Paul speaks of us being *'baptized into Jesus Christ'.* (Romans 6:3) Without baptism we are still *'in Adam'* and without the hope and assurance that being *'in Christ'* brings. Baptism is the step we take to show we're serious about God's Secret. It is the gateway to embracing it fully. It puts us in a Father-son or Father-daughter relationship with God and begins a relationship that has the potential to last for eternity.

Step One

Step one is logical. We first need to believe in God and Jesus. We wouldn't even be considering making the change unless we believed in God and in His Son. Though we need to believe in Jesus as more than just an historical figure, or even as a great

The solution

teacher and prophet. We must believe in him as the Son of God, the world's saviour, the second Adam, and as our own **personal** saviour. God wants us personally involved with His plans for the world through Jesus. He wants to include us. He doesn't want mere spectators. So we make the change to being *'in Christ'*, because we see him, and appreciate him, as our escape from the doomed lineage of Adam. But what about step two? What about baptism?

Taking the plunge

You will have heard of baptism, but you probably won't know what it's all about. If we choose to make the switch from Adam to Jesus, then to signify and settle that, we go through a symbolic death and rebirth called baptism. The word derives from an old Greek word *baptizo* which means to dip or immerse something, usually a piece of cloth you want to dye another colour. The Bible speaks of us being *'baptised into Christ'*, because that's the way we signify that we have become *'in Christ'* and we've joined his family as his brothers and sisters.

When he died, Christ suffered the consequences of being born in Adam. But because he was totally sinless and didn't deserve the consequences as we do, God raised him from the dead. God is just. He would not punish a man who'd done nothing wrong. He then made Jesus His second Adam, exactly as He'd planned from the very beginning, to set the world back on course. And now, through baptism, we can associate ourselves with the saving work of Jesus by going through a symbolic death and resurrection. We make a new start, as he did.

This is why you'll hear the term 'born again' used of believers. It's because they begin a new life *'in Christ'* after their symbolic death and resurrection through baptism. To be born again *'in Christ'* is not only the result of an emotional and intellectual decision; it's also the result of engaging in the ceremony of baptism. Without that essential occurrence, we can't properly be said to be born again.

Baptism puts believers on a new path. They were destined to die *'in Adam'* along with everyone else, but through baptism they are considered, in the divine view, to have already died. If they stay on the new path (which isn't difficult, it's a pleasure, as you'll learn), then, when actual death occurs they will one day be raised to eternal life in a world made new. This is promised to all who are faithful *'in Christ'*.

The sleep of death

The death of a baptised believer is referred to biblically not as death at all, but as sleep (more of that in Part Two). Sleep isn't used euphemistically to soften the harsh reality of death. Sleep is closer to the reality. To God believers are merely sleeping until He wakes them with the call to resurrection (again, more in Part Two). So baptism is the prescribed way of marking and establishing our induction into Christ. There is an agreeable logic and suitability to it all.

By the way, the sprinkling of a few drops of water over the head of a baby, known as christening, isn't baptism, and it's no substitute for it. It doesn't properly symbolise death and rebirth. Neither has an infant accomplished step one. It hasn't come to a belief in God and made an informed choice to be *'in Christ'*. Christening is neither sanctioned nor mentioned in the Bible. Baptism is, and it has always been, a brief but complete submersion in water, following an affirmation of belief in God and salvation through Christ.

Sacrifice

Baptism is voluntarily undertaken, and so was the death and resurrection that it symbolises. Jesus **chose** to die on the cross. It was God's will, but it was Jesus' decision. This raises the important issue of sacrifice. Why did God require it? Why did Jesus have to undergo a harrowing execution? The word 'excruciating' relates to the extreme pain of crucifixion. Literally it means 'from', or 'of the cross'. Jesus fervently prayed to God on the evening before the crucifixion that it might somehow be

The solution

possible for him not to have to go through with it. Even so, he never wavered in his willingness to go ahead, if that was what his Heavenly Father asked of him. And God did ask it of him.

But why? Isn't human sacrifice a barbaric practice?

Jesus' death was not human sacrifice in the abhorrent way that we usually, and rightly, think of it. He was human and he was sacrificed, but what happened was a long way from the appalling rites of past civilizations such as the Aztecs. Their angry gods were appeased and the safety of the nation secured, they believed, by offering multiple human sacrifices around the year. In the Bible the worshippers of a god called Molech sacrificed their children to him. God denounced this as a totally unacceptable pagan practice. He would not tolerate it among His own chosen people, the nation of Israel. So would God be guilty of such a dreadful thing Himself? No, He wouldn't.

If we go back to the divine symmetry of the two Adams, we can see that Jesus' death was necessary to resolve the situation and undo what the first Adam had set in motion. For all those who line up behind the second Adam become related to an Adam who didn't fail. But that hardly seems reason enough for Jesus to die, although it was certainly a part of completing the symmetry. The main reason, however, is that God wanted to show us how much He loves us, by making the greatest sacrifice He could – His own Son. But He didn't force it upon Jesus. That would have been wrong. This is how Christ's death differed significantly from pagan human sacrifice. It was not done fearfully and superstitiously, to placate an angry god; it was done lovingly and caringly to show us the supreme love of the true God.

The sacrifice of Jesus could only have been meaningful if it was willingly done, and for the right reasons. Jesus knew exactly what he was doing and that he was the second Adam. He'd read so many prophecies about himself in his Father's communication. Jesus had the power to free himself and walk away from the

God's Secret

Roman soldiers, the Roman governor, the Jewish authorities, and anyone else who stood in his way if he chose. But he chose not to. And his Father knew he would not walk away. Jesus wanted to play his part in setting humanity back on track.

The reason is quite staggering.
Still you might think that there was no need for Jesus' death. **Whatever** the reason for it, God could have arranged to do things differently and spared His Son. He is **God** after all. But there is a reason that made Jesus' sacrifice essential. And for every other reason I've come across for Jesus' sacrifice, it could be argued that God could have set things up differently. But not for the following reason. This made it necessary.

Proof of love
John 3:16, one of the best-known verses in the Bible begins: *'For God so loved the world, that he gave his only begotten Son…'.* Why is the second part of that statement presented as if it proves the first? How does it follow that God gave Christ to die **because** He loves the world so much? The reason most would give is that His only begotten Son was the most precious thing God had, and He was willing to sacrifice Him for us to show His love. No doubt that figures significantly in what happened. But it still leaves the question of why God would seemingly bind Himself by rules of His own making and leave Himself no choice. Was there no other way God could have shown us that He loved us, than putting Jesus through that ordeal? You might think God capable of finding a way. But I believe that verse points to another, greater reason that Christ died. And why it was the only way.

This is a personal view. But for some years it has been the only reason I've found that means God **had** to sacrifice His Son. There is another verse in John's Gospel that says, *'Greater love hath no man than this, that a man lay down his life for his friends.'* (John 15:13) No one would argue with that. Jesus himself said it. And he showed that **greater** love by giving his life not just for his immediate friends, but for all those who would benefit from it, by

The solution

laying down his life to become the second Adam. Other lesser mortals have given their lives and demonstrated this highest form of love, too. There are the occasional heroes among us. We give them medals. But here is the problem, and here is God's solution. Although God **is** love, and He is the great originator and embodiment of love, He was unable to express the highest form of love by giving His own life. God is immortal. He cannot die. But He was able to demonstrate His great love through His Son's death. Let me explain.

God knew a way to express His supreme love for us. He couldn't give His life for us, but He could show, beyond doubt, that He **would** if He **could**. In Jesus, His Son, was a man who perfectly reflected the mind of the Father. They were and are one in mind. Like Father like Son – but in a way closer than any father and son were ever alike. Jesus had the mind of God: he was in perfect harmony with God. That tells us beyond question, that if Jesus was willing to die for humanity, then so was his Father. If Jesus could demonstrate the highest form of love, then it follows that so could his Father, if such a thing were possible.

And it had to be more than theoretical. The only way to prove it beyond doubt was for Jesus to go through with it. For me the fact that Jesus loved us enough to give his life for us indicates that God would do the same if it were possible for Him to do so. They are of one mind, and would certainly be so on such a fundamental issue as their love for humankind.

To my mind, this is the only explanation that cannot be countered with the objection that God could have done things in a way that didn't entail the death of Jesus. When we take into account the things we've just considered, there was no other way. God is love, and Jesus proved it for Him, and for us, by willingly laying down his life to save the world.

Before we end this chapter, and Part One of the book, there's one last thing I want to mention.

The world's greatest love story?

As we've been looking at what the Bible says happened at the beginning of the world, and why the world is the way it is, let's indulge for a moment in a little speculation about something that might have happened in Eden. This in no way changes anything we've already said. But if it is true – and I strongly suspect that it is – then it gives us a truly remarkable insight into what happened between Adam and Eve and the ramifications of it. And I'm not entirely alone in speculating along these lines. The sense of it certainly appeals to me. Maybe it will to you.

It's usually *Romeo and Juliette* that is billed as *The Greatest Love Story Ever*. But the story of Adam and Eve could surpass it by a long, long way. Because it just might have helped determine the fate of the world in a way that has almost escaped notice.

The account in Genesis, which we've been referring to a lot, tells us that Adam and Eve were made and pronounced *'very good'* along with the rest of Creation. But they were tested to see how good they really were, by being told not to eat the fruit from a particular tree in the Garden of Eden. That tree was called *'the tree of knowledge of good and evil'*. And that might make us think that this narrative should be treated as an allegory. But the news that Jesus along with all his original followers, including those who wrote the New Testament, took it as fact, should be enough to make us reconsider that.

The account in Genesis tells us that Eve was smooth-talked into eating the forbidden fruit. She then gave some to Adam and he ate it too. But strangely the Bible tells us that **Adam** brought sin into the world and not Eve. She surely sinned first. Remember that piece we quoted from the Apostle Paul: *'by one **man** sin entered into the world.'* Shouldn't that be, by one **woman**? As it turns out, no. And the reason for it comes out in something Paul said in another of his letters. This looks like a pointer to what really went on in Eden. Paul says, *'And Adam was not deceived, but the woman being deceived was in the transgression.'* (1 Timothy 2:14)

The solution

It's slightly cryptic, but easy enough to unpack. Paul says that Eve was implicated in the disobedience because she let herself be deceived. But Adam *'was not deceived'*; he took the fruit from her knowing full well what he was doing. Why on earth would he do that? Eve had just been tricked into doing something punishable by death, so why would Adam then take the fruit from her and eat some himself? It seems an astonishingly foolish thing to do.

Unless...

Unless Adam loved Eve so much that he chose to die with her rather than live without her. This seems like quite an assumption. But what other explanation can there be for what he did? I can't think of one. And if that were so, then the ramifications may have been huge – re-directing the history of the world, in fact. Because how could God then proceed to punish them both and end the Creation, as far as they were concerned, when the disobedience of Adam was at the same time a monumental act of selfless love! In a way, the very highest form of love.

Adam had disobeyed God, yes, and there would be consequences, yes, but Adam had also shown himself to be a man of outstanding devotion and character. Was this a contributing factor in God letting things continue? Was it also a situation that God foresaw, and which made Him plan for a second Adam? – knowing He was going to let a failed world continue?

We should factor in, too, the point that in the New Testament, the church is referred to as the bride of Christ. They are the second Adam's wife, or Eve. Jesus died for the church, for his Eve. Which may be an insight into what the first Adam was trying to do for Eve when he took the fruit from her. She was created as Adam's helper, we're told, and some of the reason he brought sin into the world, and not her, was because he was considered responsible for her. Did he perhaps think that by taking the fruit himself, he would deflect the blame from her? Was he trying to give his life for hers? Are the two Adams far more alike than we thought?

This is, as I said, conjecture based on the inference of that one verse in Paul's letter to Timothy. I love where it takes matters, though some may think it takes matters too far. But it's certainly food for thought.

End of Part One

Now we can get on with talking about God's Secret. Though in laying the ground for it we've already become acquainted with some important aspects of it, and that's going to be helpful.

As you'll know from the opening chapters, we're going to be digging for treasure in Psalm 34. God's Secret is not confined to that particular place, though, as we've said, it's woven into the fabric of the entire Bible. It's either staring straight at us, or it's peering through from just under the surface wherever we read. But we've chosen to go to Psalm 34 because it approaches the subject in a direct and systematic way. It takes us quickly to the heart of the matter, in 22 short verses. In fact, as we'll explain in a moment, it is literally an A–Z of God's Secret.

If you came through Part One, rather than heading straight to Part Two, then thanks for staying with me. I hope you're now well enough equipped for the next section. I also hope that by now you feel some of the relish that I do, at the prospect of delving into some of the eye-opening and life-enhancing truths of God's Secret. Delving means digging, of course, which reminds us we have some treasure hunting to do.

PART 2

GOD's SECRET

Psalm 34

1. I will bless the Lord at all times: his praises shall continually be in my mouth.
2. My soul shall make her boast in the Lord: the humble shall hear thereof and be glad.
3. O magnify the Lord with me, and let us exalt his name together.
4. I sought the Lord and he heard me, and delivered me from all my fears.
5. They looked unto him and were lightened: and their faces were not ashamed.
6. This poor man cried, and the Lord heard him, and saved him out of all his troubles.
7. The angel of the Lord encampeth round about them that fear him, and delivereth them.
8. O taste and see that the Lord is good: blessed is the man that trusteth in him.
9. O fear the Lord, ye his saints: for there is no want to them that fear him.
10. The young lions do lack, and suffer hunger: but they that seek the Lord shall not want any good thing.
11. Come, ye children, hearken unto me: I will teach you the fear of the Lord.
12. What man is he that desireth life, and loveth many days, that he may see good?
13. Keep thy tongue from evil, and thy lips from speaking guile.
14. Depart from evil, and do good: seek peace, and pursue it.
15. The eyes of the Lord are upon the righteous, and his ears are open to their cry.
16. The face of the Lord is against them that do evil, to cut off the remembrance of them from the earth.
17. The righteous cry, and the Lord heareth, and delivereth them out of all their troubles.

Psalm 34

18 The Lord is nigh unto them that are of a broken heart; and saveth such as be of a contrite spirit.
19 Many are the afflictions of the righteous: but the Lord delivereth him out of them all.
20 He keepeth all his bones: not one of them is broken.
21 Evil shall slay the wicked: and they that hate the righteous shall be desolate.
22 The Lord redeemeth the soul of his servants: and none of them that trust in him shall be desolate.

10 An A–Z of God's Secret

A short introduction to Psalm 34

Finally, it's time to start unlocking the timeless truths of the ancient wisdom of God's Secret using Psalm 34 as our guide. We've shown the Psalm again on the previous pages for handy reference. And each verse appears at the top of the chapter as we go through the Psalm.

This is a Psalm, or song, written by a talented musician named David, who lived around 1,000 BC. Not only was he a talented musician and composer, he was also a great warrior. It's an unusual combination of talents: someone who could write and perform beautiful music, and who could stand his ground in the thick of a bloody battle. But more than this, he was a great king who started life as a shepherd boy. He was probably a great shepherd boy, too, because he was just that kind of person. He's better known as the David of David and Goliath: the young man who defeated the giant with a single stone from a slingshot.

Not that everything he did turned out well for him. He sometimes strayed from the straight and narrow, and he lived through some very difficult times, particularly when he was a fugitive on the run from Saul, the jealous king of Israel who'd heard that God had chosen David to replace him. But he survived and won through in the end. You'll find his story in the Bible books of Samuel, Kings and Chronicles.

David was special in many ways. But what set him apart from most other people more than anything else, was the high regard he had for the God of the Bible. He was someone very well acquainted with God's Secret. He lived by it. And God inspired him to compose and sing songs about it.

An inspired song
When I say that God **inspired** David, I mean something more than the word generally means. We think of poets, musicians, painters, and the like, being inspired when they are naturally gifted and draw on their innate abilities to produce something exceptional and lasting. They excel themselves and might feel as if something like an ancient muse has possessed and guided them. What stirred David to write was not this kind of inspiration. Neither was it the kind of light-bulb moment that inventors and researchers occasionally have. Those rare events that sometimes merit the accolade of genius.

No, what we're talking about here is an even more rare experience. It doesn't come from within a person, or from an imaginary muse. It occurs only when something very special influences a person's thinking from outside of them. Exactly what it would have felt like for David is impossible to guess. He was inspired to write by the direct influence of God on his thoughts.

All the writers of the Bible had this experience. Remarkably, it left room for an individual's own character to come through. God didn't completely override the mind of the writer but used it as a vehicle for the expression of divine thoughts. God even used the experiences of the writers to illustrate through them how He interacts with us. That's very much in evidence in Psalm 34, as we'll see. We touched on some of this in an earlier chapter, when we spoke about how God's communication, the Bible, came to us.

So whenever I say that David said or wrote something in Psalm 34, what I really mean is that the **inspired** David wrote it, and it is God's Word more than his. Even when he's relating his own experiences.

An A-Z of God's Secret
Those who can read Psalm 34 in the original Hebrew language will notice something distinctive about the structure. It's written in the form of an acrostic: each subsequent verse of the Psalm

God's Secret

begins with the next letter of the Hebrew alphabet. There are 22 letters in the alphabet, as there are 22 verses in the Psalm. Though there is one slight deviation from the correct alphabetical sequence, but we'll leave commenting on that for later.

The Psalm is an A–Z of God's secret. Or rather an *Aleph* to *Taw*, because those are names of the first and last letters of the Hebrew alphabet. The Psalm travels from *Aleph* to *Taw* giving us 22 snapshots of things we need to know about God's Secret.

The revelation that this Psalm is an acrostic based on the Hebrew alphabet adds another dimension to it. It's not just clever word play. For Israelites wanting to learn the verses, especially for singing them, it would be a handy aid to memory. But, more than that, the acrostic device supplies another level of meaning, because each letter of the Hebrew alphabet is also a word with a meaning of its own.

This happens in our own alphabet with letters like 'b' and 't' sounding like *bee* and *tea,* but in our case it's accidental, and the letters have no link with the objects they sound like, apart from sharing a sound. But with Hebrew letters the link is real because it relates back to the original word picture, or pictogram, from which the letter evolved. For instance, the second letter of the Hebrew alphabet, *Beth*, is also the Hebrew word for house or tent, because the written character that represents *Beth* has developed from a simple line drawing of a house or tent.

This means there's an additional layer of meaning to each verse of Psalm 34. Using the example we just mentioned, the second verse of the Psalm is the *Beth* verse, so there will be an underlying connection with the house or home.

More a luxury than a necessity

But let's leave that aside for now. We have enough to be going on with. I've provided a table at the back of the book (Appendix 2) which shows how the Hebrew alphabet lines up with the verses, and I've supplied the generally accepted meanings of the letters. The meanings of the letters change nothing that we'll be saying about God's Secret from the verses. The meanings simply provide more food for thought, that you can follow up for yourself or not, if you wish. The additional information from the acrostic is more of a luxury than a necessity.

The Bible is the inspired Word of God, so we'd expect it to operate at many levels from the simple to the sublime. It shouldn't surprise us that it sometimes goes to depths that many of us probably won't be able to, or want to plumb. But we don't need to dig deeply to discover its greatest truths. The Bible is, after all, a **communication**. We're meant to understand it. God didn't send it exclusively for theologians, or deep thinkers. It was sent for everyone.

The Bible is like the rest of God's Creation. If we want to enjoy the delights of going deeper into it, we can, and that's up to us. There's an abundance of material. And although that will add to our understanding and our appreciation of divine matters, we won't find anything deep down that will conflict with or cancel the basic truths that are on or near the surface. I say this in case you're wondering how complicated this might get. No, it's not complicated. God's Secret is very accessible. It's something God is eager to share with us, not hide from us. It's not the kind of secret that needs covering up.

We will have to dig beneath the surface a little, though, because the Bible is not for the casual reader. It yields its truths to those who are prepared to pay attention to what they are reading. But that doesn't mean it's complicated; it just means it needs thinking about. You might want to go deeper after reading this book, I hope you do, but that's entirely up to you.

Structure
As mentioned a moment ago, the overall structure of the Psalm is an acrostic, an A–Z of God's Secret. The first word of each verse

God's Secret

starts with the next letter of the Hebrew alphabet. The Psalm also divides neatly in half: the front half is about the fear of God; the back half is about righteousness. So you can see what makes this the perfect key for unlocking God's Secret. Let me just remind you, these are the two Bible verses that comment directly on the Secret:

> *'God's secret is with them that fear him.'*

> *'God's secret is with the righteous.'*

Psalm 34 addresses both these aspects, fear and righteousness, and brings them together in a way that, as far as I'm aware, doesn't happen in the same way anywhere else in the Bible. Verses 1 to 11 focus on fear; verses 12 to 22 focus on righteousness. The two sets of verses also show a similar pattern:

First half (Fear)		**Second half (Righteousness)**	
1-3	basis of fear	12-14	basis of righteousness
4-5	benefits	15-16	benefits
6	pivotal verse	17	pivotal verse
7-8	deliverance	18-19	deliverance
9-10	provision	20-21	provision
11	conclusion	22	conclusion

There's no need to dwell on the structure, and certainly no need to remember it. You probably won't anyway. But I thought it might be helpful to include it here just to show that there is a pattern and a logical progression in the Psalm. Though it's not something we'll be referring to. Except for the pivotal verses.

Verses 6 and 17 are almost identical. I've called them **pivotal verses** because they sit at the centre of each half, and act as a central and significant thought around which the others cluster. They are worded almost identically. But there is a subtle difference in the wording that we'll discuss in a later chapter. This subtle difference serves to highlight the fact that the first half of the Psalm is mostly about things that are external to us, situations in which we find ourselves, and the second half is mostly about things that are internal, our thoughts and feelings.

As we'll see later, the **fear of God** is something that comes into play more in the events and circumstances of our lives, whereas **righteousness** is something that goes on in our heads and hearts. Though there is some crossover. And that's something we'll find true of all the individual aspects of God's Secret, that they're not in rigidly fenced off compartments. They all overlap here and there, influencing and playing off one another. Which isn't complicated, it's very much like life itself, where all our thoughts and actions have a bearing on one another, sometimes subtle, and sometimes obvious.

Background

One more thing before we step into verse one of Psalm 34: a little background will be helpful. When David wrote Psalms like this one there was often a situation in his life that prompted them. Songwriters often write from personal experience, and in this David was no exception. Sometimes we can't be certain which event in David's life prompted a particular Psalm, but with Psalm 34 we are given the information along with the Psalm. It appears in the heading placed above it in the Bible.

David was a fugitive when he wrote the Psalm. He was on the run from Saul, the king of Israel, who had taken a dislike to him. The hostility arose because God judged Saul to be unsuitable to reign over His chosen people and rejected him. David was selected and anointed king in prospect while Saul was still on the throne. So you can see the problem. Once, when things became particularly bad, David fled to a Philistine city called Gath. The Philistines were Saul's enemies, so David was probably applying the principle that 'my enemy's enemies are my friends.' Not so much in this case, though, because Gath was the hometown of Goliath, the giant whom David had killed. David thought, or hoped, that he wouldn't be recognised, but he was mistaken. He was arrested and taken to Achish the Philistine king. If David then hoped that they could put aside their differences and treat him as a valuable ally against Saul, he was mistaken in that, too. So David faced execution.

According to the narrative in 1 Samuel 21, David feigned madness. The king was taken in by this and saw no point in killing him. Or, as some suggest, he was wary of a superstition regarding the treatment of mad people (which David may have counted on), so he dismissed David from his presence, and he escaped. Once he was free, he fled to a cave in the hills. Here about four hundred men of Israel who were opposed to Saul joined him and made him their leader. Psalm 34 is David's song delighting in his escape, which he probably performed for his followers by way of celebration.

David gives all the credit to God for his escape. So his clever ruse was either supplied by God, or, if it was his own idea, God helped to make it work by influencing his captors to believe him, and then by creating the opportunity for him to slip away unnoticed. It's certain that God wouldn't have allowed the execution of the one He'd already anointed to be king over His people. That must have crossed David's mind, but he clearly didn't like to presume anything. The obvious relief expressed in his Psalm, shows that David must have thought it was touch and go for a while.

David and his followers knew they faced a time of fierce persecution from King Saul. But David's Psalm is full of optimism because they now knew without a doubt that God was on their side.

David and Peter

In the New Testament, there's a letter from the Apostle Peter to the believers in his day. I mention this because Peter made a number of references to Psalm 34. He saw parallels between the persecution of the believers in the 1st century and the plight of David and his followers when Saul was pursuing them. The Christians in the Roman Empire were facing some fierce persecution from Emperor Nero. The history books tell us what a monster Nero was, so it must have been a nerve-wracking time for believers. Peter quoted Psalm 34 because he wanted to give his fellow believers the same kind of encouragement that David gave to his followers. This probably tells us, too, that the character of Nero is a fair guide to the character of Saul. We know Saul had quite a temper on him, so the parallel is probably justified.

Against this background, we have Psalm 34 before us. Out of David's deliverance came the A–Z of God's Secret that we now have the pleasure of looking into.

11 Forgotten something?

> 'I will bless the LORD at all times: his praise shall continually be in my mouth.' (Psalm 34:1)

Sometimes when you hand a youngster a present, their eyes will light up and all they can think about is getting the wrapping off and seeing what it is. At which point mum or dad will say, 'Hey, haven't you forgotten something?' The distracted child will probably then say something like, 'Huh?' At which point the parent will say, 'What do we say when someone gives us something?' The child will then work it out and say, 'Oh, yes, thank you.'

David starts his Psalm in a similar place, saying, in effect, to all of us, 'Hey, haven't you forgotten something?' – just in case any of us have begun to take things for granted. In case we're failing to take account of just how much there is to be thankful for. Because he certainly hadn't.

The Psalm begins with David telling us about his own experience of God and how happy he is with it. If you look at the verse again you'll see that it's made up of two parts which complement one another, the second part re-stating slightly differently the thought of the first. This arrangement is typical of the way in which some of the poetry of the ancient Israelites was written: the rhymes were rhymes of meaning rather than of the sounds of the words. Which gives it a very modern feel, because modern poetry has tended to move away from rhyming schemes. The ancient Israelite poets were ahead of their time. Most of the verses in Psalm 34 are rhymed like this, but not all of them.

David blesses and praises the Lord at all times, he tells us. This is what we'd expect from someone who knows God's Secret. David is someone with an exceptionally high regard for his God. He is totally in awe of Him, and can hardly bless and praise Him enough.

Forgotten something?

And, in truth, blessing and praise are the only rational response from anyone who is even partially aware of who and what God is. And 'partially' is all we will ever manage as things stand, because His greatness defies the imagination to take it in, and the language to express it sufficiently. I was obliged to say that because I couldn't find the words to do it. He is the Mind and Might behind the universe. When astronomer and physicist, Sir James Jeans wrote that 'the universe looks more like a great thought rather than a great machine' he was right, and it was God who had that great thought.

Blessing God?

With the greatness of God in mind, however, there seems to be something seriously wrong with the opening verse of David's Psalm. Surely the greater should bless the lesser. Blessings are usually bestowed in a downward direction, as from the bountiful to the needy. But here we have David saying that he blesses the Lord. For all his accomplishments, David was a mere man. Surely it's God who does the blessing, not us? We look to **Him** because there is so much that He can do for us. What can we possibly do for Him, or give Him? It's hard enough to find something to give the man or woman who 'has everything', let alone the One who truly does have it all. What could He possibly want or need from us?

The answer lies in the fact that this is not **bless** in the sense of one bestowing favour on another – which can't happen where we and God are concerned – this is **bless** in the sense that we might say a heartfelt 'bless you' to someone who has done us a great kindness. Possibly that phrase started out as '**God** bless you' and has been shortened to take God out of the picture, so that now the inference is **I** bless you; but either way, it's meant as an expression of gratitude. When David says he will bless God *'at all times'*, he's saying that he will be **grateful** to God all the time. We'll come back to that in a moment, because there's something else we want to take a look at first. It's that phrase *'at all times'*. How was it possible for David to bless God all the time'?

At all times?

That's surely not achievable. He can't have spent every waking moment in gratitude to God. The same is true about David's **praise** for the Lord being *'continually in my mouth'*. That can't literally be so because it's absurd to think that he spent his entire time, all day and every day, speaking words of praise. He must have said other things. And if we're going to be really literal-minded about this, there's also the logistical problem of blessing all the time while praising all the time. It's clear we have to understand this more sensibly.

I'm reminded of a business meeting I once attended where the chairman said that our goal for the company was continuous improvement. As I saw it, that was impossible. We'd fail every day. Because if we didn't improve for even twenty minutes a day we'd fail to achieve our goal of continuous improvement. I was obviously feeling pernickety at the time, and my colleagues pointed out that **continuous** was not meant literally, as in 'without a single pause', it was meant aspirationally, as in seeking general ongoing improvement. Which is how David was using the words **at all times** and **continually**. He meant that he aspired to do so, when in reality he was praising and being grateful whenever he could, or whenever it occurred to him to do so.

Fanaticism

David wasn't telling us that he was a fanatic who obsessively devoted every moment of every day to mentally and vocally praising God. His enthusiasm for God did not cross the line to an unhealthy obsession. That's not the way of God's Secret. Nobody wants the company of a man of woman with a pet subject they can't put down. It invades almost every sentence of their conversation. The effect they have on everyone is the complete opposite of what they think they are doing. We don't catch their enthusiasm; we just want to get away from them. They can turn us right away from the very thing they're trying to attract us to. If you read the life of David, and his Psalms, you'll see that he was no fanatic. Though he was passionate about what he believed.

There's clearly some poetic licence at work in this Psalm. It's a poem, a song, after all. What David expressed in this opening verse is that he lived in a general state of awareness of the presence of God. It was like the air he breathed. He saw the hand of God in the world about him, and in the affairs of his life, and this often prompted thoughts of gratitude and praise. Sometimes he expressed his thoughts aloud, too: they were *'in my mouth'*. David lived his life, for the most part, in happy awareness of the God who had given life to him. He knew God's Secret.

The man inspired to write Psalm 34 clearly had a passion for life: he had an air of assurance, contentment and purpose about him that had its roots in a deep trust in his Lord. Believe me, you wouldn't want to rush away from a conversation with a man like David. He was the kind of man you'd want be around and stay around if possible. At this point in his life, about four hundred people had just decided that they wanted to be around him, and many more would be doing the same in the years that followed.

An attitude of gratitude

The attitude of gratitude that today's self-help and wellbeing writers are so fond of advocating is nothing new. David was living by it and recommending it to us over three thousand years ago. In fact, when it comes to our spiritual, mental and emotional wellbeing, there's nothing that works effectively for us that is entirely new. The best advice has been on record in God's communication, the Bible, for millennia. You'll notice if you read the big names in psychology, that when you strip away the theorising and systemising, and the now-quaint ideas that were of their time, any enduring truths you have left will have been around in some form or other in the Scriptures for centuries.

There is an important difference, though, between the thankfulness of David and the attitude of gratitude put forward by the wellbeing promoters of today. And it's what makes David's kind of thankfulness a part of God's Secret. The difference is this:

who are the self-helpers thanking? – and who was David thanking?

Just an expression

We quite often hear people say that they are thankful for something when it's not at all clear to whom, or to what they are being thankful. They are thankful that something turned out well for them, or for someone else, perhaps. Or they are thankful that they had a job offer or a narrow escape. But if you asked them to whom they were being thankful for making these things happen they would look a little confused and wonder what on earth you meant. 'It's just an expression' they would no doubt say. Or they'd shrug to indicate that some vague something 'out there' was somehow responsible for the good things that happened to them.

Occasionally, of course, people are genuinely thankful to God. Whenever David was thankful for something, it was God he was thanking. That's what he'd tell us if we could ask him. In fact he does tell us in the opening words of his Psalm. It's the very first thing he want us to know about him: *'I will bless the* LORD *at all times.'*

When people say they are thankful, and that it's just an expression, it's likely they are just trying to perish the thought that there might be something or someone out there to thank when things go well. 'Count your blessings,' people will say. But blessings are things with which we are blessed, and that inevitably leads on to something or someone doing the blessing. There's a blessor and a blessee, as it were.

So, again, 'count your blessings' will be reduced to just an expression to avoid signifying a belief in someone out there providing good things for us to accumulate and count. When being thankful becomes just an expression, people have only the vaguest notion of the giver as some benign force that sometimes favours them. The rest of the time the universe is either against them or indifferent to them. How different it was for David. He'd discovered reality. For him there was Someone there to praise and be thankful to. He knew perfectly well where his blessings came from.

The realisation that there must be a God changes everything. We can enjoy and acknowledge the source of our good. When we say we're thankful, or when we're counting our blessings, we're able to do it in the way of God's Secret. Be like David and thank God for what you have and enjoy. Recognise God as the giver, and move your life to another level. Sadly, people have even managed to turn 'Thank God' into just an expression.

But who is God?

Gratitude and praise should logically go to someone. Now let's give some thought to who that someone is. We've been saying **God**, but David never uses that word in the Psalm. Every time, instead of **God**, he says 'the LORD'. He says it sixteen times in twenty-two verses, so quite a lot. Almost every verse.

When David says *'the LORD'* instead of God all the way through this Psalm, we might think he's using a rather general term. But in fact he's being very specific. Because he is actually using the name of God. In the original language the word translated 'the LORD' here is *Yahweh*, which is the name of God. More correctly, it is **a** name of God, because God is referred to by a number of different names in the Bible. But this name *Yahweh* is the most significant. We're told in the Bible that *Yahweh* is the name He gave when a man called Moses specifically asked Him for His name.

Moses, and his people the Israelites, had spent years in Egypt where gods were numerous. The ancient Egyptians had a god for almost everything, and they gave names to them all. When Moses was chosen by God to lead the Israelites out of their captivity in Egypt, Moses wanted to know God's name, so that he could properly identify God when he spoke of Him to the people. God identified Himself as *Yahweh*, and of this name He said, *'...this is my name for ever, and this is my memorial unto all generations.'* (Exodus 3:15) This is the name He was to be permanently remembered by. *Yahweh* is the name David used wherever he said *'LORD'* in Psalm 34.

Lots in a name

Names often mean something in the Bible. They can signify a person's character, origin, or destiny. We rarely bother with such things nowadays when we name our children. We think about how well a forename will go with a surname but not what it might say about our child's character or destiny. Not so in Bible times. As an example, take David's name. It means 'beloved'. It was a name that obviously had meaning for David's parents when they gave it to the youngest of their eight sons. But, as it turned out, it was also prophetic of David's relationship with God. As he grew up, he became beloved of God.

In fact, David was *'a man after his [God's] own heart'.* (1 Samuel 13:14) When we say someone's a man or a woman after our own heart, we're saying we have a close affinity with them. They understand us; they see things how we see them. And this is how God saw David: as someone who understood Him and saw things His way. It's good to know we could hardly have gone to a better person to help us understand God's Secret than to the beloved David, who was a man after God's own heart!

So, in Bible times a person's name often said something about them. David was **beloved.** Samson was **strong.** When it comes to the meaning behind the name of God, however, things are not so straightforward. Which is hardly surprising when we take into account that God's name is likely to convey something of the nature and character of the One who is eternal and all-powerful. The meaning of *Yahweh* that most people familiar with the Bible settle for, though not with absolute certainty, is: '**I AM THAT I AM.**' It's as enigmatic as we might expect. Some believe it should be **I WILL BE WHO I WILL BE**. Both are approximations, but the latter version does convey more of the eternal nature of God, and at the same time His power to express Himself in any way He chooses. Dwelling on His name for a while certainly triggers the awe that is the fear of God.

The one and only God

What God's name doesn't express, though, is a three-fold nature. There's not a hint in His name of the Trinitarian nature that many ascribe to Him. Such a concept, if it were correct, would surely be evident in some way in His name. But not only is God's name silent regarding the Trinity, but His entire communication to us is also silent about it. Support for it is from inferences, not from clear, unequivocal statements. How can this be for something that is allegedly of such major importance? How such a belief has come to dominate mainstream Christian thinking on the God of the Bible is almost as big a mystery as the doctrine itself. Something which, in the early days of Christianity, would have been heresy to propose is now heresy to deny. David, the man after God's own heart, knew nothing of it.

And should you be thinking these observations heretical – that maybe you should put this book down – I strongly suggest that first you take a closer look at the development of a doctrine that was not around in the days of Christ and the apostles. It isn't mentioned anywhere in God's communication to us. The nearest we have to it is in 1 John 5:7, which says: *'For there are three that bear record in heaven, the Father, the Word, and the Holy Ghost: and these three are one.'* This looks pretty convincing until we learn that it was added to the text much later to provide support for the Trinity. It has been removed from more recent translations because the oldest and more reliable manuscripts don't show it.

Again, we have to ask: Isn't it odd that a doctrine considered by many Christians to be the most important doctrine in the Bible is found only by inference? Something so vital ought to be in plain sight, clearly stated and unmissable. God's communication to us breaks down seriously if it takes learned theologians to piece together its most vital truth. As I've said already, God didn't address His message to the theologians of this world, He sent it to us all, and it's most vital truths will be obvious to us all.

Doctrines, principles and actions

Inevitably we are going to encounter doctrines while delving into God's Secret. I'll do my best to keep things as theologically light as possible. We are primarily looking at God's Secret to learn how best to conduct ourselves for optimal success and happiness. But how we act can't be divorced from the principles and doctrines that we hold dear. This is true not only of religion but in life generally. It's how life works. Whether we're religious or not, we all hold certain overarching beliefs about life. These are our doctrines. We might not think of them as such, but the big truths we subscribe to about life are our doctrines.

Doctrines don't have to be religious beliefs. They can be political or philosophical: in fact they can be any set of beliefs that a group or an individual might hold. Our doctrines are the worldview against which everything else in our life is set. They are the foundations on which our principles sit, and which inform and direct how we act. That's how life is for everyone.

Worldview ▶ principles ▶ actions

Our beliefs about the world (our doctrines) provide the guidelines within which we operate (our principles), which determine what we do (our actions). Our lives are structured in this way, however random we might think them. We each have an outlook on life which informs how we engage with life.

All the things that we've made up our minds about – whether we believe in God or evolution; whether we believe in Conservatism or Liberalism, whether we're vegan or meat eating – all these and many other things, large and small, combine to create our worldview. They are what we believe about life, and they are essentially our doctrines. Our principles will reflect them. And if we have integrity then what we do will be in line with our principles and the worldview that generates them.

Integrity

Integrity occurs when all three elements, our actions, our principles and our doctrines are in accord. It happens when what we do fits with our principles, and our principles fit with our worldview.

God's Secret is very much about integrity: it involves all three elements. It contains a worldview, a set of principles, and follow-through actions. When we learn and live by these elements as outlined in the Secret, we'll have **true** integrity. We'll have an integrity based on what's really going on in the world, and what we really need to do about it. We won't have an integrity based on false assumptions about the world.

The three aspects work together in God's Secret. The Bible doesn't separate them out and put them in different boxes. Doctrine, principle and practice are woven together in the text all the way through the Bible. So that's what we're going to find in Psalm 34. All three are there and we'll look at them as and when we meet them. So the doctrines aren't diversions, as such, they are essential parts of the Secret. Every time we meet a doctrine as we go through Psalm 34 it will help to inform the principles and practices that the Secret advocates. The doctrines build the worldview into which the principles and practices properly fit.

Don't get hung up on all this, though. You don't have to consciously think about the three aspects of integrity. All you need do is settle back and soak up the aspects of God's Secret as we go through Psalm 34. It will all fall into place along the way.

So, the first element of God's Secret in Psalm 34 is gratitude. It's right and proper for us to acknowledge the goodness of God towards us. And having been reminded to say 'Thank you' for the presents we've been given, the blessings we can count, let's carry on by opening another present as we look at verse two of David's inspired Psalm.

12 THE HUMBLE WHO BOAST

'My soul shall make her boast in the Lord: the humble shall hear thereof, and be glad.' (Psalm 34:2)

David moves on from telling us how grateful he is to know God, to saying that although he is humbled by knowing Him, he is so proud that *Yahweh* is his God. This is one of the few times when pride is okay. A relationship with God is like no other. We might be proud of having a friendship with someone royal, but David **was** royal, and he loved to boast of his friendship with God.

Micah, one of the lesser known writers of the Old Testament, was inspired to pen this telling and instructive verse: *'He hath shewed thee, O man, what is good; and what doeth the LORD require of thee, but to do justly, and to love mercy, and to walk humbly with thy God?'* (Micah 6:8) Whenever I read that I can't help thinking: how else could one possibly walk with God but humbly?

Picture yourself strolling along beside the most powerful person on the planet. In this picture you're very reticent, I'm sure, paying close attention whenever the great man or woman speaks, and hardly daring to say anything yourself. Now elevate your walking companion to the most powerful being in the universe. You'd probably have difficulty putting one foot in front of the other, your knees would be knocking so much. You'd be very humble at the time, and you sure would be boasting about it afterwards!

Real humility

Walk means 'way of life'. To walk humbly means to conduct yourself in a humble way on life's journey. God tells us through His prophet Micah, that those who live according to His precepts must have a humble disposition. God hates pride. There should be no

The humble who boast

place for it in us. If we saw ourselves through God's eyes we'd see how ridiculous human pride is.

But let's not get the wrong idea about humility. It's not a negative thing. Our humility is the absence of pride, not the presence of abjection or self-loathing. God wants us to be confident, secure and relaxed about life. But He wants us to have the **real** confidence and security that come from trusting in Him and not in ourselves. Humility isn't a retreat from life; it's grasping the reality of life. It's a strength, not a weakness. We can feel good about life because God is with us, and that we know His Secret, not because we mistakenly believe we are sufficient of ourselves.

When David spoke of the humble in Psalm 34, his first thought was of the mixed band of characters that had joined him in opposition to King Saul. This second verse says that the humble were glad that their leader made his boast in the Lord and not in himself. That made him the kind of man they could follow. David wasn't a shallow man after personal gain and glory by opposing Saul. They knew that. He was a God-fearing and righteous man. He just wanted to follow the destiny his Lord had selected him for. On one occasion he even held back from killing Saul when it was in his power to do so.

Tough but humble

Most of those humble men who followed David were competent warriors. They may have been a bunch of disaffected men from all walks of life, but, because a kind of conscription was in force in Israel, they would also have been men who could quit themselves well in battle. Or they would not have been willing to join David against Saul. They were tough but they were also God-fearing characters who put their trust in God. So they were in fact humble. They recognised the greatness of the Lord and their own insufficiency. We shouldn't make the mistake of associating the humility that God wants from us with weakness and timidity. I don't think anyone would have made that mistake if they'd met David's men on the field of battle – or David himself, for that matter!

God's Secret

Times have changed and believers are now peace-seekers not warriors; but nothing's changed where our attitude to life is concerned. We can still be strong characters with humility, trusting in God and not ourselves. The right kind of humility doesn't rule out strength of character, it can even promote it. Knowing God is on our side gives us good reason to be confident and outgoing. It puts our trust in the right place.

And if we're already confident by nature, we don't have to suppress who we are in order to be humble, we have only to avoid pride and put our trust in God where it belongs.

Unfair advantage?

You might think that if we're naturally mild mannered and unassertive we have an advantage when it comes to being humble. But humility still requires the same from us as it does from the naturally confident: that we avoid pride and that we trust in God. However extrovert or introvert we are, whatever temperament we have, we all have to deal with the same human nature.

Introverts might be more inclined to pride themselves in their humility. They can have a quiet pride. Extroverts may be inclined to 'beat themselves up' over their inability to take a back seat. But we don't have to take a back seat to be humble. Our humility is unrelated to the disposition we were born with. Having a strong or weak personality is neither an advantage nor a disadvantage. What matters is that we quell pride in whatever form it takes for us, and that we trust in God. That's real humility, and it will work with whatever kind of personality we have – with whoever we are.

Same beliefs, different people

While we're on the subject of personality, this is a good place to mention that believers don't all have to become identical people when they share the same doctrines, principles, and practices. We still remain essentially who we are, and nothing can really change that, nor should it. There isn't just one sort of Christian. But sometimes people think that's how it ought to be. And that causes problems, because it can make some people feel that they won't fit in with what they believe to be the standard Christian type. Think back to that mixed band who joined David and you will have a more accurate picture of those Jesus expects to join him. All kinds of people, but with common aims. Believers come in all types.

The barriers of perception

It always saddens me to hear someone say that they are just 'not the type' to be a believer. I mean, when they genuinely believe it of themselves and it's not just an excuse for not bothering. They truly cannot see themselves as Christians. They have built up a picture in their heads of the kind of person a believer is, or must be, and it's not them. But they are mistaken. And a lot of what I'm saying here is to help remove that kind of barrier.

Perception can be more powerful than reality. Because how we perceive things is **our** reality, even when it's wrong. We are all ruled by our perceptions to some extent. What we have made our minds up to believe about certain things becomes for us the truth about them, even when we're wrong. Mostly it doesn't matter very much, and we all tweak or change some of our perceptions over time when new information comes our way.

But how we perceive ourselves and Christianity matters a lot. Because we can entertain mistaken notions about ourselves and Christianity which create barriers that need not, and should not be there. And we'll never fully grasp God's Secret, and become a part of what's really happening in the world, unless we dissolve those barriers. The barriers are misbeliefs about what Christianity is, and misbeliefs about whether it's really for you, because of the kind of person you are. These two things go together, and they misinform one another in a loop.

But don't be over-concerned about this right now, if in some measure it describes how you feel. To some degree everyone has these barriers of perception to surmount when they encounter

God's Secret

God's Secret. Perceptions acquired over the years about ourselves and God often need re-evaluating in the light of fresh information. Just keep on reading, because a lot of what's in this book will help.

There is not one correct version of a believer: one look, one demeanour, one set of interests, one set of talents, one way of speaking, one way of dressing or working, and so on. There's room *'in Christ'* for everyone. Some are cautious; some are go-getters. Some are practical and some impractical. Some are serious and some easy-going. Some are formal and some informal. And so on. Whatever our personality, there's a place for us. We can all be humble believers. In fact a necessary part of being a **humble** believer is humbly accepting that other believers will be different.

The Apostle Paul, writing in a similar vein, was, perhaps, ahead of his time when he wrote: *'There is neither Jew nor Greek, there is neither bond nor free, there is neither male nor female: for ye are all one in Christ Jesus.'* (Galatians 3:28) In other words, it doesn't matter where you come from, what your status in life, or your gender happens to be, as believers we're all one *'in Christ'*.

We are who we are

Believers all follow the one great example of Jesus, that's true, and our characters will be transformed by that experience, but we can only follow him as ourselves. Be a believer, but be yourself also. A spiritually transformed character is not an entirely different person. Values, aims and worldview may change, but the essential core person is still there. The Bible likens the transition to taking off some old clothes and putting on some new ones (Ephesians 4:22-24). We're the same person, but wearing a new outlook. Don't think all believers must be the same just because they believe the same things, and follow the same Jesus.

Yourself but different

To be a believer we don't have to be someone we are not. We can still be ourselves. That's not to say that if we used to burgle houses or steal cars before we became a believer, that it's okay to continue doing that. Our new believers' worldview, principles and practices will override that. But they won't override our personality, which may be outgoing or reserved, fun-loving or serious, studious or athletic, adventurous or home-loving. You could once have been a criminal, and at the same time have been any of these things, because they are who you are. You can become a Christian and remain any of these, because they are still who you are.

We seem to have wandered a little off track, but it was worth it to get the right perspective on humility and to know that it doesn't mean those with God's Secret must all be timid. Neither does it mean that believers must all be of only one type, like paper-chain dolls. We are who we are. And we can change our view of the world while remaining who we are. We can learn to see the hand of God in our personal world and the world at large. Through God's communication we can know His Secret, discover who He is and what His plans are – all while remaining who **we** are.

Knowing God and His Secret is quite something to boast about. That's how David saw it. The God of all things was interested in him, and he wanted to shout about it. If we could be as sure of God's interest in us, we'd surely want to shout about it, too. Well the fact is we can be. That's why God communicated His Word to us. He wants all kinds of people, your kind, my kind, to know Him, and to know His Secret.

Know or know of?

When I say know Him, I don't mean just know **of** Him. There are plenty of people who know **of** God in the sense that they consider there's probably a higher somebody that they think of as God. If you ask them whether they believe in God they'll say, yes, they suppose they do, in a vague kind of way. Or they might promptly

God's Secret

say 'yes', quite confident about it, though they hardly give God a moment's thought from one week to the next. They know God as a concept not a person. Certainly not for them the continual blessing and praise of David. They know of a God, but they don't know who He is. They are certainly not in the enviable place of knowing God's Secret. Nor will they ever be if they keep God at such a distance.

The God of all sizes

So, what does it mean to know God? How is such a thing even possible given the immenseness of God and the next-to-nothingness of us? Can an insect know and befriend a person? Realistically, that's never going to happen, is it? – however fondly we might like to carry it around in a matchbox. But for God a relationship with a person is not a challenge. His omnipresence means that He is simultaneously in the farthest galaxy and inside the smallest molecule. He doesn't have to come down to our size because, in a sense, He is already **all** sizes.

'A still small voice'

A Bible prophet named Elijah was once looking for a sign of the presence of God. He was at a low point and was looking for some reassurance. So he went to a place where God had shown Himself previously, a place called Horeb where Moses had once experienced the presence of God. We're told that while he stood looking and listening, there was a fearful storm. It was very dramatic, but there was nothing in it to signify God's presence. Just a storm. Then came an earthquake, but neither did that signify anything. He could see no sign from God in it. After that there was suddenly wildfire raging among the surrounding trees and bushes, but God wasn't in that either. It told the prophet nothing; gave him no reassurance. God was not in any of these things that we might sometimes call 'acts of God'.

When these dramatic events had subsided, Elijah heard what is described as *'a still small voice'*, or literally, the sound of stillness. What a wonderful expression: the sound of stillness. It was a

The humble who boast

deafening silence, we might say, especially following on from all the noise and commotion that had preceded it – rather like the effect of walking past a workman breaking up concrete with a pneumatic drill when he suddenly switches it off, and you're hit by a wall of silence. In this case there was the sound of a silence which was the God of the universe quietly making Himself known. (1 Kings 19: 11–13). Yes, God is very restrained in His dealings with people. Necessarily so, as we would not survive an encounter with His full-on presence and power. He doesn't have to try to be impressive, because He simply is. That's what God was telling Elijah, who, as the Bible narrative about him indicates, was a prophet sometimes given to big, somewhat theatrical demonstrations of power.

Something we notice, even about truly great men and women, is that they have no need to flaunt their abilities. It's the nature of God to avoid grand gestures. He shows His power only when making an impact is necessary. The plagues on Egypt and the parting of the Red Sea (described in the book of Exodus), were employed to make an impact on both the Egyptians and the Israelites, to give them something to remember. God had no need to demonstrate His power otherwise.

Usually He works in quiet and seemingly mundane ways. Causing His communication to be written on parchments by inspired people, for instance, rather than have it supernaturally inscribed on golden tablets and delivered by archangels to the sound of heavenly fanfares. God doesn't need that kind of show. Most telling of all, with regard to God's preference for the more natural and ordinary over the supernatural and grand, is His Son's birth. *'No room in the inn'* for the Son of God says it all.

We haven't said much about Jesus so far in this second part of the book, but that will be remedied as we move on through the Psalm. Jesus was still a thousand years in the future when David wrote Psalm 34. But that doesn't mean that he didn't know of him.

A man with a woman's soul?
Before we move on to the third verse of Psalm 34, there's something that looks a little peculiar here in verse two that we shouldn't let slip by without comment. You'll notice that David said, *'My soul shall make her boast in the LORD.'* Read it quickly and you'll miss the oddness. Two questions come to mind. Firstly, why was it David's **soul** that was making her boast in the Lord, and not the man himself? Secondly, why was David's soul **female** when he was a man? This could get interesting.

Questions about the nature of the soul take us into the territory of doctrine again. As I said, this is going to happen at almost every turn as we go through this Psalm, because doctrine, principle and practice run together throughout the Bible. The doctrines provide the backdrop for the principles we practice when we live by God's Secret. And, as you'll see, they're not only helpful and essential in order for us to understand the Secret properly; they can be quite intriguing too.

What is our soul?
There are two views that dominate thinking about the soul. You probably fall into one camp or the other. You either believe that your soul is some ethereal part of you that is your true essence, and that it will live on somehow, somewhere, when your mortal body stops functioning. Or, on the other hand, you may not think you have a soul at all, and that your physical death means the permanent end of your conscious existence. I'm guessing that most people prefer to believe option number one here, but which of them is correct? It might surprise you to learn that, according to the communication we have from the God who made us, neither of these options is correct. Although surprisingly, the second one is closer to the truth than the first.

Death of the soul?

According to the Bible, the soul exists but is not immortal. Here are just two of the references that lead to this conclusion: *'The soul that sinneth it shall die'* (Ezekiel 18:20*) and 'he which converteth a sinner... shall save a soul from death.'* (James 5: 20)

The word 'soul' is used in two ways in the Bible. Sometimes it refers to the person themselves, not to some separate spiritual part of them. This is how David uses the word when he says, *'My soul shall make her boast in the* LORD.*'* He's saying simply, and poetically, that **he himself** will boast about God. But at other times the word 'soul' can refer to a person's animating life force. This may sound like something ethereal and eternal, but it still blinks out at death.

David could actually have been employing a combination of both uses of the word 'soul' in order to convey poetically that he boasted of God from all that he was, from his very soul. Going back to that verse we just quoted: *'The soul that sinneth it shall die,'* this tells us unambiguously that souls aren't immortal. The soul is basically the person, though the word can indicate the life force that God gives us – and indeed gives to every other creature on the planet, because no difference is made in the Bible between the souls of people and other creatures.

We have quite a conundrum here if we believe that the soul is different from the person. Because if the soul that sins and dies in this verse is different from the person, we have a situation where our soul can sin without us being involved (not sure how that would work), and then it could die, while you, who did not sin, presumably carry on living without your soul, which has died. This makes no sense whatsoever, I'm sure you'll agree. The truth is simply, your soul is you, and you are mortal. The words **'immortal'** and **'soul'** don't appear together anywhere in the Bible.

What's the point of it all?

When a person dies, they return to the earth and *'in that very day his* [or her] *thoughts perish'*. (Psalm 146:4) This may not be what you wanted to hear, but I'm guessing that it's what you've always half suspected, much as you'd prefer it to be otherwise. Death is death. And if you're now beginning to wonder, 'Well, if that's the case, what's the point of it all?' then you'll be pleased to hear that there is a way of escape. It's not inevitable. There's something riding to our rescue. It's called salvation. It means rescue from death – and our rescue from death is what God's communication is essentially telling us all about. It's God reassuring us that He hasn't left us all to die, with not a hope of doing anything about it. In fact it's Him telling us that He has **already** done something about it.

Salvation makes no sense if death is not really death. If we have an immortal soul, then what are we being saved from? Why would God offer us eternal life as a gift for believing certain things, and following a certain path through life, if we already have an immortal soul?

For those who believe in the immortality of the soul, the standard answer is that we have immortal souls, yes, but if we don't accept the salvation that God offers, those immortal souls will spend their eternity in hell. They claim that God has actually condoned or participated in the creation of a fiery underworld realm, or dimension, where Satan and his helper-demons can torture those who've sinned, every day for eternity. Or alternatively those errant souls go to a place called purgatory, a half-way house where they'll be given the opportunity to mend their ways. Not a difficult decision, I should think, for anyone facing an eternity of torture. None of this is found in the Bible. It flies in the face of real Bible doctrine. And it's certainly contrary to God being a God of love.

God certainly doesn't want us to love Him because we are too terrified to do otherwise. Love cannot work like that. The soul that sins is not consigned to hell; it is consigned to death, to oblivion, where '*his* [or her] *thoughts perish*'. It does not live on in another place. It dies. Hell is not a place where sinners spend eternity in torment, any more than heaven is a place where believers spend eternity in bliss. Neither of these things is threatened or promised in God's communication. Which may surprise you (doctrine being intriguing again). What God **has** said about these things, we'll come to later as and when they arise in our progress through Psalm 34.

David's female soul

The point of this doctrinal excursion is to clarify that David's reference to his soul is simply his way of saying **me**. And in case you thought I'd forgotten about it, David's reference to his soul as **her** doesn't mean he's confused about his gender. This is merely an idiomatic use of the female gender, no different from referring to a boat as she, or to the moon as female, as the poet Walter de la Mare did when he wrote, she 'Walks the night in her silver shoon'. No comment is being made on the actual gender of a boat or the moon, and no comment was being made by David on the gender of his soul. Calling it **her** doesn't raise any gender issues.

There is a more serious matter of gender, though, which we'll look at in the next chapter because it comes up in the next verse of Psalm 34. It's the matter of the gender of God. So let's move on.

13 MAKING GOD BIGGER

'O magnify the LORD with me, and let us exalt his name together.' (Psalm 34:3)

David now urges everyone to join him in praise of God. Don't hold back, he says: *'magnify the LORD with me.'*

This is another verse written in the form of ancient Hebrew poetry, where the rhyme is in the meanings not the sounds of the words. A useful spin-off from this form of writing is that, in the process of reflecting the meaning of the first part of the verse, the second part helps to explain it. So we can tell that magnifying is going to involve some exalting.

There seems very little point in making God bigger than He already is, even if such a thing were possible. But magnifying something is never done to make something bigger; it's done to make something appear bigger, so that we can see more detail.

Things don't get bigger when we magnify them. Hold a magnifying glass over an ant and it doesn't get any bigger, it just appears to. The same is true when we magnify the Lord, as David encourages us to do here. God doesn't get any bigger. He can't do that, because He's already everywhere. He just **appears** bigger to us.

Magnifying God means making Him bigger in our minds and hearts. It's making Him fill more of our thoughts, not more of the universe. David is telling us not to be satisfied with a basic level of knowledge of God, but to build on it, to enlarge it. Magnify it. Only when we do that can we truly exalt Him. Have you ever tried praising someone you know little or nothing about? Where do you start? You probably don't, because you have so little to go on. Limited information means limited praise. To magnify and exalt someone we need to know things about them, and the more the

Making God

better. David could be effusive in his praise because he ⎵ much about God. The Lord was already big in his mind and heart, so he could make Him big in his praises. By asking us to join him, David was asking us to be like him. Get to know God better.

As with many things, the more we know and understand about them, the more we become absorbed in them and the larger they feature in our lives. And there's nothing more absorbing, once we get into it, than the truth about God and His purpose with us. What could be more fascinating than that? It's all about life's big questions, after all. If we have things in our lives that are more consuming and fascinating than that, then it's probably time for some serious reassessment, because we are short-changing ourselves. Not that we shouldn't have any other interests at all, but that we could probably do with reshuffling our priorities.

God is many things

Let's start the process right now of making God bigger for ourselves by looking at some of what there is to know about Him. Listed in no particular order here are just 25 of the things that we can glean from His communication to us:

God is a creative genius	Psalm 8:3
God is the Creator of all things	Genesis 1
God is the Sustainer of all things	Job 34:14-15
God is eternal	Psalm 90:2
God is everywhere	1 Kings 8:27
God is all-powerful	Joshua 4:24
God is all-knowing	Psalm 147:5
God is all-seeing	2 Chronicles 16·

God's Secret

God is a promise maker	2 Peter 1:4
God is a promise keeper	Luke 1:72
God is love	1 John 4:8
God is light	1 John 1:5
God is compassionate	Psalm 86:15
God is forgiving	Daniel 9:9
God is patient	Psalm 86:15
God is righteous	Psalm 71:19
God is gracious	Psalm 86:15
God is good	Matthew 19:17
God is sometimes jealous	Exodus 20:5
God is sometimes angry	Psalm 7:11
God is our Father	Matthew 5:45
God is just	Deuteronomy 32:4
God is a helper	Psalm 46:1
God is a defender	2 Samuel 22:3
God is to be trusted	Psalm 22:5

re, but this will get us started. We can't dwell on each
ributes here, because that would take us away from
of this book, and is a book in itself, but it will be useful

to look at one of them, just to show how the Lord is magnified when we look more closely at something about Him.

God is a creative genius

The word 'genius' falls a long way short of describing God's creative power and flair. On this planet alone, His Creation is staggeringly varied. The taxonomists, the people who classify species of flora and fauna, are constantly being presented with new things to add to their lists. The range of plants, animals, birds, reptiles, insects and other creatures here is phenomenal. Did you know there are over 370,000 known species of beetle? I can't think why evolution would result in something like that, but I can imagine a creative genius 'playing' with an idea. 20th century scientist J.B.S. Haldane famously said, '…it would appear that God has an inordinate fondness for stars and beetles.' And we've found a lot more stars and beetles since his day.

The real artist

We call a landscape artist like John Constable a genius for the ability he had to create outstanding paintings of the English countryside. But what about the One who provided the real landscape in the first place – the scene that Constable was looking at and trying to recreate in oils? What of the One who provided the trees and bushes; the shrubs and grasses; the sky and the cloud formations; the contours of the hills and the meanderings of the streams; the seasons and the sunlight? God's genius puts the talents of our greatest artists so far in the shade. Even the shapes and patterns we find in abstract art are of limited imagination when set against the richness and variety of the designs we find in nature.

And here's a thought: If everything we see in nature was blindly brought together by an evolutionary process, and it has no creative imagination behind it, then a country scene is no different from the kind of abstract art produced when paint is thrown randomly at a canvass. By copying it, even though he didn't try to reproduce exactly what he saw in a photographic way, Constable gave us nothing more than second hand abstract art.

This also puts a question mark over our love for the countryside. In evolutionary terms that would be nothing more than, perhaps, the attraction of what is safe and familiar, because landscapes would have no intrinsic aesthetic merit. Why should we see any? More sense suggests a Creative Intelligence. I know we've had a hand in shaping some of our landscape, for both good and bad. Usually when it's bad, that's because we've given no thought to what we were doing. Usually when it's good, that's because we've kept or copied the best of what occurs naturally – we've painted using God's palette and His original designs.

Best book

In the field of literature, God has created the greatest book of all time. The Bible is the bestselling, most quoted, and most translated book ever written. And it has everything: the origin of the world and the appearance of every living thing; great millennial sweeps of history; true tales of intrigue and romance; thrilling accounts of battles and wars; heroes and villains, deceit and skulduggery; kings and queens, princes and princesses; nations and empires rising and falling; giants and sea monsters; great poetry and great wisdom; predictions fulfilled and fulfilling. And that's just the Old Testament.

Added to this we have the crowning glory of the New Testament: the account of the life of the greatest and wisest man who ever lived, and of his humble band of followers who took Christianity to the world. The Bible is not only a book of religion (how off-putting that can sound), it's a work of unsurpassed creative genius. And it belongs on the non-fiction shelf. It also belongs on your shelf at home if you don't have a copy. But not gathering dust, of course.

Homing in on just one of the attributes of God like this – His creative genius – we see so much more of Him. We enlarge our understanding of Him. We magnify Him by expanding our

Making God bigger

knowledge of Him and that inevitably increases our appreciation of Him. We can properly praise and exalt Him because we know many remarkable things about Him. He fills more of our hearts and minds.

Everywhere but somewhere

We mentioned above that God fills the universe so we can't make Him any bigger. And I'm sure no one would actually understand our magnifying of Him in that way. It's our personal universe in which we can make Him bigger. But while speaking of God's omnipresence in the universe we shouldn't lose sight of the fact that He also has a localised personality. He's right here as well as being far out there.

Solomon said of Him, *'behold, the heaven and heaven of heavens cannot contain thee.'* (1 Kings 8:27) He fills the whole of space. But we're also told that He can be in a particular place. For instance, David refers to God in Psalm 2:4 as *'He that sitteth in the heavens'* which is to say that God can reside in a particular place in the heavens. God has the unique ability to be everywhere and yet somewhere. Bringing Solomon's and David's comments together, He can sit in the heavens which cannot contain Him. I'm not sure if even our current understanding of quantum physics can accommodate that one.

God often presents Himself as a Being with personal boundaries, rather than a mind spread throughout the universe. He is depicted as a Being who is located somewhere, but whose awareness and influence encompasses all things everywhere. He can be instantly anywhere, because He's already there. He is everywhere and yet somewhere. It's a paradox, but with our limited comprehension we are bound to run into problems trying to get out heads around the nature of *Yahweh*, the Creator and Sustainer of countless galaxies. The paradox is resolved to some extent, though, if not explained, when we take the name of God into account. Y' recall that *Yahweh* means *'I Am That I Am'*, indicating the*

God's Secret

so powerful that He can be whatever He chooses to be, even somewhere and everywhere simultaneously.

Magnifying us

On the subject of magnifying, surprisingly the Bible speaks of God magnifying us. *'What is man, that thou shouldest magnify him? and that thou shouldest set thine heart upon him?'* That was from Job, who was incredulous that God would exalt mere men and women, as well he should have been! (Job 7.17). The Lord magnified Joshua (Joshua 4:14) and He magnified Solomon *'exceedingly'* (1 Chronicles 29:25), so much so, that Solomon became the wisest and probably wealthiest man of his time. We won't necessarily achieve that level of wealth and wisdom, regardless of what the advocates of prosperity theology might tell us. Though such people are not entirely wrong. Because God does respond favourably to those who magnify Him, and He exalts them. When we make more of Him, He makes more of us. It works both ways.

God will magnify us when we don't magnify ourselves. This is important to remember. We already know from the previous chapter how vital humility is to understanding God, and to having a good relationship with Him. Any self-magnifying will distance us from God and will only make us smaller.

In the New Testament, we have Mary's song of joy over being chosen by God to be the mother of Jesus. Mary illustrates perfectly how our meekness and our magnifying of the Lord rebound favourably upon us to our own magnification. She begins, *'My soul doth magnify the Lord, and my spirit hath rejoiced in God my Saviour*... *e hath regarded the low estate of his handmaiden: n henceforth all generations shall call me blessed.'* She magnifies the Lord because she has been n. And that she was already humble, of *'low* ιat she was already one to magnify the Lord, been an essential part of the Lord's reason for he mother of Jesus. When we exalt His name,

He exalts us. Then we have more reason to ex... upward spiral.

Gender and God

As we are asked to exalt **His** name, let's pause briefly and take a look at this matter of the gender of the God of the Bible. God is referred to as male in the first verse of Psalm 34, but we didn't comment on it then because we already had enough to think about at the time. But as it bothers some people, we ought to give it some thought before we go any further.

There are those who are not comfortable with God being male, or with God always being referred to as male. They prefer the idea of a female God – or goddess, I suppose that would be – and they like to speak and write of God as **her**, or they confusingly track back and forth from **him** to **her** so that God is not exclusively one or the other for them. Which is fine if what they are doing is right, but it's not fine if it isn't right. A preference for something to be other than it is, doesn't make it so, no matter how strong that preference may be.

Equality

Over recent years much good work has been done to remedy the social evils of inequality with regard to men and women. Men have certainly had things too much their own way for too long, and that needed to be addressed. We needed a much fairer society, and in many ways we now have one in much of the world. Though it's still a work in progress. But there is always a danger when pushing for change that the pendulum will swing too far in the other direction: the worthy enthusiasm of the reformers will be taken beyond what is fair, sensible and correct. Which is where we are these days with queries over the gender of God.

It's easy to understand why the idea of a male God became an issue. The thought is that a male God is the product of a m... dominated religious history. The gender of God is seen as ? case of male bias that has no basis in fact. What that gh, is that quite a lot of the ancient gods in our male ominated history were female: Aphrodite, Artemis, Athena, and more. So if God were man-made, then he or she was almost as likely to be female as male.

Jesus said that all those who enter the Kingdom of God will be transformed and become like the angels: *'they neither marry, nor are given in marriage, but are as the angels of God in heaven.'* (Matthew 22:30) Gender is something that God created along with everything else in this world, and it may not exist outside this present arrangement. That's something we have to take into account.

What we also have to take account of is that the God whose communication to us is the Bible has presented Himself to us as male. We can't get away from that. He has made it clear that He wants us to consider Him as our Heavenly Father, not our heavenly mother, or our heavenly anything else. That is the way He requires us think of Him, and we cannot *'exalt **his** name'*, as David encourages us in this Psalm, in a way that honours Him, if we ignore something as basic as the way He asks us to address Him. We wouldn't be so discourteous as to do that to another person, so let's not do it to God.

Like an Egyptian

Believing God to be female may be fashionably correct, but it's not factually correct. So best avoided. Unless, of course, when you talk of god you are not talking about the Creator whose communication to us is the Bible. In which case your god can be anything you chose. You're free to be like the Egyptians of old and think of your god as whatever you prefer: male, female, animal, bird, fish, insect, sun, or moon… whatever you wish. But if it's the ...le you mean, then He has chosen to be understood ...e should respect that. And if we want to access His e reverential fear that His status requires will mean should address Him in the way He chooses.

Making God bigger

Actually, if you've grasped anything of His character and magnificence, you'll be more than happy to comply.

What about Satan?

It may seem a little mischievous to say this, but it occurs to me that we never hear voices clamouring for Satan to be female. For some reason, everyone is happy for him to remain him. Remarkably, though, as you'll see when we spend a little time in a later chapter looking into who the devil and Satan really are, these two characters can be either male or female. As I say, doctrine can be very intriguing.

14 No fear

'I sought the LORD, and he heard me, and delivered me from all my fears.' (Psalm 34:4)

What are you afraid of?
All the usual things, probably, plus one or two things that are peculiar to you, but by no means rare. David had quite a few fears, it seems, but the Lord delivered him from them all. Clearly we are talking about a different kind of fear now, from the fear of the Lord that is reverential. We don't want to be delivered from that. We want to be delivered from the wrong kind of fear that destroys our happiness, and is the source of so many of our problems. We introduced the subject of the right kind of fear in Chapter 5, because God's Secret *'is with them that fear him'*. It's a key element of the Secret. Now we have the opportunity to look at the wrong kind.

Can you imagine being free from all your fears? Not having a single thing to worry about? That was the enviable position in which David found himself after he'd *'sought the LORD'*. He had a lot to be fearful of at the time while evading King Saul, who would kill him if he found him.

Seeking the Lord means going to Him in prayer. It can also mean going to His communication for guidance, but here it would have meant prayer. David prayed, the Lord heard him, and now he was delivered from all his fears. Simple. Amazingly so. Can it really be that easy? When your life is aligned with God's Secret, yes, it can be that easy.

Sensible fear
We've said there's good fear and bad fear, but there's also sensible fear. It's another kind of good fear really, though very different from a reverential fear of God. It's the fear that keeps us

from doing dangerous and daft things. Not everybody has it in sufficient quantities, it has to be said. We all do rash or stupid things occasionally. Some people even do them deliberately. They like to override their sensible fear, take risks and enjoy the heady rush they get from it. And some of them pay dearly. The fear that promotes caution is good for us. People who say they fear nothing are not being sensible, and probably not being truthful either. Ask them to share an enclosure with a dozen hungry lions and I'm guessing they'll suddenly recall an earlier appointment.

The fears that keep us from physical harm are valuable instincts. They don't make us cowards, they make us sensible and keep us safe. If we were in a burning building looking at an approaching wall of flame, fear would kick in and we would do our utmost to get out of there, not wait around out of curiosity to see what happened. That's a positive fear that works in our favour.

Caution and precaution are both low-grade versions of sensible fear. It's right to think of such things as fears, and all the time they stay at a sensible level they are not fears we'd want to eliminate. It's good that we put on a seat belt, and that we wash our hands before eating. It's only when these sensible precautions cross the line into obsessions or compulsions that they cease to serve us well and become the kinds of fears we want to lose.

Fear is many things

In everyday speech, we're sparing in our use of the word fear. You may not have noticed, but we're inclined to avoid using it when talking of things which really are fears. We prefer to give our fears other names – names that make them more tolerable and less threatening. We don't like to think of ourselves as fearful, or to have others think of us that way. The problem with that, though, is all the while we re-label our fears as things more acceptable, things we can live with, we are less liable to get rid of them and more likely to become stuck with them. Being free of our fears starts not so much with facing them, but with facing the fact that they really are fears. And, as for facing them, we don't have to do that alone, as David tells us.

The following are some of the things that are fear hiding behind another name; the list might surprise you:

Anxiety	Worry
Stress	Anger
Envy	Negativity
Insecurity	Superstition
Addiction	Boastfulness
Blaming	Pride
Intolerance	Shame
Neuroses	Pessimism
Denial	Grudge bearing
Passive aggression	Uneasiness
Unfriendliness	Easily offended
Self-justifying	Need to be right
Resentment	Overly critical

All these things, and many more like them, are fear, or aspects of fear. Dr Lissa Rankin, who writes on the subject of psychosomatic illness, has a paragraph in her book *The Fear Cure* headed *The*

Masks That Fear Wears, where she writes: 'In our culture, fear tends to masquerade as a lot of other emotions.' She says that we seem to be more willing to admit that **stress** is what plagues us, and we might even wear it as 'practically a badge of honour'. 'We parade our stress,' she writes, 'as proof that we are busy, productive valuable people leaving our mark on the world. But for many people being "stressed out" is just code for being really, really scared.'

We prefer other words, because to admit to fear is to show weakness – and that's something else we fear. So instead we are anxious, because anxiety sounds better. When we are afraid of what others may be thinking of us, we can repackage that as being very upset about it. If we're not very friendly, or not good at socialising, we're content to be labelled as aloof or shy, rather than admit that it's because we fear rejection. I may be over-simplifying it a little, but you get the point, I'm sure.

Spiritual 'insurance'

So many things are traceable to fear. We can even add religion to the list, because people sometimes turn to it from fear rather than love. For the fearful, religion can be more like spiritual insurance than enlightenment. Better to get on the right side of things in case there's a God, or in case there's a hell. Shamefully some preachers will prey on such fears to get and keep converts.

There are some Bible passages that were once the stock-in-trade of those who used to be called the 'hellfire and damnation' preachers. They misused these verses to scare people into salvation – as if such a thing were possible. What they did in fact was scare people away from the truth. I'd thought such a practice had died out long ago, but sadly it's still out there. Watch some of the religious channels and you'll still find them sternly glowering and wagging a finger at the camera. And the reason it's still out there is that sometimes the preachers themselves are fuelled by fear. They are sadly driven by their own anxiety that if they don't 'save souls from hell' they themselves will wind up there. It's a sad travesty of the truth, and the preachers themselves are often its worst victims.

God doesn't want people to fear Him in that way. As David found, God wants to remove all anxiety from our lives. He wants to give us security and peace of mind. He wants to be our *'rock'*, our *'shield'*, and our *'strong tower'*. It must severely disappoint Him when we misunderstand Him and misrepresent Him so. It's our respect and our love for Him that God wants and deserves not our fear and dread.

Love and fear

You probably think that hate is the opposite of love, but hate is just one of the many expressions of fear. The true opposite of love is fear itself. And love is the antidote for it. Love obliterates fear. When we love God we don't fear Him. We reverence Him, appreciate Him, show Him our gratitude, praise Him... we don't fear Him. Not in the wrong way. Love and fear are mutually exclusive.

On this subject, there is an absolute gem of an inspired truth in a New Testament letter written by the Apostle John. He wrote, *'There is no fear in love; but perfect love casteth out fear: because fear hath torment. He that feareth is not made perfect in love.'* (1 John 4.18)

This truth is at the very heart of God's Secret. All worriers should have the opening half-dozen words of this verse framed and on their wall: *'There is no fear in love.'*

Because God is awesome and all-powerful we're prone to make the mistake of **tempering** our love for Him with some fear. It seems only right. We're apt to hold back on the love, not get too close or presume too much. But we can't be positive and negative about God at the same time. Whenever we try that, it's always love that loses. Our love should eliminate fear, but if we hang onto a little fear, because it **seems** right, it will detract from and weaken

No fear

our love. That's not how it's meant to work for us. *'There is no fear in love.'* None at all. There is awe and respect, but not wariness or dread, or any of the other things that are actually fear.

Making a difference

Believers sometimes make the mistake of letting their reverential fear of God turn into the wrong kind of fear. It can be such a subtle development that they don't realise what has happened. They'll claim to have a reverential fear, but in practice it differs hardly at all from a dread of God. Reverence may simply be fear by another name in this case. They are motivated by apprehension rather than love. And they think of this apprehension as a legitimate part of reverence, when it's nothing other than a fear which is diluting and even negating their love for God.

There is a knock-on effect for the whole of their spiritual lives when this happens, because their trust in God is weakened, and they might doubt their salvation and the grace of God. Our reverence for God must be an entirely positive thing. It's about awe, respect, high regard and love. We need to keep anxiety out of it. It's not meant to be there.

David adds to this

Not only is our wrong fear of God cast out by our love for Him, David tells us that, through a loving relationship with God, **any** fear that troubles us can be cast out. If we go to God in faith as David did we can be released from all our fears as he was. The only barrier to this is our own habit of fearfulness. God delivered David because he was willing to believe he was delivered. He was willing to trust.

I know that sounds a little close to the believe-and-achieve psychobabble of the self-help and popular psychology writers. But, as we've said before, these people sometimes connect with the truths of God's Secret. It would be strange if they didn't, considering that they are studying the human mind that God created. David rejoiced that he was delivered from all his fears, even though he was still evading Saul's soldiers. We'll say more about this in a later chapter, when we talk specifically about trust. God wants us to trust Him, and God's Secret shows us that we can and should.

But it's hard to break the fear habit. We can grow oddly comfortable with our fears, and reluctant to let them go even when we don't want them. And when we've been worrying for years it's not going to go away overnight. There's sometimes even a superstitious element to our fears. We worry that if we don't worry, then the thing we're worrying about is more likely to happen. We can believe that our worrying helps to ward it off in some way. But the realisation that God can and will alleviate all our fears when we go to him, and when we learn to live by His Secret, is seriously life changing. Freedom from fear, and real peace of mind is possible.

And what price can we put on peace of mind? We'll learn something extremely helpful about obtaining peace of mind in the next chapter when we talk about a remarkable insight that God has given us in His communication. He tells us how to achieve **perfect** peace. I wasn't aware of this insight until I started working on this book. I couldn't see how the perfect peace God spoke of was attainable, but now I can.

A problem with perfection

Speaking of perfection, there's what looks like a problem with it in that verse about fear and love we quoted earlier. In case you didn't notice, John said that it's not simply **love** which has the amazing power to cast out fear, it's *'**perfect love**'* which *'casteth out fear'*. That seems to throw a whole set of spanners into the works. Love we might manage, but *'perfect love'*, that's something else entirely. Who can manage that?

To the really accomplished worrier this might explain, of course, why they still have, and always will have, their fears. It's because their love isn't perfect, and never will be. And we might all be thinking a little along these lines. So is that it? Do we walk away, back to the dubious comfort of the fears we say we don't want? We knew it was too good to be true. How on earth do we set about making our love perfect? What's the secret here? What are we missing that David so obviously found? How are you and I going to make our love so perfect that we don't fear anymore? Is that even possible? Well, it must be, because God doesn't ask impossible things of us. What would be the point of setting us up to fail? The more we learn about God, the more we learn that He's doing all He can to 'set us up' to succeed.

Growing up

The welcome news is that it really isn't perfect love that this verse is talking about. What's intended is **mature** love. That's what the word really means, and that's how it should be translated. It's not an absolutely faultless and unwavering love that's spoken of here. It's a mature love that is meant.

Unless and until our appreciation of God **matures** we'll be hampered by fears. Until we learn enough about who God really is, and how He relates to us, we'll be wary of Him. Fear is a sign of spiritual immaturity. That's what we're being told. If we're afraid of God, a more mature understanding of Him will overcome that. And if we have all kinds of anxieties, a proper understanding of what God can do for us will help us to overcome them. David is an example of someone with mature love, someone capable of being delivered from all his fears.

But we don't have to be mature in the sense of much older before our love matures. David certainly wasn't **old**. Because John called it mature love doesn't mean it happens only when we get older. It's a progression from an immature kind of love that lacks understanding, holds onto fears, and finds all kinds of reasons to do so, to a mature love that fully trusts and believe. And it can happen at any time we're wise enough to make the transition.

God's Secret

God's Secret is aimed at nurturing mature love and spirituality in us. It gives us grown-up answers to life's questions and problems. It presents us with a worldview, and a set of principles and practices that have stood the test of time because they originate from an eternal mind. True solutions that are as old as the earth. David had the right, mature attitude to God.

Awe-inspiring though He is, God doesn't want us quaking in our boots at the very thought of Him. He wants us to love Him in return for the love that He has already lavished on us. He gave us life and love in the hope that we would do something with them. He communicated His Secret to us in the hope that we would learn and mature spiritually. Truly, as the Apostle John said: *'We love God because He first loved us.'* (1 John 4:19 NKJV) Loving God is a response. We're wrong to think that we initiate it by going to Him and declaring our faith. Any such declaration is a response to what God has already set in motion.

Where love comes from

'The fear of the LORD is the beginning of knowledge' (Proverbs 1:7) and *'The fear of the LORD is the beginning of wisdom.'* (Psalm 111:10) Knowledge and wisdom both begin with the fear of the Lord. They are initiated by the fear of the Lord. When we are truly awed by God, we want to know all we can about Him, and that thirst will lead us to wisdom. And wisdom (which is the marriage of knowledge and understanding) will lead us to loving Him. So it's also true that the fear of the Lord is the beginning of love. There's a progression from fear to wisdom to love, or from reverence to understanding to love.

The right fear leads to love. We start with awe and wonder and perhaps by feeling smaller than ever, but the more we understand and the wiser we become, the closer to love we move. Eventually fear resolves into love. We don't lose our profound respect for God, but it becomes a part of something greater. We will always be God-fearing, but we will grow to love His awesomeness as much as we respect it. So it is that our love matures from its beginnings in the fear of the Lord. And so it is that the fear of the Lord is a key element of God's Secret.

Grace and fear

The more we understand about God from reading His communication, the more we realise how much God understands us. He knows us better than we know ourselves. He knows exactly how we tick, what we are capable of, what we lack and what we need. He's fully aware of our individual deficiencies, so He knows that for a relationship to work between Him and us, He's going to have to make a lot of allowances for us. And He does that. Love is about making allowances after all. But the kind of allowance He has to make for us is **far** greater than any allowance we have to make in our love for one another.

We're looking at one another from the level of one failing human being to another, so for us to make allowances is only fitting. That's how it works between those who profess a love of any kind, be it romantic, brotherly or sisterly, or of deep and enduring friendship. We're either blind to each other's faults and transgressions, or we're not bothered by them. That's how love works among us. We make allowances, there's give and take, because we're all on an equal footing. But we're not on an equal footing with God, and so for our relationship with Him to work something more is needed.

He's looking at us from the standpoint of perfection. So for there to be any kind of relationship, God is going to have to make a huge allowance for us. Or how can He possibly love us? He can't ignore what we are. From His point of view there's an awful lot **not** to love about us. We only see one another partially, but He sees and knows **everything** about us. Which is hardly to our advantage! And so He has introduced something called grace into His relationship with us. Grace is Allowance with a capital A.

Grace is probably the most misunderstood and under-appreciated doctrine of the Bible. Grace is a component of love – a large component. Arguably it's **the** most important part of it. And more than anything, grace is the key to eliminating our very worst fears. It means that God is making a very big Allowance for us. I don't want to say more about it here because we have two chapters on it later in the book. Grace is a big part of God's Secret, and David understood it long before anyone sang about how amazing it is.

Too good to be true?

Returning to our verse in Psalm 34, when David said that he sought the Lord and the Lord heard him and delivered him from all his fears, he wanted us to know that we can experience that same freedom. He wasn't saying 'This worked for me, because I'm David and I know God's Secret.' He was saying that we can have what he had. A life free of the wrong kind of fear is available to all.

It seems too good to be true. Because, after all, we're all natural-born worriers, some of us more than others. We grow up learning to be anxious from almost everyone around us, because fear is contagious. And the worry habit becomes entrenched over time. We become addicted to our fears because they have 'helped' shape our reality; they've become an integral part of the way we think. We can come to believe they are a necessary part of who we are. Shedding them, much as we might want to, feels like losing a part of ourselves. So it's scary to lose them. We fear the world may not make as much sense without them. The truth couldn't be more different. You weren't born with any of the fears that now plague you. You collected them along the way to where you are now.

The fear-free experience of David is open to us all. It's part of God's Secret. With each of the verses of Psalm 34, we'll be adding a new piece to the picture. The more pieces we add, the more spiritual tools we'll have for overcoming our reluctance and for living by the Secret (the counsel, the guidance) of the Lord. So let's not have a defeatist attitude to our fears. They are not us.

'But if not'

I have a confession to make. When I spoke earlier about the good fears that keep us safe, I mentioned a fear of being in an enclosure of hungry lions and a fear of being in a burning building. Those examples weren't chosen at random, but for good reason. The Bible tells us of a man named Daniel who was thrown into a den of hungry lions, and of his three friends who were thrown into a raging furnace. They were being punished for not renouncing their worship of *Yahweh* and for not bowing to the idols of Babylon. All four of them were remarkably fearless, and they all came through their experience unscathed. This shows, **truly remarkably**, that if our love and understanding of God go deep enough, we can trust God and be unafraid, even in the direst of circumstances.

Something the three friends said when they were threatened with being burned alive has stuck in my mind ever since I first read it many years ago. They hoped God would save them, and they were fairly confident, *'But if not...'*, they said – if God wasn't going to intervene for them – it didn't affect their resolve one bit. Those three little words spoke volumes: *'but if not'*. God might save them, or He might not, but either way their love for Him was unshakeable, just as they knew His love for them was too, whatever happened.

They loved and trusted God too much to bow down and worship a heathen god. The outcome was that they were all rescued. An angel of the Lord stepped in – literally in the case of the three friends, because one stepped into the furnace with them to protect them. Another kept the hungry lions away from Daniel.

You'll be pleased to hear that believers are not generally called on to exhibit this heroic level of faith. But what happened to Daniel and his friends does show us the level of trust that is possible for those who know and live by God's Secret. It is possible to be **completely** unafraid when you trust in God completely. That level of freedom from fear is attainable. Something to bear in mind here, though, is that Daniel and his friends had this situation forced upon them. They weren't seeking out danger for the thrill of it, or being reckless because they knew they had God's protection so it didn't matter what they did. The freedom from fear that comes with loving God and living His Secret will never lead us down that path.

Angels and miracles

Daniel and his friends experienced miraculous interventions by the angels. I know that miracles can provoke scepticism (as do angels, though not so much). The Bible records a lot of miraculous events. And if that should make you doubt the Bible, then try to imagine a Bible without miracles: a Bible in which God or His angels or His prophets or His Son never did anything out of the ordinary. I don't know about you, but for me such a Bible would be a lot less like a communication from a divine Being. I'd expect to find supernatural events in a communication from a supernatural Being. And, taking it a step further, in a world that is still watched over by that same supernatural Being, I would expect there still to be supernatural events.

Miracles still happen. The angels may not be as overt in their dealings with us nowadays, but they are still at work on behalf of the God-fearing. And they are the subject of a later chapter.

15 Happiness

'They looked unto him, and were lightened: and their faces were not ashamed.' (Psalm 34:5)

Back in 1978, Dr Frank Minirith and Dr Paul Meier wrote a book called *Happiness is a Choice*. It was a great success, though many people were irritated by the idea that their unhappiness was their own fault. The concept of happiness being a choice lingers on to this day, together with the irritation. If you want to point out to someone that their unhappiness is their choice, then be ready to make a quick exit. I wouldn't recommend the experiment, so please just take my word for it.

Surprisingly, *Happiness is a Choice* is a religious book. In addition to being clinically qualified, Drs Minirith and Meier both have degrees in theology. And they say quite a lot about the difference in approach they have to make in their clinical practice towards believers and non-believers. For them, a believer has less excuse for unhappiness than a non-believer.

There's a lot of truth in what they say. We do have more control than we might think, or care to admit, over our moods and emotions. And a believer is more likely to be happy, and has less excuse not to be. But it's not as clinically clear-cut as the two doctors make out. The book's title harks back to something Abraham Lincoln said, and said far better: 'Most people are about as happy as they choose to be.' His version is better because it's more relaxed and doesn't come across as a fixed law of life. And although it doesn't make for such a snappy book title, the use of the phrase 'about as happy' makes it a lot closer to the truth. Because where our happiness in concerned, there are factors apart from choice to be taken into account – factors like our nature and our nurture: who we are and what we've been through to get

When you're happy and you know it

In his Psalm, David says of certain people that *'They looked unto him* [the Lord] *and were lightened.'* If you've ever seen somebody really pleased about something then you'll know exactly what he means. The glow on the face of a student, for instance, who just learned about her excellent grades. I'm reminded that years ago, after I'd just passed my driving test, I tried to fool my family into thinking that I'd failed by walking into the house with a glum expression. But as hard as I tried, I couldn't wipe the grin off my face.

When you're really happy about something it shows – you beam – and that's what happened to those people David saw. They looked to God and they beamed because He'd come to their aid. The people David was referring to were most likely the band of followers that joined him after his escape from Gath. They'd been longing and praying for his safe return.

Looking to God

But when David's followers looked to God, they took more than a brief glance in His direction. They hadn't just turned religious in a crisis. There's a temporary kind of 'religious conversion' that I've heard called fox-hole Christianity. It's the prayer of desperation in a tight corner, of an unbeliever who will subsequently explain away their escape, should it come, as incredibly lucky, and then carry on in their unbelief. The experience will maybe produce a deep sigh of relief after the adrenaline rush of the situation, but not the happy glow of appreciation that comes from knowing in your heart that you looked to God and He was there for you.

A more literal translation of *'were lightened'* is 'were made radiant'. That's not just 'Phew! Lucky escape!' It's the glow we feel inside that spreads all over our face when we know something marvellous has happened for us. That's probably why we call them

Happiness

facial expressions, because they express on our faces how we feel inside.

For those who know God's Secret, looking to God becomes a way of life. Not for them the expediency of fox-hole Christianity. Those people David mentions who looked to God and were made radiant, were friends of his who already knew and believed in *Yahweh*. We know some of the story behind Psalm 34, but we need to bear in mind that the truths David wrote about under inspiration are bigger than the events of his life which prompted him to write about them. They were true for him in his situation, and they are true for everyone in similar situations. They provide a pattern for us, to show us how God interacts with us, which is why God included them in His Word.

It helps us today to share in the delight of David's friends when their prayers were answered and he was returned safely to them. Their radiance was not because they'd now discovered God, but because they'd been reassured that He would act supportively for them and for David. In the normal way, as believers, they enjoyed a certain ongoing level of happiness from knowing God in their day-to-day lives. But occasionally they were made radiant by some especially good God-sent event. This is how life is when we know God's Secret. We are generally happy, and sometimes we are radiantly happy.

Made for happiness

Happiness is what we all want for ourselves. We often want it for others, too. And that can be either altruistic, or it might be because the happiness of others, especially those closest to us, contributes so much to our own happiness. It's harder to be happy around miserable people, so we prefer them to be happy, too. Happiness is one of our most basic drives, perhaps the most fundamental and necessary of them all. Without happiness what is life? There's hardly any enjoyment in anything. Life becomes mere ex
not living. For life to be worth it we need to have a reasonal
of happiness. It's what God wants for us, too.

God's Secret

We are made to be happy. Which is a simple deduction from Proverbs 3:13: *'Happy is the man that findeth wisdom, and the man that getteth understanding.'* God wants us to find wisdom and to get understanding. These things bring happiness. So it follows that He wants us to be happy. Specifically, He wants us to be happy in the only way that happiness can properly be achieved and enjoyed. He doesn't want us chasing rainbows for an illusion of happiness. He goes to great lengths in His communication to provide us with the necessary wisdom and understanding that will make us truly and lastingly happy. So, yes, we are made to be happy.

God's wisdom and understanding – the things we are looking at in God's Secret – ensure a good day-to-day level of happiness. Way above average. Unlike those gloomy cartoon characters who have rain-clouds following them around, we carry some portable internal sunshine with us everywhere we go. Occasionally, as with David's friends when he was returned to them, we experience times of exceptional punch-the-air happiness. But for them, as for us, the joy runs down after a while, and we drop back to a more sustainable level of happiness. We can't live in a state of perpetual glee. That's not normal for anyone, and not what we should expect from being a believer.

If you meet someone in the queue at the supermarket, who is usually excitable and demonstrative when in their place of worship, you're likely to find a more demure character, I'm sure. Which is as it should be. (And, incidentally, it's not the norm for **everyone** to be animated in church. Some are, some aren't. As we've said, we're all different.)

To be permanently bubbling over about the joys of the Christian life is not actually an attractive quality. Nor is it symptomatic of the kind of peace that believers enjoy. It suggests a more restless state of mind. I've encountered people like that and noticed that over time it can drain them and leave them low, because they can't work out why, when they've given their all, they can't maintain it and they feel so unhappy. God seems to have let them down. But He never does that. Sometimes we need to learn that God already knows how much we love and appreciate Him and His Word, without us having to demonstrate it continually to Him, to others and to ourselves. Enthusiasm is great, but not when it's without let up because of some underlying insecurity. That's nothing like the happiness God wants for us.

Of course, some people are naturally enthusiastic in whatever they do, and they have the energy to match, and it's great when they bring that to their religion. They don't tire us they inspire us, because they have the ability to relax and operate at a lower setting whenever they want to. They are connected to the peace as well as the power of religion. Perhaps their general happiness level is set a little higher than most. Which, to get back to it, is what we're talking about here: general happiness. For believers, happiness is like an emotional true north, towards which their inner compass is always trying to point them.

Accept no substitutes

The right to pursue happiness is written into the American constitution. I'm not sure how that works, or whether the government gets complaints from those whose pursuit has been thwarted. But the concept of the **pursuit** of happiness doesn't seem quite right. It seems to put happiness forever ahead of us and never in our grasp. We know what it means, and it is a noble sentiment that the highway to happiness should be open to all, but it doesn't help us to think of happiness as something we have to pursue. It can make us think it's not something we can ever catch.

Solomon says, happy is the one who **finds** wisdom and who **gets** understanding, rather than the one who chases after them. It's a little pedantic, maybe, and sometimes pursuing things like peace is as good and legitimate as attaining them, and doesn't mean we won't ever attain them, but I just want to get across that the Bible is positive about our ability to be happy **now**. As I said, we're made to be happy.

God's Secret

But we're not made to be any kind of happy. We're made to be happy in a way that's good for us and true. Our happiness needs to connect with reality. That's what God wants for us. It's what He's showing us in His Secret. Real happiness comes through the wisdom and understanding He gives us. That's the important thing to remember about happiness. There's only one genuine version of it. We should accept no substitutes.

It's a common belief that happiness comes in all shapes and sizes. Happiness is reckoned to be as varied as the people who have it. We're all different. We all like different things. So happiness is different for each one of us. That seems right. But it can't be. Because, if God tells us where happiness is to be found, and many people think that they have found it somewhere else, then what is it that they have found? They must have found something else, something which has the appearance of it, but which isn't real happiness.

Because our drive for happiness is so strong and fundamental (we're made for it, remember), it follows that when we reject the genuine version, we're not just going to go without, we're going to look for a replacement. We're going to manufacture our own. Though what many people create for themselves is not even their own, it's more of a consensus happiness. It's the agreed version, with variations, that a lot of people have settled on.

A worldview that leaves God out of it will disconnect us from reality. Without the understanding and wisdom that God offers, our understanding of the world will be limited and faulty, and any so-called wisdom arising from that understanding will be likewise. So the general principles by which we live will be adrift. Even if we have integrity because we live rightly according to our principles and our worldview, it will be of no real value. All it will mean is that we act consistently with our wrong view of things. Any happiness we derive from living with wrong ideas about life will be precarious because its foundations are shaky. It can't be real happiness because it's based entirely on the unreal things we've been telling ourselves. This may sound harsh, but I can't think of a gentler way to put it.

Where real happiness comes from

But that's enough discussion for now, let's get practical. We're about to look at something remarkable that believers can do to promote their happiness. God's Secret is very much about the promotion of real happiness, both for God and ourselves: '... *for thou hast created all things, and for thy pleasure they are and were created.*' (Revelation 4:11) The very word 'gospel' means good news. Everything we look at in His Secret is another piece of an overall happy picture that God is showing us.

Real happiness comes from knowing these things, but it also comes from putting them into practice. Many of the things that make up God's Secret are not only truths to take on board, they are activities to engage in. The activity may sometimes be mental or spiritual, rather than physical, but it's nonetheless an activity. It's something we do. We're about to look at a particular thing we can do that has remarkable benefits.

In Part One we mentioned that one of the meanings of the word 'secret' is the ability to do something really well. You may have the secret of propagating roses effectively. Well, now we're going to look at one of the secrets of real happiness. We're going to look now at a verse of the Bible, not from David this time, but from a man named Isaiah. You may have heard of him. He was a prophet (meaning a teacher as well as someone who speaks of the future) who, like David, was also inspired to write a song. Here's the remarkable second line from that song:

> '*Thou wilt keep him in perfect peace, whose mind is stayed on thee: because he trusteth in thee.*' (Isaiah 26:3)

At first glance that may not appear too special. But this is a truly remarkable verse. It's one to keep in your heart and reflect on

God's Secret

regularly. I'd certainly recommend it to you if you want a lifetime of personal happiness. The verse has a generally good feel about it. But there's far more to it than that. It's a recipe for perfect peace in seventeen powerful words. And I can tell you now that one of those words is hiding an insight that's extra special. One of those words could be better translated, in fact **ought** to have been, and knowing its proper meaning will furnish us with the means of attaining personal happiness. But we'll come to that shortly.

The first thing to notice about the verse is that it's not just God telling Isaiah that He will keep him personally in perfect peace, and so on; it's the prophet telling all believers everywhere something that he knows God will do for any of them: *'Thou wilt keep him* [whoever they may be] *in perfect peace, whose mind is stayed on thee: because he trusteth in thee.'* It's something Isaiah had learned from personal experience. When he kept his thoughts on God and trusted in Him, he enjoyed perfect peace. He didn't have to worry about a thing.

But Isaiah's personal experience was elevated to a universal truth when the prophet was inspired by God to write it down and it was included in God's communication to us. His words became inspired scripture. And notice that there are no modifying clauses of the 'yes, but' sort attached to what he said, to lessen the impact of it. It stands exactly as Isaiah wrote it. When we centre our thoughts on God and put our trust in Him, God will do for us what He did for the prophet: He will give us **perfect** peace. By the means that we'll come to in a moment.

The reverse is also true
It's very useful to look at this verse from another angle. Turning it around, the verse tells another story. It tells us that if someone doesn't have perfect peace, it's because their mind is **not** stayed on God, and they are **not** trusting in Him. There can be no other reason for their lack of it, because there is no other real and lasting way to perfect peace. It doesn't come from relaxing or meditating, or from anything else like that, pleasant as these things may be.

Happiness

It rarely if ever occurs to most people that they don't have perfect peace because they are not thinking of God and trusting in Him. That would scarcely ever cross their minds. Although it's the truth about their situation. If you ask them what's wrong when they're down, they'll give other reasons. They'll say it's because of something that happened to them, or the bad breaks they've had, or because of what 'he said' or what 'she did', or what 'those people' are doing. These are the kinds of reasons they'll give for their cheerless state, and they most likely genuinely believe them to be the causes. There are 1,001 reasons for being unhappy – almost all of them avoiding the real reason. (I say 'almost' here because there are certain mental conditions which may preclude happiness. Not that such conditions necessarily rule out someone knowing and living God's Secret as well as they are able. We dare not say **anyone** is beyond that.)

Our happiness is not dependent on other people or on things that happen to us. If we are going to wait for people and circumstances to change in precisely the way we want before we can be happy, then we're probably going to have to wait indefinitely. Do we want to put off being happy indefinitely? It makes no sense. Unless we're of that sorry brigade who seem to relish being unhappy. The ones who constantly complain and feel hard done by. It might make them feel better to believe they are right when so much else is wrong, as well it might be wrong, but that's a high price to pay for the loss of real happiness. So don't wait for the world to change around you. Real happiness is an inside job.

Though aren't we veering towards 'happiness is a choice' here? Hold that thought, because we've put off revealing one of the secrets of perfect happiness for too long already.

Imagine that!

One of the keys – no, **the master key** to real happiness is found in what Isaiah said in that verse we looked at: *'Thou wilt keep him in perfect peace whose mind is stayed on thee.'* As we said, one of the words in that verse is hiding the key, because it was not correctly translated. The word that appears as *'mind'* in that verse is quite a rare word in scripture and should be translated 'imagination'. What we are being told is that we will have perfect peace when our **imagination, not simply our mind,** is centred on God. That's an important difference.

Imagination is a wonderful thing. It can take us mentally anywhere we want to go. Someone once made the comment that they preferred radio to television because the pictures were better. The imagination is amazingly versatile. Without it the arts and sciences would be struggling, or more likely non-existent. But there is a down side to it. It can work both for and against us. And all too often we allow it to work against us. We let it rob us of our peace instead of using it to bring us peace. We let our thoughts churn over and over on negative situations and outcomes. Catastrophising somebody aptly called it. It's letting our imagination run riot, working overtime on how bad things are and how much worse they could get. That's the way to kill happiness – and every chance of it, I would think.

Worry is the work of the imagination. It doesn't exist outside our imagination. So we have to take charge and use our imagination differently. When we lack peace of mind, when we lack happiness, the secret is to make God the focus of our thoughts. Trust Him for a good outcome whatever your situation, however bad things might look. Don't abuse your imagination by feeding it with negativity; use it to your advantage by fixing it upon the God you can trust. We need to intercept our imagination whenever we catch it setting off on a journey of worry and send it down a more positive road.

Don't think: What could go wrong? How much worse could this get? I can't see any way out of this. Think instead: How will God get me through this? How is God working right now to make things turn out well for me? Fix your imagination on God and all the things He can do in your favour. And not just once in a while. Make it a habit. Make it your permanent mindset.

Happiness

But don't just insert this right way of thinking into a wrong worldview. The perfect peace that comes from using the imagination this way is compatible only with the right worldview. You'll probably realise that this won't work outside, or independently of God's Secret. There may be a moderate 'placebo effect' from using the imagination this way, because our minds and bodies are designed to react favourably to a positive outlook. But this is more than positive thinking, or what the New Age movement calls 'the law of attraction', by which we are supposedly able to use our imaginations to manifest whatever we want for ourselves.

What God is telling us through Isaiah is that we must use our imaginations to demonstrate the trust we have in the God we believe in as a part of our worldview. God responds favourably to our trust in Him and our reliance on Him. But if we use our imaginations negatively that shows we don't trust Him.

Happiness is a choice

Yes, our happiness **is** a choice. But it's not a simple decision to be happy or not. Such a decision will be about as effective as most New Years' resolutions. It won't last. The real choice is whether to trust God or not. The choice is whether to learn and live by His Secret or not. The choice is whether to use our imaginations in ways which demonstrate we trust God or not. These are the real choices we have to make when it comes to having real happiness or not.

Real happiness **is** a choice, but it's more than just the choice to be happy, it's the choice to trust God, and to do that within the worldview that His Secret provides. David and his followers made the right choice, and they were beaming.

Not ashamed

When David said that those who looked to God were beaming, he added that *'their faces were not ashamed.'* He meant that those who looked to God had no reason to regret it. They'd not put their faith in someone who'd let them down and so now they were ashamed. They were not hanging their heads for having trusted in someone who couldn't deliver; they were holding their heads high and beaming. They'd trusted God. In their hearts they knew He would come to their aid, even when things had looked bad, and God had responded.

Stopped in my tracks

A simple message on a day-to-day tear-off calendar many years ago changed my perception of religion. Often those things are banal and cringe-worthy, but this one stopped me in my tracks. It said: 'A man's religion should be the happiest thing in his life.' At the time, mine wasn't, and this woke me up to the fact that it should be, and set me on the path to finding out why and what I could do about it. In fact a lot of what I did about it is in this book and in previous books. Religion is meant to be a happy thing. Not necessarily singing-and-dancing happy, though why not if that's how it affects you, but lifting the spirits. If religion's message is depressing you, then you're getting the wrong message. You're not looking at the same God that David was looking at. He found that when people looked to his God, their faces became radiant with happiness.

Sorrow

Before closing these thoughts on happiness, let's not ignore the fact that sometimes unhappiness is appropriate. In some situations it is the only healthy response, and we must go along with it. I don't need to elaborate. Though the right word here is sorrow rather than unhappiness. I don't believe it's insensitive for me to say that real happiness can run deep enough to accompany and survive sorrow. And that it can be our pathway through and out of it. The comfort of God's counsel can help us through times of sorrow. Especially the secret of perfect peace from Isaiah. It can give us something positive to hang onto and look forward to when things seem anything but positive.

16 NO TROUBLE

'This poor man cried, and the LORD heard him, and saved him out of all his troubles.' (Psalm 34:6)

When David described himself as *'this poor man'* in this verse, he wasn't referring the state of his finances; he was talking about his mental and emotional state – what is better described as his spiritual state.

We know this is about his spiritual state because the word for *'poor'* in the original language points to oppression not poverty. When David wrote this he had been in a low place spiritually. He was being hounded and oppressed without just cause by a king who wanted him dead. But as we saw in the last verse, there was still much to be happy about. And in this verse he continues to give God thanks and credit for his recent deliverance from Achish king of Gath.

In the first five verses of Psalm 34, David has told us about being grateful and humble, praising God, being delivered from all our fears, and being made radiantly happy. Now he goes on to say that he's been rescued from **all** his troubles. Knowing his situation, that he was still in danger from King Saul's men who were hunting him, and that he had only a few hundred men with him, it seems a little premature for him to say he'd been delivered from all his troubles. But things were looking up. He now had this band of men. And small though it was, it was a start. And he'd escaped what looked like certain death at the hands of the Philistines. His situation had certainly improved. It was still quite a stretch, though, for him to say that all his troubles were now behind him. David must have known that he was a long way from being out of danger.

God's Secret

Not in denial
But David wasn't deluding himself. In a very real sense, his problems **were** behind him. Because if he'd ever had any doubts at all about God being on his side, those doubts were gone now. The oppressed man had cried to God and He had come to his aid. The man in a low spiritual state, disheartened and afraid, had looked to *Yahweh* and had experienced His direct help. God was with him. Now he was absolutely sure of that. So, however bad his situation still looked, he had every reason to believe that all was in fact well. He had been saved from all that was troubling him.

David had more problems in his life than most of us will ever have to deal with, and yet he was able to find complete contentment. With God's Secret as his guiding light, he was able to see beyond his problems to the reality of the hand of God in his affairs. He knew he could trust God to see him through whatever lay ahead. How true it is what somebody once said:

> 'Those who leave everything in God's hands will one day see God's hand in everything.'

That's how it had turned out for David. And now he wanted to make a song and dance about it. Well certainly a song, because that's what this Psalm is, and perhaps also a dance, because he was known to dance around when he was exhilarated by the things God did. He didn't do it just to get it out of his system; it was to let everyone in the vicinity know about his amazing God. It wasn't, 'Hey, look at me!' it was 'Hey, look at God!'

Why do troubles happen to righteous people?
The fact that David was delivered from his troubles tells us that he had troubles to be delivered from. Which sounds a bit obvious, but it's important to remember that those who live by God's Secret are not shielded from everything that might go wrong. They are not sealed off in a trouble-free cocoon of protection. They live in the same world as everyone else. Therefore they have the same things to deal with as everyone else.

No trouble

Peter, one of the New Testament writers, had to remind his fellow believers that they shouldn't react to their problems *'as though some strange thing happened unto you'*. (1 Peter 4:12) And Paul, the most prominent of the New Testament writers, told believers that: *'There hath no temptation taken you but such as is common to man.'* (1 Corinthians 10:13) In other words, don't be surprised, as believers, that things still go wrong for you, or even that you still have impulses to do the wrong things.

But if that's the case, what advantage is there in being a believer? Why should we bother with God's Secret if it changes nothing with regard to what happens to us?

Well, for a start, that's not entirely true. It does change things. But the motivation for becoming a believer is not primarily to avoid problems. Insofar as it does protect us, that's a side effect. If that's the main attraction, then we're going to be disappointed.

The reason we become believers is because we have grasped that there must be a God – we have recognised that the book we call the Bible is His communication to us, and from that communication we have learned who He is and what He is doing. As a consequence, we are in awe of Him, and we want to praise and magnify Him. As our wisdom and appreciation grow, our fear diminishes and love takes up more room. Added to which, as someone who had reached all these conclusions about God and travelled this same spiritual path once wrote: *'We love him, because he first loved us.'* (1 John 4:19) We don't start the process by loving God; He started it by loving us. It's our awakening to His love which inspires our response of love.

God's Secret is not a magical formula that will make everything always go right for us. The easy ride is not good for us because it will leave us untried and lacking depth of character and spiritual maturity. God doesn't want us to miss out on the experience of real life by steering us around every obstacle. Partly, I should think, because He doesn't want to be the Heavenly Father of children with no real experience of the world. Most parents know that it does children no good to shield them from every adverse circumstance, give them all that they want, and make life too easy for them. That's the way to produce spoilt children. And our Heavenly Father doesn't want the spiritual equivalent of spoilt children.

Believers get problems, but, as we've already seen, they also get the spiritual skills to handle them effectively. Perfect peace is still possible even in the midst of problems. That's what David illustrates by telling us he's been delivered from all his troubles. His troubles were still there but he'd been delivered from them! In the midst of troubles is where we learn most about the value of God's peace and where we can find the incentive to cultivate it. Most of us would settle for less than perfect peace. Just a little more peace than we have would be good. How close we get to perfect peace is up to us and to how committed we are to centring our minds on God's care for us, rather than imagining all the things that might go wrong, or what seems to have gone irreparably wrong already.

A way to escape

We're going to learn a lot more about this in the chapters ahead, especially in the next two chapters, one of which is about the work of the angels among us. Before we move on, though, there's something else we should look at regarding believers having similar trials to everyone else. We are helped by focusing on God, which is a great advantage. But how we fare in times of trouble is not all down to us. Something else happens when a believer gets stuck in a problem. And here lies one of the answers to the question 'what advantage is there in being a believer?'

We didn't finish that quotation from Paul we made a few paragraphs ago. Here's the whole verse: *'There hath no temptation taken you but such is common to man: but God is faithful, who will not suffer you to be tempted above that ye are*

No trouble

able; but will with the temptation also make a way to escape, that ye may be able to bear it.' (1 Corinthians 10:13)

That throws more light on things. When God allows problems to come our way that are difficult to handle, and when we seem to be getting a lot more than we can cope with, there is a limit to how severe, and for how long, God will allow those problems to remain. Even though a difficult situation may continue for some time, and there may seem no end to it – even then, a believer knows that they will not be pushed beyond their ability to handle it. A point will be reached, and something will happen to alleviate the problem. And this will be God providing *'a way to escape'*. *'God is faithful,'* writes Paul. He won't desert us when our need is greatest.

When we've turned our imagination away from all the bad places to which our situation might be leading us, and when we've centred our thoughts on God, and yet matters are still not improving, Paul says, hang on, don't despair, a way of escape will come. Wait and watch.

What Paul was getting at

God has no desire to push us so far that we fail. He takes no delight in punishing the wicked (Ezekiel 33:11), so He certainly won't want to bring harm to those He loves. He is faithful to us. He will step in if and when we can't cope. The essential thing in those situations, though, is to **let** Him in. We can become so wrapped up in our little personal world of problems, so immersed in fearful imaginings and misgivings that we fail to see the big helping hand extended towards us. God might leave us a little longer in our situation so that we get some experience and spiritual maturity from it (to help our trust in Him to grow), but not for so long that we give up on Him. Because that is the worst consequence of unrelenting problems: we might lose faith and doubt that God really cares, or even exists.

It was to help prevent believers turning away from God that Paul revealed what he did about the *'way to escape'* from temptations.

The believers he wrote to were suffering persecution from the Roman authorities, and it was severely trying their faith. Paul didn't want believers to become so overwhelmed by their inability to handle the problem that they gave up trying to be righteous and turned away from God. That was potentially the most calamitous temptation they faced. Help handling temptations is not usually, if ever, about God reducing the attraction of things like greed, lust, or revenge. He doesn't influence our minds so we're less greedy, lustful or vengeful. That's for us to work on, not Him, using the tools He has given us.

The way of escape Paul mentions is a way of escape from the temptation to abandon God because of our problems, or how badly we think we're managing them. That's what he was getting at. In dire circumstances, a way of escape will open. But that doesn't mean God will alter a believer's thinking to reduce temptation. Again, it's a matter of believers using the spiritual tools God has already given them. In fact this is about them using the most powerful and versatile tool in the spiritual tool box. In addition to using their imaginations positively, which is a great help in dealing with troubles, believers are offered a way of escape that will open up for them whenever they turn their attention on it.

Though it's not so much **a** way to escape, it's **the** way to escape that will open. That's what the verse really says. Paul used the definite article, **the**, because he had a particular way to escape in mind. It's the way which is perfectly designed to eliminate the temptation to give up and abandon trying to live the righteous life. But more of that later – much more. We have two chapters up ahead, called *The grace escape* parts 1 and 2, that will explain the *'way to escape'* more fully.

Do you really love me?

This is a question we sometimes put to those we love, and which may put them on the spot. Though hopefully not. Do you really love me? We may have doubts because of the way they've been acting towards us. Or maybe we haven't heard the three magic

No trouble

words in a while, so we want to hear them again. Usually there's nothing to worry about, and it's just us feeling a little insecure. We like to know that we are loved by those we love. God is the same in this respect. He loves us, and He wants to know that we love Him in return. Not that God is ever insecure. That's never going to happen. But He does want to see some evidence of love in those who profess to love Him. Is there any depth to our love, or is it shallow, and will it evaporate in the heat of problems?

God wants to know that we really do believe in His presence and that He loves and cares for us. And He finds out these things by making it seem for a while as if He is not there and that He doesn't care. We know this from the experience of the nation of Israel. After God brought them out of slavery in Egypt, they were made to wander in the wilderness for many years before settling down in their promised land. We're told in the New Testament that these very things were put on record in the Old Testament to help us understand how God works with believers. (1 Corinthians 10:11)

God allowed the people to get thirsty or hungry, or be under serious threat from the neighbouring peoples. He didn't sort out everything in advance – let them know in good time that water would be made available (which it would be), food was on the way (which it was), and there was nothing to fear from the people around them (which there wasn't). None of that. God stood back and watched. He waited to see how they would deal with the situation.

Did they believe in His presence? Did they trust in His care? Did they love Him? Or were they fair-weather believers – only okay when things were going well for them and God was giving them all they wanted? Was their love little more than a love for the things God gave them? – present only when they could see no end or interruption to the food supply? God's intention was not to harm them, but simply to discover the true condition of their hearts concerning Him.

And wisdom tells us that God will sometimes deal with believers today in the same way on their journey through life. When we understand what's going on, we're better able to handle it. When God seems far away and uncaring about our situation, these are the times we need to pause and think of Israel in the wilderness. We are being watched. God **is** there, and He cares, and He will demonstrate that as we continue to show Him that we believe and trust. That way of escape that Paul mentioned will open up for us.

And just to be clear, it wasn't the complaints of the people of Israel that brought the food and water they needed. Those things were already on the way. God hadn't brought the entire nation out of Egypt so that they could die of hunger and thirst in the wilderness. Though that was what they sometimes thought. God just wanted to hold back a short while to see if they truly believed and trusted in His love and care. As it turned out, most of them didn't – but the food and water still came.

What about omniscience?
Objectors like Richard Dawkins argue that if God knows everything why does He need to test us to find out whether we really love Him. Surely He already knows. Of course God knows how people are thinking and feeling, and how they will react when He tests them. When He tests people it's not so much for His benefit as theirs. The reason is to bring the truth He already knows about us out into the open, so that we can see it, too. God wants to make us as aware as He is of our spiritual condition. Testing us in appropriate ways brings about this shared awareness, and will hopefully improve relations. That's why we get tested with troubles sometimes.

Time to move on.
The righteous will get troubles, pretty much the same as everyone else gets them. We live in the same world so it's going to happen. The important thing to remember is that God is always faithful and will provide a way of escape when we need one. As mentioned,

we're going to be talking a lot more about this in chapters 27 and 28 when we get to the subject of grace.

Knowing that we are saved from all our troubles, even when those troubles are still with us is a paradoxical and essential part of God's Secret. David certainly understood it. It means we can look beyond our troubles and trust God to steer us safely through them. David also knew of the very practical means by which God sometimes does the steering. We know that, because in Psalm 34, immediately after talking about being saved from all his troubles, he goes on to talk about the work of the angels. So that's where we'll go, too.

17 Angels

'The angel of the LORD encampeth round about them that fear him, and delivereth them.' (Psalm 34:7)

I've always been daunted by novels that have a cast list of a page or two to help us keep track of who's who. But that's nothing compared with the roughly eight billion lives and stories that are running concurrently here on God's Creation, all of which He can keep track of.

The angels are the ones God employs to help in this work. They act on His behalf to steer people and events generally in the way they need to go in order to stay in line with God's overall plan for the world. A lot of what they do is fairly passive, allowing people to get on with their lives and not interfering unless they really have to. But, as we can tell from what David says in this seventh verse, the angels have a special interest in those who fear God. The angels' role in their lives is more active.

God's messengers

The word angel means 'messenger' or 'agent', from which we can tell that much of their work is about communication, and acting on behalf of others. They are constantly relaying information from one to another in order to maintain some order across a world that might seem chaotic at times. But, because of what they are doing continually behind the scenes, it's a lot more organised than we might think. In addition to keeping in touch with one another, they communicate with God, and sometimes, when it's really necessary, they'll communicate more openly with individuals. Though they generally keep a low profile among us.

In the past the angels were more openly active, meeting and talking with people, involving themselves in people's lives on

Angels

God's behalf. But whenever they did this they always had a specific purpose in mind, they were on a particular errand, as, for instance, the angel Gabriel was when he visited Mary to tell her of the baby that was to be born to her. These kinds of personal visits, though, were few and far between. The angels' work has always been mostly invisible. But that doesn't mean it's always unnoticeable.

The chief function of the angels, as David knew, is to look after those who fear God: the ones who understand God's Secret. The Bible describes the angels' function in this way: *'Are they not all ministering spirits, sent forth to minister for them who shall be heirs of salvation?'* (Hebrews 1:14) Their work is to minister to, to assist in every way they can, those who will ultimately be the *'heirs of salvation'*. That last phrase might seem a little obscure but it means simply those who will inherit the eternal life that God has promised to those who fear Him. They are the ones in which the angels have a particular interest. We'll take a closer look at this verse about the angels' work in a few moments. First let's clear up some popular misconceptions about them.

A web of misinformation

Most bookstores these days have a set of shelves allocated to Mind and Spirit. Here you'll usually find a selection of New Age books about angels. According to this genre, the angels are at the beck and call of anyone who knows the right words or rituals to summon them, and they'll do almost anything we ask. This is about as far from the truth as it can possibly get. There are usually some passing references in these books to the angels in the Bible, but clearly the books' sources are more New Age pagan than they are biblical.

I have such a book in front of me as I write: *The Power of Angels,* by Wendy Hobson. Its opening remarks sum up remarkably accurately the problem with such books. She writes: 'Although mentioned frequently in the Bible, [angels] are only occasionally named and so, like the 'three wise men' of the Nativity, a web of information has been spun around them.' Here lies the problem. The 'web of information' goes far beyond what is known and extends into guesswork and fancifulness. People are now more familiar with these imaginary angels than they are with the real ones.

It's ironic that the author should speak of the web spun around the 'three wise men', when she has inadvertently been caught in it herself. It's only tradition that there were three of them. They brought three gifts to the infant Jesus, so it's assumed there must have been three of them. But the Bible never refers to three wise men. There may have been only two. Some sources suggest more than three.

Books such as *The Power of Angels* abound with conjecture, providing angels' names, their particular qualities and skills, the colours and crystals associated with them, and much more. They give us every unknowable detail they can. The web of information spun around the angels has become, for many, more familiar and plausible than the original biblical truth about them.

This kind of book leans heavily on anecdotal evidence. There are always stories about seemingly miraculous angelic interventions in people's lives. Most of the stories can be accounted for by natural occurrences. In a world of around eight billion people, someone is going to be prevented now and then from boarding a plane that crashes. It's a matter of numbers more than miracles. The world would be an odder place if these things didn't occasionally happen.

Though I'm not saying that we should dismiss **every** account of angelic intervention as mistaken or fabricated. There are bound to be fraudsters and attention seekers among those claiming some kind of angelic intervention in their lives. And there are bound to be people who have had something extraordinary happen to them that could be interpreted as help from an angel, and they've convinced themselves that it must have been, though it probably

Angels

wasn't. But, even allowing for the mistaken and the deceitful, there are still going to be occasions when those who claim to have had an angelic encounter are right. Most of those who are right will, of course, be believers, but by no means all of them.

For example, a little girl saved from drowning by a mysterious stranger who just happened to be in the right place at the right time and who slipped away unnoticed afterwards – that little girl could have grown up to be a believer, or to become the mother of a God-fearing righteous person, which was foreseen by the angel. Or in some other positive way she could have impacted the life of a believer. In any number of ways like this the angels must surely intervene in the lives of some of those who are not believers, and who may never be, in the process of looking after the righteous. The angels are helping to oversee an entire world of intersecting lives, billions of stories criss-crossing, interfacing, helping and hindering one another in a myriad ways, subtly and sometimes conspicuously. The angels' main task is to look after the righteous ones in the midst of all this, as the Bible says, but that is bound to have a ripple effect across much of humanity.

The angels also have the work of helping to keep God's plan and purpose with the world on track. That means they have a hand in steering into place those who govern the world, the leaders and politicians, and even the dictators where necessary, for we're told *'the most High ruleth in the kingdom of men, and giveth it to whomsoever he will.'* (Daniel 4:32) It's not inconsistent with all this that the angels will sometimes have to intervene directly in the lives of people other than the righteous, in the process of looking after the righteous. Such interventions might seem random to us, and happen sometimes to people with no particular religious leanings, but the angels can see a far bigger picture, and they are aware of all the influences we each bring to bear on one another, knowingly or otherwise.

God's Secret

Public servants

We can learn a little more about the angels by returning to that verse we quoted earlier about them being *'ministering spirits, sent forth to minister'* to the God-fearing. In the Greek of the New Testament, that word translated *'ministering'* is associated with public service. In the UK we're already used to associating ministering with public service because we refer to our leading politicians as ministers, and the head of government as our Prime Minister. They are appointed to serve the country. This is the sense in which the angels minister.

Their public service is to serve the world by looking after the God-fearing. And they are in truth serving the entire world when they do this, because without the presence of the God-fearing, God would probably be finished with this present world. Which would not bode well for anyone who found themselves living in such a Godless place.

You may have heard what happened to the cities of Sodom and Gomorrah. What you might not know is that before God destroyed those cities, a man named Abraham pleaded with God to save them. He asked God's angel who'd been sent to destroy the two cities, whether he would still go ahead if there were some righteous people left in them. The angel said no, even if there were just a few righteous there he would not do it. What happened then was that the last few righteous people left Sodom and shortly afterwards fire rained down on the cities of the plain and destroyed them (see Genesis 18).

The situation at the time of the flood in Noah's day was similar. But for the presence of righteous Noah all flesh would have perished. When he and his family were removed from danger, God proceeded to eliminate the rest of mankind from the world.

Accounts of such events in the Bible are not put there for historical interest; they are preserved to help us understand the ways in which God works. They teach us about God. And the lesson from

Angels

these stories is alarmingly clear. Going by this, it's no overstatement to say that the world needs the righteous. Without them the future of humanity might be precarious, to say the least. And so the great and very worthy public service that the angels provide is to keep the God-fearing righteous safe. And in so doing they may well be helping to keep humanity from destruction.

Angels encamped around

David expressed his understanding of this poetically when he wrote: *'the angel of the LORD encampeth round about them that fear him.'* David was both a poet and a soldier, we remember. Here he referred to something from his military experience to express how he felt about the protection the angels gave him. In military terms it was like having an army encamped around him. Rows upon rows of tents on all sides, occupied by trained and battle-hardened warriors, armed and at the ready. Something he was familiar with. That was the feeling of safety it gave him when he thought about the presence of the angels. And he saw that as something God provides to all *'them that fear him'*.

How incredible it is, and how privileged we are, to be able to peep behind the curtain and see something of what is really going on in the world. That's what knowing God's Secret allows us to do. Whatever is happening, however random and perhaps threatening it appears, the angels are at work guarding and guiding the God-fearing. This verse in David's Psalm is most likely where the notion of 'guardian angels' originated. Though that phrase doesn't occur in the Bible, it does make sense that a believer's individual safety should be assigned to a particular angel who keeps his eye on them right through their life and gets to know them.

How else might it work? The only alternatives I can think of are a kind of shift-work system; or a pool system of supplying whoever is available as and when required; or no system, where all angels keep a general eye on all believers. None of these seems either likely or appropriate. *'For God is not the author of confusion'*, as the Apostle Paul said (1 Corinthians 14:33). So individual guardian

God's Secret

angels are more likely, and there are hints in the Bible, like our verse in Psalm 34, which draw us towards that conclusion.

Jacob's ladder

We're told in the Bible of a man named Jacob who was given an insight into the work of the angels. Sleeping outside one night, he had a dream from God in which he saw a ladder stretching from the ground where he slept right up into heaven (See Genesis 28). On the ladder he saw angels continually ascending and descending. When you know that the angels are God's messengers, the dream makes perfect sense as a representation of the angels about their business of passing information back and forth from earth to heaven. Not that they do it on a ladder!

And while you still have that image in your mind of angels moving up and down on a ladder, you might ask yourself why would angels **need** a ladder, even in a dream? The answer is that nowhere in the Bible are angels spoken of as having wings. And although the ladder in the dream is not meant to be taken literally – it's just a way of conveying the idea of a link between God and man through the angels – it would still be incongruous for Jacob to have seen angels with wings climbing up and down this enormously long ladder.

Angels have the power of flight because they are spirit beings whose abilities are not bound by flesh-and-blood limitations, not because they have wings. Admittedly, it's still a little incongruous for them to be using a ladder, but not quite so much as winged ones doing it. Jacob would have seen real angels, not the winged fantasy beings who could never be mistaken for people, as the angels in the Bible regularly were. And as they still are according to Hebrews 13:1 where believers are advised to be kind to strangers because they may unknowingly be dealing with angels.

Running errands

As the word angel means messenger, it's appropriate that the phrase *'sent forth'* in that verse we quoted about them, carries the

Angels

idea of sending someone out on an errand. That's the meaning behind it. The angels are running the errands that God has sent them out to do. That might sound fairly routine and pleasant, a little mundane even, and sometimes no doubt it is for them. But bear in mind also that it was an angel who discussed the fate of Sodom and Gomorrah with Abraham, and who finally rained fire on both cities. Some of God's errands can be spectacular and devastating. Not that that should trouble the God-fearing, though.

Angel's delight
The work of the angels brings them great delight. There is nothing grudging or half-hearted about their service to God. They were not taken away from what angels might otherwise be doing and pressed into service on God's new Creation unwillingly, but were overjoyed to be appointed to the work. They are also eager to see what God is doing here: things of a kind never seen before, it seems, *'which things the angels desire to look into'.* (1 Peter 1:12)

Part of their work of looking after the God-fearing is helping them to find God in the first place. The Bible tells us that God calls people to Him. God would love **everyone** to be called and righteous, of course, but realistically, He knows that isn't going to happen. He knows the ones who are likely to respond favourably to His message. The angels help by bringing about circumstances that can nudge the right people in the right direction. They help to make them aware of God's Secret. Hence *'there is joy in the presence of the angels of God over one sinner that repenteth.'* (Luke 15:10) Who knows? if you're not already a committed believer, or have never properly encountered God's Secret before, then perhaps an angel was instrumental in getting this book into your hands. It's the kind of thing they do, after all.

The angels and Jesus
The angels experienced tremendous joy at the birth of Jesus. They played a key role in communicating what was happening to Joseph and Mary and others as The Nativity unfolded. And their joy was unbounded in the song that the astonished shepherds

God's Secret

heard in the fields around Bethlehem: *'a multitude of the heavenly host praising God, and saying, Glory to God in the highest, and on earth peace, good will toward men.'* (Luke 2: 13,14)

As Jesus grew up and began his ministry, the angels' greatest joy must have been looking after the most God-fearing and righteous man ever; *'for it is written [of Jesus], He shall give his angels charge concerning thee: and in their hands they shall bear thee up, lest at any time thou dash thy foot against a stone.'* (Matthew 4:6) That's from a Psalm expressing poetically how close the angels would be to Jesus. And it seems to show that he had more than one guardian angel – but, then, he is rather more important than the rest of us.

It must have been hard for them to back away and leave Jesus at the time of his crucifixion. Perhaps this helps explain Jesus' cry from the cross: *'My God, my God, why hast thou forsaken me?'* (Psalm 22.1) Was Jesus sensing the angels' temporary departure from him, we wonder? They would not have been allowed at this point to intervene and carry out their work of looking after Jesus as they always had. They must have been made to draw back, to allow God's plan for salvation through Christ's sacrifice to proceed.

But we can be sure that Jesus knew in his heart that God would never truly abandon him. That's apparent, too, from that very Psalm Jesus quoted from the cross. Psalm 22 is another of David's, written at a time when his life was in serious danger. But the Psalm goes on to show that David had that unshakeable trust that we've spoken of before. Even though he was desperate, David knew that God had not *'hid his face from him; but when he cried unto him, he heard'.* (verse 24) By quoting the Psalm Jesus was identifying with the feelings of David. God would never leave him. Doubtless Jesus' words would have been a comfort to the angels while watching the one who had been in their constant care suffer. They could not intervene, but God was still present. And Jesus knew it.

Angels

This has turned into a more detailed look at the angels and their work than originally intended, but the subject is such an enthralling one, and such an important part of God's Secret that it's as well we've devoted this space to it. And it gives us a good grounding for what's to come in the next chapter.

18 Taste and See

> 'O taste and see that the LORD is good: blessed is the man that trustest in him.' (Psalm 34:8)

In this eighth verse of his Psalm, David presents us with one of the most intriguing aspects of God's secret. It's a way of experiencing God for ourselves. We might have thought this kind of thing didn't happen anymore – that it only happened long ago, when people like David had a very real two-way experience of God, but not today. David approached God, and God responded. He never had to wonder whether or not there was a God. The question would never have crossed his mind: he knew God exists from personal experience. We might not think this sort of experience, or this level of certainty, possible these days.

But David, on God's behalf through divine inspiration, sends out the invitation: *'O taste and see that the LORD is good.'* This is a life-experiment that we can carry out, and through which we can satisfy ourselves beyond question of the existence of God. If we thought that there was no way to prove God's existence, and that a belief in Him could only ever be built on what we might think of as the uncertain foundations of faith and hope, then here's a way to plant it on solid ground.

Believing in the unseen

We all believe in things we've never seen, and things we most likely never will see. We have to, because we simply can't experience everything. Life would be unworkable if we could believe only in the things we could verify first hand. I've never been to China, and probably never will go there, but I'm absolutely certain it's there, just below Russia. I believe it's there because I've seen pictures, I've met Chinese people, and nobody I know denies the existence of the place, and insists that I'm foolish to believe in it. So, as far as I'm concerned, it's there, and no question about it.

Things are not as simple when it comes to determining the existence of God. I've never seen God, and neither has anyone I know. There are no pictures or videos of Him, and there are plenty of people saying that He doesn't exist. Normally, in a situation like this, we would have to concede that He probably isn't there. No sense believing in Him.

But sometimes, in order to verify the existence of something, we have to go beyond the usual conventions. Sometimes we have to rely on an indirect experience of something rather than a direct one. There are occasions when we can tell that something exists even though no-one can see it. We can tell it's there because of the effect it has on what we can see. For instance, we knew long before we found the planet Pluto (now demoted to a dwarf planet) that it existed, because of the effect it was having on other objects in the solar system. The effect alone was enough to tell us it was there, and to guide us where to look for it.

Also, while we're in space, so to speak, there's something mysterious out there called dark energy. Apparently, around ninety-five percent of the universe is made up of dark energy. Yet we can't actually find it. It's an invisible force that dominates the universe. We know it's there because, so the cosmologists say, something is making the universe continue to expand when, according to them, it should be showing signs of slowing prior to collapsing back on itself.

Let's not argue the rights and wrongs of the expansion/contraction theory here, I just use this as another example of something that we cannot see and yet does seem to be there because we can observe an effect it is having. This is such a perfect example, too, because it concerns something we cannot see which is vast beyond our imaginations. Rather like God Himself. By the time you read this, the scientists may have found dark energy, which will confirm everything I'm saying about being able to detect something is there because of the effect it's having. The same is true for something the scientists call dark matter. This also fills much of space, and we know it's there only because it interacts with gravity.

Back down to earth, and on a smaller scale, knowing that things we **cannot** see exist because of the effects we **can** see, occurs quite a lot. No-one has ever seen electricity, for example, but we all know it's there. We know very little about it really. We know it only by the effect it has of powering our civilization. Take a battery apart and you won't find the electricity that was stored in it. Knowing something that we can't see is there by the effect it's having, is also how medical diagnosis often works. It's how criminal investigation often works, by piecing together the clues. It also seems to be the way the mechanic who fixes my car sometimes works. He can tell what's wrong by the effect it's having on my car.

It's personal
When David tells us to *'taste and see that the LORD is good'*, he's saying that we should prove for ourselves that God is good. Tasting is, after all, something we have to do for ourselves. It's a very personal thing. We can't sample something by giving it to someone else to try. Even the most florid descriptions of the wine connoisseurs will never match the experience of tasting the wine by sipping it ourselves. And the food tasters who once sampled food and drink for kings and queens, didn't taste the food on behalf of their employers to give their views on the flavours of the dishes, they did it to check for poisons.

So we are invited to taste God's goodness for ourselves, and the outcome of this is not only do we learn how good God is – because He responds favourably to us – but we also confirm for ourselves that He is actually there. We'll see in a moment what this tasting entails. But first there's something we need to bear in mind.

It may disappoint you to know that someone with no belief in God whatsoever cannot use tasting and seeing that He is good to prove that He exists. God is not going to be 'tricked' into showing His hand like this. This may seem to invalidate the procedure. After all, what use is it if we can only prove God is there if we already believe that He is? But when you think about it, it makes perfect sense. We have to believe in God **before** we can taste and see whether He is good. Tasting and seeing will **confirm** it beyond doubt. But you only get the confirmation of His existence if you already believe in it. And this is why.

Tasting, Testing and Trusting
Let's not confuse tasting with testing. When we taste and see we're not setting up a test for God to show His hand and prove He exists. That's almost certainly going to backfire. By which I mean that nothing will happen, and we will be given 'confirmation' of any doubts we might have about God's existence. God will not play games like that with us. Jesus called it tempting God, and he said we shouldn't do it.

What exactly does David mean by taste and see? What is he saying we should do? The answer is in the structure of the verse. It's another of those rhymes of meaning, where the second half helps to explain the first half. And this is what David says in the second half: *'blessed is the man that trusteth in him.'* That's telling us that we are blessed when we trust in God. The two parts of the verse reflect one another like this:

Tasting = trusting

Seeing = blessing

so

Taste and see = trust and be blessed

God's Secret

This means that tasting is about trusting God and not about testing Him.

Unconditional trust (or trust and see)

When I checked, I half expected to find that the word translated 'taste' in the Psalm is usually translated differently. I thought it would turn out to mean something different from tasting in the usual sense of what happens when we eat and drink. But it mostly means simply tasting food. Which means it's a metaphor that we're dealing with. Tasting is a metaphor for sampling something, for entering into the experience of something to see what it's like.

David is telling us that we should put our complete and **unconditional** trust in God. No doubt you've heard of unconditional love, well here we have unconditional trust. It means putting our situation, ourselves, our lives, fully in God hands, without any stipulations added. This is the only kind of trust God wants from us (see Proverbs 3:5). You probably know what I mean by stipulations. We generally **think** them rather than say them. We say that we'll trust God totally with our situation, but in the back of our minds we're thinking we know how things should turn out, or how soon we should get results, or any other such condition. We probably have a Plan B, too.

That all amounts to conditional trust. And that's not enough. Forget all the conditions. What we need to do is place everything in God's hands and trust Him completely for the outcome. We need to be fully convinced in our own minds that whatever He does for us will be absolutely the right thing. This is the right way to taste and see that God is good.

Unconditional trust is best reserved for God, by the way. Trusting this fully is not recommended between people because even with the best intentions we let one another down. There is no-one apart from God (and Jesus, of course) who warrants this level of trust.

As Hezekiah, another psalmist and king mentioned in the Bible, once wrote, *'Put not your trust in princes, nor in the son of man, in whom there is no help.'* (Psalm 146: 3) He knew first-hand about untrustworthy princes because he'd been a prince himself. He also knew that what was true of princes, who were in privileged positions and should be setting an example to others, was true of all men and women. It's best not to put our trust unreservedly in them; because we may regret it. Try as we might, we all fail sometimes. But God doesn't. We can trust Him completely – unconditionally.

I'm not suggesting we should mistrust everyone, have no faith in people, and expect the worst of them. That's a sad and bleak outlook on life. Not recommended at all, certainly not in the Bible. This is not to promote cynicism towards our friends, family, neighbours, colleagues, and everyone else we encounter. I'm just highlighting, as does the Bible, that trusting in God is very different from trusting in people. We are inclined to let people down now and then, and people let us down, because that's the way we are. We can't always follow through even when we plan to and want to.

So it's unwise to place too much of our faith, our hopes, or our lives, unreservedly in the hands of other people. But we can have complete confidence in God about everything. What Hezekiah had in mind was that we shouldn't trust others so much when it comes to the big things, rather than the little day-to-day things which are not so critical.

Let go and let God
So, taste and see means trust and be blessed. When we taste something there's only a minimal amount of labour involved. We can hardly call tasting a physical activity. We don't roll up our sleeves to get on with a bit of tasting, do we? We lift food to our mouths, we chew, and the tasting happens. It's something we engage in, rather than work at. Which makes it a good analogy for trusting. We engage in trust rather than labour at it. We look at the

situation we are in, or the path our life is on, and we commit it to God. You may have heard the saying 'Let go and let God'. It means to stop worrying about things and allow God to help you with them. That way you open the way for Him to bless you and show you that He is good.

You might think that 'let go and let God' is just a catchy saying with no basis in the Bible. And it sounds like a recipe for laziness. We could stand back from any situation and excuse ourselves from action on the grounds that we are letting go and letting God deal with it. But that's not the idea behind it. And the saying has biblical backing. In a passage from one of the Psalms the Lord urges us to *'Be still, and know that I am God.'* (Psalm 46:10) It sounds as if it God is saying simply sit quietly and still your mind. Meditate on Him, perhaps. That might help, but that's not what we're being advised to do here. The original Hebrew phrase for 'be still' is more often translated 'let go' (as in, release your grip on something and let it fall to the ground). And the circumstances in which Psalm 46 was written tell us more about what this letting go means.

It's a Psalm from the same man, King Hezekiah, mentioned a moment ago. It was written at a very worrying time for the king. The Assyrian army was at his city gates, demanding surrender or else. Assyria was a superpower at the time, so the situation looked bleak for Hezekiah and his people, who were under siege in Jerusalem. But Hezekiah turned to God in prayer. His prayer was one of desperation, yes, but nothing like the prayers of the 'foxhole Christians' that we mentioned earlier. The king was a righteous, God-fearing man. And the answer that came back from God was *'Be still, and know that I am God.'* In essence, Hezekiah was told to 'let go and let God'. He was told not to worry. Even though the situation looked disastrous, he was to let go of it, and know that God was there to deal with it.

Letting go and letting God isn't being lazy, it's actively engaging in trust. It's about knowing our limitations and remembering that God is there for us when we trust Him. The same God who reassured

Hezekiah says *'O taste and see'* to us. He will be present for us, too, whatever our circumstances. So it's perfectly right, when we have difficulties, for us to 'let go and let God'. It's in complete accord with what the Bible tells us. It's exactly what God wants from us in some circumstances. Allow Him into your situation.

Fathers like their children to go to them when they have problems, and in that respect, our Father in Heaven is no different. Though, in point of fact, God wants us to take it a lot further than running to Him only when we have major problems. He wants us to trust Him at all times; *'taste and see'* is not something to fall back on, it's a way of life. Trusting and being blessed as a result is the enviable way of life of those who know and live by God's Secret.

Back to the angels

In case you're wondering what happened to Hezekiah and his people, let's revisit the scene of that siege of Jerusalem. Hezekiah had been told to 'let go and let God'. So he did. He stepped down and put his complete trust in God. That night *'the angel of the LORD went out'* into the camp of the Assyrian troops and slew 185,000 of the men who were threatening to slaughter most of the people of Jerusalem and enslave the remnant. This one angel dealt with the Assyrian army as though it was nothing to be reckoned with at all.

We might think it severe of God to deal them such a blow, but the narrative in 2 Kings Chapter 19 tells us the whole story. The Assyrian superpower was not only forcing its rule upon the surrounding nations, it was also imposing its gods on them. Which was all very well when the gods they were deposing and replacing were worthless idols no better than their own, but at Jerusalem they were presuming to dispose of and replace the only living God, *Yahweh* himself! As we've said before, God usually acts in covert ways, and only reveals His might when really necessary to teach us something. It's clear that the Assyrians needed to be taught something. And take note of the fact that God sent only one angel to decimate an entire army. How do you feel about the prospect of having a guardian angel now!

A believer's experience of tasting and seeing that the Lord is good will almost certainly be a lot less dramatic than Hezekiah's or David's. I certainly hope so for all our sakes. God will respond when we trust Him unconditionally. Most likely we won't see an angelic being working for us, and neither did Hezekiah or David, as far as we can tell. But the angels were there all the same. What we'll see is the results of what they do, as did Hezekiah and David. The blessings that follow the trusting.

We do need to be the kind of people that the angels are assigned to look after, before we experience their direct attention. David makes that clear in Psalm 34. We need to be among the God-fearing around whom the angels will encamp. These are the ones who interest the angels more than anyone else. That doesn't mean, though, that God has no interest in others. He's very interested in those who want to understand His Secret, and who aspire to be righteous and God-fearing, but haven't yet found their way to Him. The story of Cornelius in the Book of Acts (Chapter 10) gives us an example of a man blessed by God before he fully understood and was baptised into Christ. God notices these things.

It's probably true to say that Cornelius tasted and saw that God was good even before his commitment to Christ. He already fully believed in God and trusted Him sufficiently, so it's extremely likely he was on the angels' radar, so to speak. He just needed exposure to the full Secret of God, so that he could take the final step into Christ. And this might surprise you: those who take that final step are known in the Bible as saints. And they are the subject of the next chapter.

19 Everything You Want

'O fear the LORD, ye his saints: for there is no want to them that fear him. The young lions do lack, and suffer hunger: but they that seek the LORD shall not want any good thing.' (Psalm 34:9–10)

These next two verses of the Psalm are so close in meaning, and complement one another so well, that we'll take them together in this chapter.

But before we get to the main points in the verses, there's something we shouldn't let slip by without comment. When David says *'O fear the LORD, ye his saints'* he hasn't started speaking to an entirely new group of people. He's still addressing the same people he's been speaking to all along. But he's now calling them saints.

Aren't saints very different from the usual run of people? – rather exceptional beings? Well, yes, they are, but not in the way you might think.

The word saint means **called out person**. Nothing more. But that's really quite a lot. Saints are exceptional people. But they are exceptional because they have responded to the call of God, not because they are an elite group of immortal super-believers. Remember, part of the work of the angels is calling people to know God, guiding them as deftly as they can without interfering with their freedom. Angels won't turn anyone into a believer against their will by manipulating their thoughts and feelings; all they can do is make sure that suitable people are presented with the opportunity to become believers. The angels are actually trying to make saints of us. When you become a believer you automatically become a saint. You will have responded to the call of the angels on God's behalf, which makes you a called out person, hence a saint. Saints are regular believers, not a higher ranking group who wear halos. Incidentally, halos are the invention of classical religious artists and stained-glass window makers. The halo was a convenient way of identifying the more holy characters in pictures, but it has no basis in fact. Saints don't wear them.

Sainthood

The mainstream churches have introduced the strange and unbiblical practice of canonising those of their number that they deem to have led outstandingly holy lives. Always dead people these days. Saints now emerge through a process of ecclesiastical bureaucracy rather than the calling of God. But the creation of this imaginary elite (which some people even worship and pray to), goes far beyond what we're told about the saints. Every bona fide believer can rightly assume the designation of saint. I doubt, though, whether any of them will be using the word formally as a title. I certainly won't be referring to myself as St. Colin any day soon; though I do believe I am a saint in the proper biblical sense of the word.

David knew exactly who the saints are. He knew he wasn't encouraging a select band of believers in heaven to *'fear the Lord'*. And, one might reasonably ask, why would he or anyone need to do that? If such a group of believers existed they would have no need of his encouragement; they would already be streets ahead of the rest of believers, David included, when it came to fearing the Lord. In addition to that, David was exhorting the saints to fear God because *'there is no want to them that fear him.'* Which makes no sense if these saints are immortal believers in heaven. What could they possibly lack?

The truth of the matter is that the saints David encourages in the fear of the Lord are people who have responded to the call to be believers. He knew his small band of followers qualified, so that's who he was initially addressing as saints in his Psalm. But what he says is applicable to all saints, all called out people. Having cleared that up, let's press on and think about what else is in these two verses.

God knows best

Those who fear God and who are called to be believers will lack nothing good. That's a bold claim from David – though he made it on God's behalf, of course. And if everybody knew about it, and took it at face value, the queues to join churches everywhere would probably run down the road and round the corner. The reality is, however, that believers are not always, and without exception among the most well-off people we know. Occasionally they are; but generally they aren't.

When David said *'there is no want to them that fear him'* he wasn't saying that all God-fearing people would have everything imaginable. He wasn't promising large bank accounts, big houses, luxury cars, yachts, and private jets. But neither, I should add, was he saying that none of them could have such things. There are certainly some God-fearing rich people mentioned in the Bible. Solomon was probably the wealthiest man alive in his day. But despite what the preachers of prosperity theology tell us, David's words don't mean that great wealth automatically flows towards the God-fearing.

What David is telling us is that believers can have all they **want.** Which might sound like they have an Aladdin's lamp. But what believers want will be governed by the fact that they are believers. Being a believer changes our perspective and priorities. It gives us a new and different worldview. Anyone who is spiritually smart enough to know the counsel of God (His Secret) knows better than to hanker after things that could draw them away from it. Their goals in life will not include the accumulation of wealth and its trappings. Believers have a '**God knows best**' policy. The accumulation of wealth is not necessarily the best thing for them. It can also be a symptom of insecurity. Believers are freed from such fear. They know they are looked after. So they can get on with enjoying their righteous, God-fearing lives, and leave their welfare and security to God.

A saint will try to avoid anything that is likely to adversely affect his or her spiritual wellbeing and their relationship with God. Augustine, who is known as St. Augustine, but perhaps I should avoid that after what I just said – he gave this piece of sound advice: 'Love God and do whatever you please.' It's very cleverly put. He seems to be saying one thing while he's actually saying another very different thing. He's not saying that if you love God you should not restrict yourself from doing anything at all. Deny yourself nothing! He's saying that if you love God you will want to restrict yourself to doing, as far as possible, only those things that someone who loves God would want to do. You'll take God's counsel.

In full, Augustine is saying, 'Love God and do whatever it pleases you to do as a God-loving person.' In a similar way, those who fear the Lord won't lack for anything because they'll want only what is compatible with them being God-fearing people – and God will see to it that, in the main, they have such things.

Any good thing

David makes this even clearer in the next verse when he says: *'they that seek the LORD shall not want any **good** thing.'* As believers we won't lack anything that is **good** for us. That's the essential game-changing piece of information here. If wealth is good for a believer then it may come. And if it isn't, then it won't, and we'd be foolish to long for it or chase after it. The decision on things like this is best left in God's safe hands. This is where unconditional trust comes in again. Believers don't strive for riches regardless of what God's will for them might be.

But how do they recognise His will for them in a thing like this? That's easy. Leave it to Him. Put their situation firmly in His hands. Pray about it. Ask for guidance. *'Taste and see.'* Whatever they then experience is His will. It's as straightforward as that. We have to take the 'small print' into account though. As the advertisers of investments usually tell us 'the value of your investments might go up or down', so might our situation change. God's will for us might change over time, as our character develops for better or worse, and our prosperity may diminish or grow, because at different stages in our lives we are likely to need dealing with differently. We might become able to handle more than we once could – or less.

It's a great relief to me to be able to leave my financial state in higher hands. It doesn't mean I can be reckless. I still have to keep an eye on my affairs. God would do us no great service if He took away all our responsibilities. We don't do that to our own children; and neither does He. But I can relax in the knowledge that ultimately it's not all down to how I am with money (or without it). It's down to the One who knows a great deal more than I do about everything, and has my best interests at heart.

And when we think about it, He owns everything, the entire world. Whatever anybody else might think they own, He actually owns everything and can distribute it however He sees fit. As He tells us poetically in Psalm 50:10–12: *'For every beast of the forest is mine, and the cattle upon a thousand hills. I know all the fowls of the mountains: and the wild beasts of the field are mine. If I were hungry I would not tell thee: for the world is mine, and the fullness thereof.'*

Believers are still fallibly human, of course, and, like most people, they might still quite like the idea of being better off or 'having it all'. But unlike most people, they generally know better than to go for it regardless. They are aware of God's Secret, which shows them a better way. As we say, His Secret is essentially His counsel, which, we remind ourselves means His guidance, support, advice, direction, and so on. Knowing God's Secret means allowing ourselves to be guided by His counsel in all matters, including our prosperity, or lack of it. Saints will read His

God's Secret

Word, acquaint themselves with His wisdom, talk to other saints about it, and pray about their situation.

We might all prefer to be well off, but wealth can lead to disaster if we're foolish enough to chase it to the exclusion of what matters more: namely our peace of mind, and our relationship with God. Eagerly pursuing money, at the expense of other things, rather than letting wealth happen if and when it will, is almost certain to lead us away from being God-fearing and righteous. It's foolish to want what isn't good for us, because *'the prosperity of fools shall destroy them.'* (Proverbs 1:32)

Riches without sorrow

The Bible doesn't say that riches of themselves are bad. It speaks of them as a blessing. But they are only a blessing for those who can handle them without harming their spiritual wellbeing. The Bible say, it's the **love** of money that is the root of so much evil, not money itself (1 Timothy 6:10). Money is neutral. It's what we do with it, and what it does to us, that makes it good or bad for us.

When God knows a believer won't be spoiled by wealth, then it may come to them. It will be a good thing. In these circumstances, we're told that: *'The blessing of the LORD, it maketh rich, and he addeth no sorrow with it.'* (Proverbs 10:22) That's an interesting insight. That must be because He makes rich only those people He knows can handle it. Those who have riches with sorrow added are those who put the making of money before more important things. They want wealth regardless of what God wants for them. And He knows better.

When God gives wealth He makes sure no sorrow goes along with it. The troubles and sorrows of the wealthy seem to fill many a news report most days. And we hear that those who win vast sums sometimes end up worse off in many ways than they were before. Some even finish up with huge debts. Some require professional counselling to help them cope with the problems of their unaccustomed wealth. We're not all able to cope with it. But when wealth is from God, the recipients are spared such problems, because He already knows they can handle it. And they will have His unerring counsel to see them through.

Another verse from the Book of Proverbs supplies this piece of wisdom: *'give me neither poverty nor riches; feed me with food convenient for me: Lest I be full, and deny thee, and say, Who is the LORD? Or lest I be poor, and steal, and take the name of my God in vain.'* (Proverbs 30:8-9) The middle course of having neither too much nor too little is probably the best and safest way for most of us. Most of us can handle that quite well. We're not so good with too much or too little.

Hungry lions

As he often does, David recommends trust. It's a major component of God's secret, as I'm sure you are starting to realise. God won't see us destitute when we trust in Him. He says *'The young lions do lack, and suffer hunger'* but the God-fearing won't. Even a top of the food chain predator like a lion can experience lean times when its cubs will go hungry. But that's not going to happen to those who put their trust in God.

David will have seen his share of hungry lions prowling around his father's flocks when he was a young shepherd. He'd have watched them eyeing up the choice lambs on the edges of the flocks in his care. And as far as he was concerned they could go hungry. His expertise with a slingshot usually sent them scampering away empty, or felled them, just like he later felled the giant, Goliath, with a single well-aimed stone. So, yes, even the young lions suffered hunger from time to time. But no one who seeks the Lord will be kept from the good things that they need.

It tallies with something David said in later life: *'I have been young, and now am old; yet have I not seen the righteous forsaken, nor his seed begging bread.'* (Psalm 37:25) Those who fear God and who are righteous will not lack for what they need.

Serious problems and insensitivity

I'm fully aware that all this talk of prosperity and the lack of it might sound insensitive, to say the least, to those who are really struggling. The same applies to all the talk of happiness and peace of mind in previous chapters. Those with serious and seemingly chronic and irresolvable problems might feel that if I lived in **their** world, walked in **their** shoes for a while, then I wouldn't be making such optimistic comments on life. Far from being inspired and encouraged by what I'm saying in these pages, they might begin to feel worse about themselves and their situation.

Let's be clear, these observations on how life works for believers are not mine. Which might seem like just a convenient way for me to dodge criticism, but a moment's reflection on what we've covered in Psalm 34 will show it's the truth. This is not my secret we're talking about in these pages; it's God's. And I'm doing my best to keep all my comments well within what His Secret reveals.

When reading Psalm 34, we have to bear in mind that David was in a particularly good place when he wrote it. A bad-looking situation had just turned out very well for him. Indeed, as they did on many other occasions, because of his reliance on God. So it's a perfect place for David to teach us about God's Secret, which is essentially positive.

But there are other Psalms written in very different circumstances, where we find David pouring out his troubles, and telling us how low and wretched he feels. But we notice that even in these Psalms he is still looking to God and trusting God whatever is going on in his life. He doesn't only trust God when things are going well, he trusts God when he's at his wits' end, depressed, and even in peril of his life. God's Secret is a constant in his life: he doesn't switch it on or off according to what's going on for him. He has that unconditional trust that we spoke of earlier. And he recommends it to all.

20 Has everybody got that?

'Come, ye children, hearken unto me: I will teach you the fear of the Lord.' (Psalm 34:11)

We've reached the half-way point in the Psalm. The subject so far has been the fear of the Lord. Verses twelve to the end are about righteousness. When David says listen to me and I'll teach you the fear of the Lord, he's not saying that the fear of the Lord is what he's **about** to teach us in the verses that follow. He's saying that if you give your attention to what he's already been saying you'll learn something about the fear of the Lord. We're half way, which means this is a good place for a recap.

Listening

When we tell children they need to do something and they ignore us, we usually tell them off for not listening. But they usually hear us all right. Youngsters' hearing is a lot better than most other people's. The problem is that they sometimes don't take any notice of what we say. They don't take it on board. They have other things going on in their heads, more appealing things that they'd rather be thinking about and getting on with. We all know this first hand from having once been inattentive young people ourselves. What parents say doesn't always fit with what youngsters want to hear right at that moment. So, we tell them again, probably a little more forcefully.

So it's appropriate that when David pauses to say, in effect, 'Are you listening to this?' that he should address us as children. Even as grown-ups we can be a bit like children when it comes to taking on board the things that are good for us. We hear them all right, and we may even sense that they are the right things for us to know and do, but when it comes right down to it, we're just not really listening. The sound waves go in our ears, but the thoughts they carry don't reach our brains. They get scrambled into so much

God's Secret

static. We're not properly tuned in. So, in case any of David's listeners are beginning to tune right out by this half-way stage of his Psalm he stops, like the teacher in front of the class who can see a few faraway looks among the faces in front of him, and he raises his voice a notch or two and says: 'Right – has everybody got that?'

In fact, when David used the term 'children' he would have meant it in precisely the way of a teacher talking to his students, because that's the way the term is often used in the Bible. The Book of Proverbs uses it this way to describe the relationship between the giver of wisdom and his listeners. The teacher and student have a kind of father and child relationship. Though we can detect another meaning behind David's reference to children. Knowing that his words were written under inspiration from God, this can also be the Lord coming through in David's writing as our Heavenly Father. Because this Psalm is more from God than it is from David.

Coming or going?

At all events, this is the time for those of us who are beginning to lose our way to get back on track. I'm not suggesting that this necessarily describes you. It's simply how human nature works, we can only take in so much at a time, so it is going to be true for a good many of us. And, anyway, it never hurts to pause and take stock of where we are, even if we have been paying attention.

That word 'come', at the beginning of the verse, is mostly translated by the exact opposite word, 'go'. It really means to **go** someplace. Translated as 'come' it gives the impression of moving forward with David into what he's going to say next. But translated 'go', which is more likely to be the case, it turns us around to look back at where we've already been. David is telling us to go back and ponder what he's been saying before we move on to what he has to say next.

This changing of 'come' to the more likely 'go' is one of the reasons I believe David is referring back to what he's already said, not to what he's about to say. The main reason, though, is the subject matter of the two halves of the Psalm. In addition to the general content of the two halves being about fear and righteousness respectively, the first half makes specific mentions of the wrong and right kinds of fear, and no direct mention of the righteous; the second half makes specific mentions of the righteous and no mention of either kind of fear. If David was going to use verse eleven to introduce what he was going to say next, then I suggest he would more appropriately be saying: 'I will teach you the righteousness of God.' So, as I say, it seems more likely he's referring back to the first half of the Psalm. In fact, I'd say he certainly is.

Those first ten verses were about the fear of the Lord. They don't tell us absolutely everything we need to know about it, but they give us plenty to work with. Certainly they tell us enough to profoundly affect our lives if we make good use of what we've been taught. From these verses alone we can secure a very good understanding of this side of God's Secret: *'the secret of the LORD is with them that fear him.'* As we know, this is one of the two verses in the Bible that define the Secret. And having reached this point in Psalm 34, we've garnered enough information to give us a working knowledge of half of the Secret. So let's summarise.

Half the Secret

What have we picked up so far? How much do we now know about the fear of the Lord? Well, here goes. And we've actually discovered more than these things because we detoured into some doctrines along the way. This is how it's been unfolding for us from the Psalm:

1 Be grateful

David begins by saying that he blesses the Lord at every opportunity. He is so grateful for everything the Lord gives him. And he's telling us this not only because he wants us to know how **he** feels about God, but also, and more so, because he wants us to know how we should all feel! We should all be grateful. The Lord gives us life itself, and everything necessary for it: food and drink, clothing and housing, family and friends, and so on. Being grateful for what we have is an essential part of the Secret and our essential response to knowing it. And if David could be so grateful for all that he had while a fugitive, living in a cave, and not sure where his next meal was coming from when he wrote Psalm 34, then it should be possible for us, whatever our situation.

2 Be humble but proud

David is humbled by his knowledge of how great his God is. At the same time it makes him proud and he loves to boast about it. He loves to boast about his relationship with God. He wants to sing out about all the good things his Lord does for him. Part of the Secret is having this same humble pride concerning God. God hates pride. In the normal way it has no place in the God-fearing heart. When we know God, we know how puny and foolish humankind is at best when compared with Him. But we can legitimately take pride in knowing Him, and it's especially appropriate that we boast about what God does for us. This dovetails perfectly with gratitude, because it means we give Him the credit when things work out well, especially when we've asked for His help. Exactly as David did. We don't pat ourselves on the back for what God does for us.

3 Find out more

David magnified the Lord. He exalted God. He placed God at the very centre of his life and thinking. He made God larger in his own mind by finding out as much as he could about Him. He learned so much of God and His ways that he became *'a man after* [God's] *own heart'*. (1 Samuel 13:14) His greater understanding magnified his praise to exaltation. It took his praise and worship of God to new heights. The more we learn of God and His ways, the more we appreciate and love Him.

4 Overcome your fears with love

David said he took all his fears to God and God delivered him from them. All the worries and anxieties that plague our lives can be lessened to whatever degree we are willing to love the Lord in return for His love and care for us. This is a major part of God's Secret. We start our spiritual journey with a fear, an awe, of God; and the more we learn about who He is and what He does (by magnifying Him), the more that fear, that awe, is displaced by love. We never lose the awe completely, of course, but it slowly shares space in our hearts with more and more love and appreciation. Knowing how much God loves us stops us fearing Him in the wrong way. And knowing God is on our side, stops us worrying about our everyday troubles, big and small. Above all, God's love is brimming with the grace that takes away our fear of ultimate failure as believers.

5 Be happy

Religion is a serious business because it addresses the biggest questions about life. But when our religion answers those questions in a life-affirming, positive way, it should make us happy. It's okay to be happy. We are made to be that way. Those who look to God are happy. They have a lot to be happy about, as just the first few verses of Psalm 34 show us. It's important that we are happy. Someone once said that 'A person's religion should be the happiest thing in their life'. When I first came across that simple statement on a tear-off calendar page it turned my life around. I realised my religion had not been making me happy, and that led me to look for reasons. Needless to say, a better understanding of God's Secret was the answer.

6 Escape from trouble

God delivers us from all our troubles. We can even be delivered from them when they haven't yet gone away. That's the seeming paradox David gives us. The God-fearing can take their troubles to God and leave them there. Once we realise that He is on our side, we don't have to fret about our situation, however serious things might look. Whatever happens, He'll provide a way of escape.

7 Angels are looking out for you

Angels are assigned to look after those who respond to the call of God. David says they set up camp around them that fear the Lord and deliver them. Memories of his recent deliverance from his own enemies were still fresh in David's mind when he wrote this. That's the kind of thing the angels do for us. They protect us **from**, and sometimes they protect us **in**, difficult situations, and from difficult people. We all have enemies from time to time, not usually out to kill us like David's were, but out to do us harm in other ways, like being unkind or unpleasant, unhelpful or obstructive.

We can't always hit it off with everyone; someone is bound to take a dislike to us now and then. As believers we try not to give offence, but we can't tiptoe through life forever wary of treading on anyone's toes. And sometimes, people will just take a dislike to us for their own personal reasons: we're just not their type, or we do things differently.

Believers needn't worry about such things, though, because the angels are never far away. We can help them in their work, of course, by remaining friendly however badly we are treated. Proverbs 16:7 tells us that *'When a man's ways please the LORD, he maketh even his enemies to be at peace with him.'* That would be part of the angels' work on our behalf: when we're living in ways that please God, they can help to show us in a favourable light to those who might be against us.

8 Taste and see (unconditional trust)

This is about trust. It's **trust** and see. When we put our unwavering trust in God we will see good outcomes. We can trust Him in any and every situation. This links with other parts of the Secret: with being grateful to God, and with not taking personal credit and congratulating ourselves, when we've asked for God's help and we get it. There's no point in tasting if we don't acknowledge God in the outcomes we see. The tasting should lead to the seeing. Which will confirm beyond doubt that God is there.

9 and 10 Have everything you want

As called-out saints of God, believers can rely on Him to provide everything they need. They will not lack for any **good** thing – which means anything that's good for them to have. And why would we want anything that's bad for us? Okay, we do sometimes want things that won't really do us any good, it's in our nature. But it's not in our nature so much when we become God-fearing and righteous. We tend to want more of what's good for us then, and we are far more likely to decline what's not good for us. It's all about having a 'God knows best' attitude to what we need and don't need. We get better at that over time as we learn more of God (magnify Him) and as we become more familiar with His Secret from His communication, the Bible.

11 Listen

Lastly, David tells us to pay attention. These aspects of God's Secret are so important that we should do ourselves the huge favour of listening to and learning about them. Giving these aspects our proper attention is in itself a part of the Secret. The Bible is not for the casual reader, and neither is the counsel of God that it contains. Hopefully you'll want to read this book again to help these things sink in. And hopefully you'll want to read the Bible for yourself, too, if you're not already doing so.

All together now

Before we move on, there's one final point we should make. We've touched on this, and now we want to emphasise it. None of the aspects we've looked at is an independent, stand-alone feature. They all work together. They are all interconnected and interdependent. They overlap and shade into one another. None of the parts is of real value to us if we don't have all the others. Brought together, they combine to make up much of the counsel of God regarding our proper fear of Him. These aspects of fear also slot together perfectly with the aspects of righteousness that we are now going to look at in the rest of Psalm 34.

21 RIGHTEOUSNESS IS THE WAY

'What man is he that desireth life, and loveth many days, that he may see good?' (Psalm 34:12)

Who wants to live a good and long life? Looking around I can see that everyone's hand is up.

This seems like an unlikely opening line for an explanation of righteousness. But it's leading us in exactly the right direction. It's a rhetorical question. David knows the answer the same as everyone else. Who desires a good and long life? – we all do. All of us on life's journey are hoping it's a good one, and a long one. What man is he? Or what woman is she? – they are you and me and everybody else.

David is saying that if this is the kind of life you want, then I'm about to tell you the way to get it. Righteousness is the way. There is in fact no other way. And in the verses that follow he explains what he means by righteousness. He provides us with a collection of aspects of it.

Journey's end

Life is often likened to a journey. But it differs from most journeys in a significant way. Usually journeys are just a means to an end. Now and then we travel just for pleasure, for the scenery, or to enjoy some pleasant company along the way, but mostly we just want to get somewhere. We have a place to be, a task to complete, or something to enjoy waiting for us. Usually we just want to get there.

But life's not like that. It's not a journey that people are eager to finish. Because for many people the end of the road is exactly that. Especially if they've taken on board the creed of what seems to be the new religion of scientism. They don't believe there's anything

Righteousness is the way

beyond this life. Or if they do, they're not at all sure about it, and they're not anxious to find out one way or the other. They'd really rather not think or talk about where their journey is taking them. For them the following rather morbid observation from a seemingly world-weary king of ancient Israel (Solomon) sums it up: *'All go unto one place; all are of the dust, and all turn to dust again.'* (Ecclesiastes 3:20)

Are we there yet?

For the righteous, though, life is a very different journey with a good and worthwhile destination in view. They know they're on the way to somewhere special. It's not all about the travelling with no thought for the destination. Quite the reverse. For the righteous the destination is the focus. It gives life's journey meaning and purpose. The righteous are actually looking forward to getting where they're going. And like excited children in the back of the car, heading for a long awaited, much desired destination, they are often asking, 'Are we nearly there yet?' And their patient Heavenly Father has to assure them that it won't be long now. Just a little longer. So they settle back down to enjoy the ride, only to be asking the same question 'ten minutes' later.

That doesn't mean believers are all eagerly looking forward to their own deaths. Nobody in their right mind would be doing that. Believers run to the doctor at about the same speed as everyone else when something is wrong. But for them the fear of death is greatly diminished, so they can relax and enjoy the journey more than most. As David says, the righteous love the idea of **many** days, not few. What they eagerly anticipate is not their own demise; it's the dramatic change in the world that God has promised that they are looking forward to.

Faithful believers know one of two things awaits them at the end of their journey. They will either die and later be resurrected when God's Kingdom is about to be set up world-wide. Or they will be among those who are already alive when the Kingdom is announced, in which case they will escape death completely; their lives will be extended into and beyond that coming Kingdom.

'Thy kingdom come'

A little doctrinal diversion will help explain what the righteous are looking forward to. Writing about what will happen to believers at the return of Christ and the establishment of God's Kingdom (as we will be doing more of later), Paul put it like this: *'we who are alive and remain until the coming of the Lord will by no means precede those who are asleep… the dead in Christ will rise first.'* (1 Thessalonians 4:15–16 NKJV)

When God's Kingdom is about to be established *'the dead in Christ'* will be raised to life again, and then they'll be joined by all those *'in Christ'* who are already alive when Jesus returns to establish the Kingdom, so that the God-fearing righteous can all set foot in the Kingdom together. These are the two possible outcomes for believers. Either they'll die and later be raised to life at the threshold of the Kingdom of God, or they'll be among those who are alive when Jesus comes to set up the Kingdom.

That's what believers are looking forward to at the end of their journey. One way or another they are anticipating life in the new and better world that's referred to biblically as the Kingdom of God. Every day takes believers nearer to it. It's not an intangible, ethereal kingdom somewhere beyond the clouds; it's a physical realm to be established here on earth sometime in the near future. That's how the Bible explains it. And that's why believers pray to their Heavenly Father, saying, *'Thy Kingdom come. Thy will be done* **on earth** *as it is in heaven.'*

You might recognise that as part of what's known as the Lord's Prayer, a model prayer Christ taught his first followers. We'll have more to say about this Kingdom of God in future chapters. And like many of the things we've considered so far, while looking into God's Secret, what the Bible says about this Kingdom will probably not be what you expect to hear. The simple original truths of Christianity are often far more reasonable (and remarkable) than the mound of theology that has been heaped on them over the years.

This opening verse of the second half of Psalm 34 is precisely the right place to start the conversation about righteousness. The righteous have a particularly strong attachment to the three things David mentions in this verse, which add up to the desire for a long and good life. It's what most people want, yes, but most people aren't willing to take the only route that will actually take them there – the way of righteousness – the way David is about to describe in the verses that follow. Before we join him there, though, let's have a look at the three things he mentions in this twelfth verse. The verse breaks down into three phrases, like this:

> 'he that desireth life,
> 'and loveth many days,
> 'that he may see good.'

He that desires life

The Hebrew word for *desire* here appears a number times in the Bible, though mostly it's translated as 'delight', and sometimes as 'to have pleasure in' – because that's the feel of the word. Desire falls short of conveying the strength of feeling. The righteous don't just have a desire for life, which is what most people have anyway, they take **delight** in it, they take great pleasure in it. We might say they have a zest for life. They see more deeply into the mystery of life because of the understanding they have from the Creator's message. Knowing God is everywhere at work behind the scenes through His angels, they know that they are connected with a bigger reality, and they travel a more secure and better-defined path through life.

That seemingly world-weary voice we quoted near the beginning of the chapter was probably Solomon's. He's the one most likely to be the inspired author of the Bible book called Ecclesiastes where that quote came from. Whenever I quote Ecclesiastes, I

God's Secret

assume it's Solomon. And I guess if anyone had cause to sound a little world-weary it would be him. He was a man who had seen it all and done it all. He was most likely the wealthiest man of his day with a personal fortune comparable to a tech multi-billionaire today. God blessed him immensely because he'd been a wise and righteous man. And when Solomon made that comment about life going nowhere but the grave, he wasn't offering his own philosophy of life, he was mimicking a prevailing mistaken one. That's how many people saw life back then, and still see it now. Going nowhere and therefore meaningless. But Solomon was a man who knew God's Secret, so his personal take on life was better informed than that.

He was King David's son and heir. In his long life as king over Israel, Solomon experienced great favour with God. He also experienced His displeasure, too. Because despite his great wisdom, he made some foolish choices over the years and caused problems for himself and his people. But in his later years he seems to have come to his senses. The book of Ecclesiastes is an inspired reflection from someone who'd experienced most of what was possible for anyone to experience, then or now. One of his observations was that *'there is no new thing under the sun'*. The scenery on the world's stage may change for each successive generation, but for the actors who strut and fret their hour upon the stage, to borrow Shakespeare's imagery (in Macbeth) life is essentially the same in whatever era they live.

Solomon's conclusions about life were not at all downbeat as he looked back. In connection with what we're looking at now regarding taking delight in life, his personal view was, '*I know that there is nothing better for* [people] *than to rejoice, and to do good in their lives, and also that every* [one] *should eat and drink and enjoy the good of all* [their] *labour – it is the gift of God.*' (Ecclesiastes 3:12–13 NKJV) Bibles may often be black and forbidding on the outside, but they can be very bright inside. God wants us to take delight in the lives He has given us. One of the rewards for the righteous and God-fearing is that they are truly able to enjoy life. They are uniquely positioned to appreciate and enjoy all the good things that God has made available to us, especially the simple things like happiness (the meaning behind rejoicing), working, eating and drinking, and doing good.

And they can do that in the knowledge that all the things that come their way, good and even bad, are under His control. They trust that God knows what He's doing even in those times when they can't properly understand what's going on, and why things should be as they are. They have that unconditional trust we've mentioned, which means they don't need everything to be exactly as they'd like it to be, or as they might think it ought to be, before they can trust Him and be happy. They can just trust, and that takes a load off their minds.

Failing completely

The righteous have a passion for life, but we know that doesn't mean they never have their low times. David went through some down periods, as we gather from reading his story and from some of his other Psalms. So if you come across a believer or two who seem pretty glum and don't exhibit much zeal for life, don't let that give you a distorted view of their Christianity. And don't imagine, either, that they are failing in righteousness. They may be saints, but they're not superhuman. Not yet, anyway.

Though the righteous do have a kind of super power when it comes to dealing with their low times. One Bible verse says, *'for though the righteous fall seven times, they rise again.'* (Proverbs 24:16 NIV) The righteous don't generally stay down. Their understanding of how life works, their ability to look behind the scenes, means they aren't likely to stay low for long. Their unconditional trust helps them weather life's storms.

Seven is not a random number, by the way, in that verse about falling seven times. Seven is often used in the Bible to suggest completeness or perfection, in much the same way as we might speak of 'the seven seas' when we mean all of them even though there aren't exactly seven. The Bible sometimes uses seven in this symbolic way. So when that verse says the righteous might fall seven times and yet still get up, that means they might fall massively, completely, and yet still get up. Which is probably true of King Solomon himself, in fact, who went wildly astray, but if he was later inspired to write Ecclesiastes, as many believe, he found his way back onto the right path.

The righteous know that all is never lost however far they might wander. Whenever bad things happen and get them down, God's reassurances are always there to pick them up again. And even though the righteous might sometimes seriously doubt themselves, they have no reason to doubt God. They know that God's love for them is crammed full with grace, too, so they need never feel that their personal failures, total or otherwise, can rob them of their destiny in God's Kingdom.

So, as David says in the opening phrase of verse twelve of his Psalm, the righteous are those who can take delight in life. Now let's see what he says in the second phrase: *'loveth many days'*.

Loveth many days

A work colleague who'd recently started reading the Bible, came up to me one day a little confused and asked me, 'Why do some words in the Bible have to be read with emphasis?' I didn't know what he meant until he added, 'You know: those words in italics that show up every now and then. It doesn't make sense to me to emphasise them when I read.'

Ah, I realised what he meant, and I could see why it didn't make sense to emphasise those words. It would be baffling. Those words are italicised in the Bible, not to add emphasis, but to let the reader know that they are not in the original Hebrew or Greek text. They were added by the translators to convey the sense better. Things don't always line up word for word when translating something. So, helpfully the translators have owned up to adding words, whenever they've done it, by showing the added words in italics.

I mention this because the phrase 'loveth *many* days' appears like this in the Authorised Version of the Bible. The middle word is in italics. So the original Hebrew says *'loveth days'*. The translators have added *'many'* because they felt from their experience of the language that it would bring the phrase closer to the intended meaning.

Mostly they are justified in doing this sort of thing. It's helpful. It not only clarifies the meaning, it also helps the words flow better. Sometimes, though, it doesn't help. Sometimes it can even mislead us. That's when they do it because they're trying to bias the meaning in the direction of their own beliefs. They want to nudge a phrase or a sentence into saying what they'd prefer it to say. Not always consciously or with bad intent, I'm sure: often it's more a matter of thinking that they are being helpful by steering the sense in the direction they believe it should go. This sort of conscious or unconscious manipulation doesn't happen often, and it's usually pretty obvious when it does, so it needn't trouble us unduly.

And as we're talking about translation, I should mention that what we have in translations like the Authorised Version is a reliable reflection of the original language. It's best to avoid versions that are paraphrases and not proper translations. In their enthusiasm to be more modern or colloquial the translators are inclined to forgo accuracy.

Also, with regard to digging deeper into the Bible with the aid of concordances and dictionaries, and other study tools, rest assured that the deeper meanings we find when we delve into the Bible don't contradict the clear surface message, they enhance it. There's not a hidden message lurking underneath what we read that turns the plain surface message on its head. Nothing like that at all. And I really must also say here that the age-old allegation that you can make the Bible mean anything you want to, is simply not true. That's often an excuse for not reading it, from critics who probably haven't, and not the experience of those who have.

Whether we accept the translators' addition of the word *'many'* doesn't make a lot of difference to this verse. But it does give us two ways of looking at the phrase, both of which are valid. Treated as '**and loveth many days**, *that he may see good'* it tells us that the righteous love the idea of **many** days because with the accumulation of lots of days there will be more and more good to see and enjoy. They will also have in mind their own lives continuing endlessly into the many days of God's Kingdom.

Treated as simply '**and loveth days**, *that he may see good'* it tells us that the righteous have good reason to love their individual days as they happen. Their acquaintance with God's Secret is likely to make them want to greet each new morning with words like these from Psalm 118:24: *'This is the day which the* LORD *hath made; we will rejoice and be glad in it.'* The Psalmist had the day of the arrival of God's Kingdom in mind particularly when he wrote that, but his words can help us appreciate and make a good start to any day. They certainly convey the right attitude with which to open your eyes on the world every morning.

So, in this case, it doesn't matter whether we let the translators' modification stand or not. It makes good sense either way.

Seeing good

The last phrase in this twelfth verse is *'that he may see good'*. It means that he may experience good things. The New International Version of the Bible gives the sense much better by linking it more closely with the verses that immediately follow. Verse twelve should flow directly into verses thirteen and fourteen like this: *'Whoever of you loves life and desires to see many good days, keep your tongue from evil and…'* David is saying that if you want a good long life then this is what you must do: follow the path of righteousness that he's about to describe.

Cautionary thoughts
Being upbeat, positive, optimistic, is great. We probably all feel we could do with more of that. But always we have to remind ourselves that being upbeat all the while is not possible, or natural, or even desirable. We can be both relaxed and positive at the same time. We can even be not so happy and yet still hang onto our positivity. A believer's belief doesn't vanish because they are a bit down, even very down. When we grasp God's Secret of what life is really all about we can circumstance-proof our belief.

Don't lean on yourself
Those with God's Secret have a distinct advantage when it comes to the down times in life. They might lose sight of the Secret occasionally because they are only human. But if they've understood and lived by it then they'll know that the only answer is to get back to it. They'll realise they've nothing to fear and they should stop relying on themselves for solutions. A major part of the Secret concerns depending on God, not on ourselves. Depending on yourself is like anchoring your boat to your boat. You are going to drift. The wellness and motivational gurus will often promote self-reliance as the answer to many problems. But self-reliance is a problem in itself, and never a solution.

> There's a verse about this in the Book of Proverbs that makes me smile, because of the image it conjures up: *'Trust in the LORD with all thine heart; and lean not unto thine own understanding. In all thy ways acknowledge him, and he shall direct thy paths.'* (3:5–6) I get a mental picture of someone trying to lean on themselves and falling over. And in a way that's what that verse is telling us: lean on your own understanding and you'll fall over. You'll get it wrong. So take up God's offer to lean on Him.

God's Secret steers us away from being self-reliant and takes us to a place where we can be God-reliant. We become assured but not **self**-assured.

God's Secret

The self-assured will inevitably become plagued by insecurity and doubt, because, at heart, they'll know, or will wind up knowing, that they don't have the answers to everything that life will throw at them. The righteously assured, as we might call them, will be blessed with ongoing security, through the trust they build in God.

So, let's take a look at some of the things that will help us love our days – things that will produce righteousness in us.

22 WATCH YOUR TONGUE

'Keep thy tongue from evil, and thy lips from speaking guile.' (Psalm 34:13)

So what's first on the list of things we need to know about being righteous? Where does David start? Surprisingly he begins by talking about watching what we say. Or is that really so surprising?

This is actually a weighty subject. It's hard to overstate the importance of what we say and how we say it. Though it looks like the following verse from the Bible might have done just that: *'Death and life are in the power of the tongue.'* (Proverbs 18:21) That seems a bit heavy. But the Bible isn't given to exaggeration. If it says that what we say is a matter of life and death, then it means it. And by way of confirmation, if we need it, the Book of Proverbs, from which that quote comes, is packed with many more references to the tongue, mouth and lips, all warning us to watch what we say. The clear message is: it's **really** important.

Keeping our tongue from evil, and our lips from speaking guile, amount to almost the same thing, which reminds us that we're looking at the Hebrew poetic form again, where meanings rhyme rather than sounds.

The tongue and lips are synonymous with talking. But these days, because so many of our communications and conversations happen via keypads, we should probably add thumbs and fingers, too. We need to watch what we say on devices as much as what we say by mouth. This is about paying proper attention to what we say, **however** we communicate.

Every communication matters

It's a part of God's Secret for successful living that we use the gift of speech for good and not evil. What we say and how we say it is the master key to good relationships, whether with close family and friends, or with casual acquaintances, or even with someone we might only ever speak to once in our entire lives. We need to be consistent about it. Every communication matters. In every relationship, however enduring or brief, we need to use our words wisely and well if we want to stay happily connected with people. Nearly all of what makes up a relationship is verbal communication. Without it relationships peter out or never get started in the first place. We connect with one another by sharing ourselves with one another, by sharing who we are, what we know, and what we do, with them, and this happens mostly through what we say to them.

We are what we say

You've probably heard the saying that we are what we eat, and no doubt there's some truth in that, but it's even more true to say that we are what we say. Our speech gives the measure of our heart. The things we say don't arrive in our mouths from some isolated speech centre within us; they arise from what's going on in our minds and hearts. What we say broadcasts who we are. These words from Jesus explain it perfectly:

> *'A good man out of the good treasure of the heart bringeth forth good things: and an evil man out of the evil treasure bringeth forth evil things.'* (Matthew 12:35)

Whether we like it or not, our words are the betrayers of who we really are. If we are basically good or basically bad it will come out in what we say. And this has nothing to do with how we sound: whether our voice is considered upmarket or downmarket or anything in between. Neither is it about whether our grasp of grammar is good, bad or middling. And it makes no difference what language, dialect or accent we use. These things say something about us of course, about out origins and back-story, perhaps, but they say nothing about how good or bad we are as people. The many and varied sounds of our voices don't matter to

God, just as they shouldn't matter to us, when it comes to how good or bad, righteous or otherwise, we think someone might be.

Content and intent

Two things matter most when it comes to what we say, and they are **content** and **intent** – what we talk about and the intention behind it. These are the factors that determine whether our speech is good or evil – and by extension whether we ourselves are good or evil. Because our speech is such an integral part of who we are. Our speech is a projection of who we are to everyone about us. It's that part of us that we launch out into the world, and the point at which we interface with it. It reveals us in either a good or bad light. Our speech tells other people what's going on inside us. Or, as Jesus put it: when our heart is good it projects good things, and when it's not it projects bad things. It's a simple matter of cause and effect. We are what we say. And we can't escape that. Not even with guile, which we'll come to in a moment.

Let's take a look at some of the evils we can put our tongues to, if we're so minded. This is a brief list, but it's plenty long enough:

lying	gossip	betrayal	sowing discord
slander	blasphemy	deceit	mocking
meanness	crudity	coarseness	belittling
aggression	abuse	libel	scaremongering
insults	enticement	seduction	flattery
boasting	pride	false witness	discouraging

That's enough to be going on with. Notice how everything on the list adversely affects our communication with others. All these things disrupt and sully our relationships with people. This is why our speech is such a powerful force in our lives for good or evil.

God's Secret

And if you still think that it's putting it too strongly to say that how we use our tongues is a matter of life and death, then try this from the Apostle James (Jesus' brother, no less), who wrote: *'The tongue is a little member, and boasteth great things. Behold, how great a matter a little fire kindleth! And the tongue is a fire, a world of iniquity: so is the tongue among our members, that it defileth the whole body, and setteth on fire the course of nature; and it is set on fire of hell.'* (James 3:5–6) James doesn't hold back, does he?

We're jumping ahead of ourselves a little here I know, because it's not till the next chapter that we get to talk about the devil and hell. I suppose I should say 'spoiler alert', but when we understand that hell is simply the grave, not a place of eternal fiery torment, the imagery James uses in those verses connects perfectly with the idea of our speech being a matter of life and death. James is likening the effects of an unbridled tongue to the fire that continually raged, in his day, at a place called Gehenna. That's the word from which hell has been translated there.

Gehenna was the city of Jerusalem's waste tip, and it was constantly burning and consuming everything that was dumped into it, including sometimes the bodies of criminals. James is saying that the tongue can have that kind of all-consuming effect on relationships. He called it *'a world of iniquity'* because when we're using it badly, that's a pointer to the world within us and the world we're creating around us. That's going to make a relationship with God very unlikely, or damage it if we already have one, so it really is no exaggeration to say how we use our tongue can be a matter of life and death.

So James doesn't hold back in his denouncement of the evils that the tongue is prone to. The misery and mischief it causes can sometimes be damaging in the extreme. The tongue is something we really have to take control of, or reap the consequences. Especially if we want to live righteously in the way of God's Secret. Our speech is top of the list of things we should give our attention to. It can bring out the best in us, or it can bring out the worst. And one of the very worst things the tongue is capable of is guile.

Guile

Guile is the thing that David rhymes with evil in his piece of Hebrew poetry. It's a form of evil so dire that it calls for special mention. Guile is what people use when they want to try and derail the cause and effect process that Jesus spoke of. Instead of bringing evil treasure from their evil hearts, with guile they try to convince us that they are bringing good treasure from their evil hearts. They want to convince us that they are not who they really are, and not for good reasons.

Guile is deceit. It's what bad people use to appear good. It's the weapon of choice for the con-man or con-woman. A scammer, for instance, will use it when trying to appear genuine. Out of the badness of their heart they are trying to bring something that will pass for good.

So David singles out guile for special mention in verse 13: *'Keep thy tongue from evil, and thy lips from speaking guile.'* Among all the evils that the tongue is capable of, guile is up there with the very worst of them. This may even be David's way of telling us that it **is** the very worst of them. It's certainly a destroyer of trust. Speech is meant to be our builder and maintainer of relationships, but whenever guile creeps in, relationships are subverted. Guile fosters doubt and mistrust in people. Even worse, it's used to prey upon the weak and the needy, those who are among the most vulnerable in society.

Guile was also the means by which Eve was deceived in the Garden of Eden, so it played a part in humankind's original downfall. Which is probably another reason it calls for mention as an especially evil use of the tongue. Eve was beguiled through subtlety we're told (2 Corinthians 11:3), which corrupted her simplicity. That's the problem with guile: it's subtle, deceitful and devious. It can masquerade so convincingly as good.

God's Secret

A little devious

There are milder forms of guile that we can drift into ourselves because we think they don't matter very much. We don't class them as guile, they seem just trivial deceptions, and so we cut ourselves some slack. It's true we shouldn't be too tough on ourselves, and a little slack needs cutting now and then, but we have to tread carefully where guile is concerned. The essence of guile is its subtlety, and that works both ways. We can use it to fool others while at the same time fooling ourselves by thinking that it's okay to do that.

Guile is not only found in the gross offences of the truly deceitful; it can worm its way into our own communications. And if it's in what we say, then it's in **us**. We are what we say, remember. Lesser forms of guile happen when we're not as open and straight with people as we could be. We're evasive, perhaps, and we hide our real motives sometimes. Maybe we pretend to be who we are not, we try to give people a different impression of ourselves, because we think people will like us more and think better of us if we do that. It's all a low-key form of guile really.

Don't get me wrong, a little pretence is sometimes a good thing. It's far better to assume a friendly attitude when someone delays us when we're in a hurry, or is a little rude to us, than it is to be unfriendly because we're not in a particularly good mood, or we're feeling a bit down over something. In fact, that's a piece of minor heroism, without a hint of guile in it. That's not what this is about. Neither is it about the occasional lapses we all have, when we momentarily slip out of character. Nor is it about those times when we feel like frauds in certain situations – that's a recognised psychological problem called Impostor Syndrome that gets many of us from time to time. Typically, we might seriously doubt our abilities and suitability for the work we are doing, no matter how qualified and competent we are. None of this is guile, because guile is something more calculated and frequent or ongoing.

Watch your tongue

What can we say then?
God's Secret shines a light on our situation and advises us to use our tongue and lips to say good and honest things. This is the way of righteousness.

We listed some of the ways we should avoid using our tongues, now let's look at some of the ways we should use them. Let's reverse all those evils and see what kind of a list that gives us.

truthful	friendly	non-judgemental	peacemaking
praising	reverential	honest	positive
kindly	tasteful	well-mannered	building up
gentle	caring	sympathetic	calming
complimentary	attentive	instructive	respectful
self-effacing	humble	accurate	encouraging

That's a healthier set of words by far. Not all of them are the exact opposites of those on the earlier list, but where we couldn't be precise we've come close.

Back to front?
Verses 13 and 14 of Psalm 34 seem to be the wrong way around. Verse 13 tells us to watch what we say, and then verse 14, that we'll look at in the next chapter, tells us to *'depart from evil, and do good'.* If our speech is the indicator of who we truly are inside, then surely we should pay attention **first of all** to departing from evil and doing good? That way our speech should take care of itself, because we will *'out of the good treasure of the heart* [bring] *forth good things'*, as Jesus said. So shouldn't David have advised us first to give our attention to getting some good treasure in our hearts by departing from evil and doing good? Our tongues would then automatically follow through with good things, and we

wouldn't have to concern ourselves so much with keeping them from evil and guile. That sounds right. But God must have inspired David to write it in that order for a reason.

The reason is that we're not only being told what righteousness is in this Psalm – how to recognise it – we're being told how to get it. God through David is showing us how to **become** righteous, and He's letting us in on some of the secrets of how to do it.

Act as if

If you want to be a righteous person then start acting like one! This may sound like the kind of criticism that gets hurled at someone for not 'walking their talk'. But in this case it's actually the expression of a spiritual and psychological truth. Popular psychologists and self-help writers have picked up something they sometimes refer to as the 'act as if' principle. This is another of those occasions when they've inadvertently connected with higher wisdom. If we want to be a certain way then it helps if we act as if we are already that way. If you want to be more confident, then start acting like someone who is confident. I remember leaning to swim this way when I was a kid. I kept pretending I could swim and after a while I realised I was swimming. You can probably recall similar experiences, because it's a part of the way we are made.

'Acting as if' is a good way of removing any mental barriers we may have to doing whatever it is we want to do. It's a way of helping us to change ourselves into the kind of person we want to be, and it's a way of reinforcing that change. This is nothing like the pretence of guile. There is no shadowy deceit involved.

On the road to righteousness it helps enormously to act like someone who has already arrived. Keep yourself from saying bad things and from being deceitful, and you are practicing righteousness. Your heart may not be there yet, but you can help it along the way to where it ought to be by acting as if it's already there. There's a kind of spiritual and psychological feedback from speaking in a righteous way that starts affecting who we are. We begin to see ourselves differently when we speak differently. This in turn reinforces the desire to *'depart from evil, and do good'* that David talks about in the next verse. And keeping our *'lips from speaking guile'* is a **powerful** way to train the heart in righteousness. So David certainly put these two verses in the right order.

On being religious

We might worry that watching what we say is going to have a negative effect on others, especially those who don't like us in the first place. If we keep our conversation positive and pleasant, people are going to think of us as being 'too nice' perhaps, or worse still 'religious' in the worst sense of that word that so many of us dislike. But this is not about putting people's backs up by seeming 'holier-than-thou'. The things we learn from God's Secret enable us to live in a sane and healthy way: a way that brings peace to ourselves and which spreads peace and harmony around us. No one likes the tag 'religious'. Not when it's used to identify them as killjoys and goody-goodies. No one wants to think of themselves that way either.

But truly religious people aren't like that. They aren't self-appointed judges of humankind. That's confusing the righteous with the self-righteous. Jesus himself wasn't like that. Keeping our conversation clean and caring, positive and honest is not going to make us 'religious' in that way, it's going to make us people who stand out in a good way, as people others can trust and be relaxed around. The righteous are trying to be right with God, not trying to impress or shame others by elevating themselves to a higher moral ground. People followed Jesus in droves, not because he was aloof and joyless. He was at ease with himself, charismatic and friendly. He also had a powerful message about what life is really all about. He knew the Secret of it.

Part of the package
But let's put the brakes on for a moment. This might be looking a little onerous. How on earth can anyone keep a check on everything they say? That's surely not possible. And wildly obsessive. We'd need to be so scrupulous. And we'd get ourselves into such a state of nerves that we'd become frightened to say almost anything at all. We certainly wouldn't come across as an oasis of calm in our immediate vicinity. So an impossible moment-by-moment editing of everything we say is not what's called for. Because watching our tongue is not something we focus on in isolation. It's part of a bigger package.

Everything else we do to bring God's Secret into our lives supports us. All the elements of the Secret work together, they overlap and interlock, so that each of them is made easier by the presence of the others. Things like praise and gratitude, appreciating and trusting God, cannot fail to have an effect on who we are and, as a direct result, an effect on what we say. What we say and how we say it are an important part of the package, but they are still just a part of it.

Expressing yourself
If you have some kind of speech difficulty, or a total inability to speak, then I'm guessing that you're not sitting there thinking that none of this applies to you. You have other ways of expressing yourself (such as thumbs and a keypad, or signing), and what David says about watching what we say will apply to you no matter what means you use to communicate. Whatever means you use is an expression of who you are, just as a voice would be. So this verse of the Psalm and this chapter are meant for you the same as anybody else, just as the other verses and chapters are, the ones on praising God and giving thanks to Him. They are also more about what's going on in our hearts and minds than they are about what's going on with our tongues and mouths.

Toneless

A major problem with written communication between us is that the tone of what we say is difficult to convey on a screen or page. The intention behind what we say is as important as what we say, and that intention can be lost or confused where there is no inflection in our voice or expression on our face to make it more obvious. Emojis can help sometimes. The addition of a smiley face can save us from misreading something as seriously intended when it isn't. But it's not foolproof and can even add to the problem sometimes.

I received an email once from a colleague which, to me, seemed unnecessarily critical of something I'd done. I was pretty sure he was using an opportunity I'd given for comments from people as an excuse for 'having a go'. A few days later we met up and I mentioned I didn't like the tone of his email. He looked aghast and said, 'There **was** no tone. I just quickly listed a few things that came to me and sent them over.' When I looked again at the message, I could see that, really, 'there was no tone'. I'd imagined it. But it was easy to imagine because the prose was sparingly business-like.

Since that incident, if I'm ever in doubt about the tone of something I'm sending, I'll re-word it or occasionally even go so far as to add a brief note saying: 'please read all the above in a friendly voice.' And sometimes I'll add a ☺ . Because it's so easy to give offence in print where people can't hear your tone. Or your lack of it.

We need to be more careful in this area of communication where we are all tending to be more casual. Remembering that we are what we say, might help us keep our thumbs from evil as well as our tongues.

23 You're a Bit of a Devil

'Depart from evil, and do good; seek peace, and pursue it.' (Psalm 34:14)

This chapter could be plain sailing or it could be a problem, depending on what religious background, if any, you bring with you to this book. But it should certainly be interesting, whatever your religious and moral viewpoint. The opposing forces of good and evil are the poles between which we all operate. This is where we spend our lives. Two forces are vying for our attention, and often we are left hanging between them like a metal ball suspended between equally powerful magnets. But sometimes the pull gets stronger in one direction, sometimes in the other.

What we notice in what David says in both verses thirteen and fourteen is that, whether we move in one direction or the other is entirely up to us. Grammatically, the unspoken subject of both of these sentences is **you**. He says **you** keep your lips from speaking guile, **you** depart from evil, and **you** seek the peace that comes from doing good. This might come as a breath of fresh air to you, as it did to me when I first realised the truth about good and evil in the Bible. Because unless you know differently from reading verses like this, you might think that the Bible tells us that, to put it crudely, we each have a little angel sitting on one shoulder and a little devil sitting on the other, whispering conflicting advice in our ears.

Cartoonists have drawn it like this for years, and many people, Christian and otherwise, believe that something like this actually happens. They experience conflicting thoughts, and this battle on their shoulders fittingly represents how they feel. It is as if two external forces are pulling us one way or the other. This has the advantage, of course, that if we listen to the wrong voice we can conveniently say 'the devil made me do it.' Though I'm guessing that few will give credit to the 'angel' when they make the right choice.

David, however, has none of this in his Psalm. This man who knows God's Secret says that good and evil are our own personal choice. We decide for ourselves, unaided or unhindered by any outside agency. Though in our case that's not entirely true, because we do have David pulling us in the right direction. In fact we have the whole of God's message pulling us this way. But what I mean is, and what David means is, we don't have a personal angel or a personal devil vying for our attention every time we have a moral decision to make.

We know something about the work of the angels among us, and it doesn't include fighting the devil over our daily decisions. And as for the devil himself – I'm pleased to tell you he simply doesn't exist. That's the breath of fresh air I mentioned just now. I'd always felt the idea of a devil was outmoded superstitious nonsense, and that made me wary of the Bible, where I thought the idea originated. On better acquaintance with the Bible I found I was wrong, and that removed a major barrier to me accepting the book as from God. So maybe what I'm about to say here will help remove a similar barrier for you.

Let's take a little doctrinal detour into who or what the devil and Satan really are. It'll be worth it, especially if it helps you clear up any misconceptions and misgivings you may have about the devil and Satan in the Bible.

The devil is a very misunderstood character
It's handy to be able to blame someone else for our mistakes and wrongdoings. We pick it up early in life, especially when we have siblings. As we get older we tend to do it less, and if we have a religious turn of mind, it might develop into blaming the devil. If we can say the devil made me do it, then that gets us off the hook. But is it right to blame the devil, or Satan? The terms are pretty much interchangeable in the Bible, and certainly in everyday

speech, though the meanings of the words are a little different. I'm not trying to encourage some sympathy for the poor devil, who is getting the blame for what so many people do. But we do need to challenge the traditional concept of the devil.

When I became more familiar with the Bible, I was able to drop the notion that Satan is a fallen angel out to trick me into doing bad things so that he can grab my soul and keep me in hell forever. Not only was this hugely at odds with what I felt an all-powerful and loving God would do or allow, it was also desperately at odds with common sense, and looked more like dark-ages superstition than genuine religion. It was a relief to discover from the Bible that it isn't true.

If you're from a traditional Christian background, then, before you put this book aside in the belief that Satan already has me, please hear me out for a few pages more. I'm guessing that you may never have taken a close look at what is written, because most people haven't.

A tricky devil?

It's sometimes said by those who believe in Satan, that one of his cleverest tricks is to convince us that he doesn't exist. I'm not sure why that's so clever, or what it would achieve apart from leaving us no-one to blame but ourselves when we go wrong. The thinking behind it is that Satan doesn't want to frighten us into doing good, or steer us away from hell, by his very existence, so he lets us think he's not really there. In that case, he's in perfect agreement with God, because God doesn't want to frighten us into doing good either. As we covered in an earlier chapter, God wants our love for Him to cast out fear. God doesn't want us to love Him because we're so frightened of the consequences of not loving Him. So He is certainly not going to allow a devil to do exactly the same thing and scare us into the arms of God.

This won't be an exhaustive study. (And I like to think of what we're doing here as more like having a chat than engaging in study.) We

You're a bit of a devil

don't want to get side-tracked for too long on this. But it needs addressing because, for many people, ideas about the devil and Satan tarnish the image of the Bible and relegate it to myth and superstition for them. So let's clear the ground. The idea of a supernatural being trying to snare immortal souls and cast them into hell to be tortured forever **is** myth and superstition We won't find it in the Bible – not if we read it with due care and attention.

The idea is significantly missing from the Psalm of David that tells us about God's Secret. This is where we would expect to find a mention of it. We don't, so we are right to question it. We should also be wary of the notion of hell as a place of eternal punishment. That, too, is missing from this Psalm about God's Secret where we would expect to find some mention of it. If these things existed they would surely have been brought into play as powerful motivators to righteousness. But they have no part in God's Secret.

The blame game

Our wrong thoughts and actions come from ourselves, much as we'd like to blame other sources: our upbringing, our circumstances, our education or the lack of it, our colleagues or companions, or the society we live in, or the devil, or… you name it. We have a natural bias towards wrong thinking. We were all infected with it when Adam disobeyed and we were downgraded as a species. We call it human nature.

Evolution has no explanation for it. It doesn't look like something good for the ongoing survival of the species. In fact it looks more like it could prove to be the extinction of the species. We don't have to work too hard at messing things up, do we? It happens with very little effort on our part. And we know perfectly well that we have to work at things like integrity and righteousness. Good attitudes and characteristics don't come naturally to us: they are things we have to cultivate. And we have to **keep** working on them or they slip away from us. The Bible agrees with this one hundred percent. It doesn't see our problems as being anywhere outside us.

Take a breather

In case we seem to be wallowing in too much negativity about the human condition, we should pause here and take a breath. The Bible doesn't say we're all irredeemably bad and there's not an ounce of good in anyone. That's not what this is about. The Bible tells us God loves us, and Jesus gave his life for us. As we'll see in a later chapter there **is** a sense in which all of us are bad – it's when we're measured against absolute perfection. But there's much good in us, and we're capable of much good, even though we're not perfect. The fact that so many of us aspire to be better than we are, proves that we're not all bad. But we are seriously hindered by our nature – that must be obvious to us all – and God's communication to us tells us so, and tells us why. It doesn't blame a supernatural devil. And it tells us the way out of our predicament. God's Secret.

A lazy devil

We have a natural resistance in our heads and hearts to being truly wise and righteous. So we have to start by recognising this and doing something about it. But that doesn't mean a fight with the devil in the traditional sense. It means a struggle with our own natural inclinations. Jesus himself said, *'For from within, out of the heart of men, proceed evil thoughts, adulteries, fornications, murders, thefts, covetousness, wickedness, deceit, lasciviousness, an evil eye, blasphemy, pride, foolishness: all these evil things come from within, and defile the man.'* (Mark 7:21–23) If we're personally responsible for all these things then what is the devil doing all day? He must be pretty unoccupied and bored.

Jesus' brother James added, *'Every man is tempted, when he is drawn away of his own lust, and enticed.'* (James 1:14) Again, the devil seems to be on permanent vacation. Temptation arises naturally from within us. We simply don't need him, do we? When

You're a bit of a devil

it comes to crossing the line into bad thoughts and behaviour, we're perfectly capable of doing it on our own.

Crossing a line

Crossing a line is the idea behind the word devil. It comes from the Greek *diabolos* from which we get words like devil and diabolical. Years ago, before even my time, there was a toy called a diabolo, which involved spinning a wooden reel on a string held taught between two sticks. It's so old my spell check's never heard of it. But the name was appropriate because the toy involved a string or a line. And that's the idea embedded in the word *diabolos* that's translated devil. Something devilish is something that crosses a line. And we still refer to someone who goes too far as having done that. To be a devil is simply to cross the line into bad behaviour of some sort.

Satan is a word that means **adversary**. So a Satan is someone or something that opposes us. That's how it's meant to be understood in the Bible. For confirmation of this there's a verse that actually calls an angel **doing God's work** Satan (Numbers 22:22, where the translators have shied away from putting Satan and have put *'adversary'*). It makes sense only if we see God's angel as an **adversary** in the situation in which he appeared. That's the sense in which he is Satan. But let's explore it further, to reassure you that this is the right way to view it.

Satan's old address

Satan's centre of operations used to be located in a city of Asia Minor called Pergamum. It was quite a cultural centre back then, prosperous and well situated, not too far from the eastern coast of the Aegean Sea. A good place to visit. Not too much like hell, really. So it's not an obvious choice for a demonic residence. How do I know he used to live there? I know Satan used to operate out of Pergamum because it says so in the last book of the Bible, the Book of Revelation. In the opening chapters of Revelation there are seven letters that Jesus wrote to seven churches back in the 1st century. One of them was to the people in the church at

God's Secret

Pergamum. And in the opening words of his message to them Jesus says, *'I know where you live – where Satan has his throne.'* (Revelation 2.12 NIV) Anyone who believes Satan to be an evil superhuman creature must wonder why he chose to rule from Pergamum instead of some hellish sulphurous abyss where he might feel more at home.

If he did have a throne there, then he would surely have had a palace and plenty of demonic servants flitting around doing his bidding. You'd think the people of Pergamum would have spotted a huge gothic palace with scaly creatures guarding it and running errands, not to mention Satan himself popping in and out on occasions. But there's nothing in the history of the town to suggest that anyone knew about it. The town's history does, however, bring something else to light. Pergamum was the headquarters of the Roman authority in Asia. The whole region was administered from there.

Anyone can be Satan

What many readers fail to notice is that the name Satan is not a name that belongs to one particular individual. The word Satan can be applied to almost anyone or anything that is an adversary. Anyone who opposes you for who you are, or what you are doing, is an adversary – a satan. There's really no need to give the word a capital letter. That only confuses the issue. Once you realise how the word should be used, all the Bible verses where it appears make sense, and you can dispense with the idea of the odd character with horns and a tail.

The Roman government in the 1st century was the greatest adversary to the spread of Christianity. There was wholesale persecution of Christians at the time. The Roman governor of the region had his headquarters in Pergamum and so the city was justifiably the throne of the adversary. From a Christian standpoint, there's nothing supernatural about it being the location of the satan's, or the adversary's throne.

You're a bit of a devil

When Jesus said *'get thee behind me, Satan'* (Matthew 16.23), he was talking to Peter, one of his disciples. Peter wasn't Satan in the traditional sense, but he was a satan in the proper sense. Peter was trying to dissuade Jesus from doing something that was necessary. So Peter, in that instance, was Jesus' adversary. In fact what Jesus said to Peter clarifies where this satanic influence comes from. He told Peter at the time, *'thou savourest not the things that be of God, but those that be of men.'* He meant that what made Peter his adversary was that he was using natural human reasoning, and not true understanding. Peter was seeing things from the human standpoint not from God's. It's in human nature that the devil and Satan reside, not the imaginary pits of hell.

This is why neither the devil nor Satan put in an appearance in Psalm 34 where David tells us about doing good and evil. As malevolent entities that are out to lead us into evil they simply don't exist. What we find instead in the Psalm is our own innate tendency to cross the line into bad ways or to act in opposition to our own best interests and the best interests of others.

Now you know why, back in chapter 13, when we were talking about gender, I said that the devil and Satan can be either male or female. We all cross the line into wrong thoughts and actions, and we're all adversarial at times.

Hell has no fury at all

As we've taken this little diversion to talk about the real meanings of the devil and Satan, we ought to add a few thoughts on hell. Maybe you've entertained the same childish thoughts as me about hell. As a child it occurred to me that if hell was beneath the ground then we might one day have the engineering skills to dig down and free everyone. Actually, I still don't see a lot wrong with that if that's where hell really is! But the traditional concept of hell comes from the same dark ages of myth and superstition as the wrong notions of the devil and Satan.

What helped me to this more enlightened conclusion is the real meaning of the word 'hell'. In the Old Testament it's the Hebrew word *sheol* which occurs sixty-five times. Three times it's translated as *pit*, and the other sixty-two times are split evenly between *hell* and *grave*. And often where it's translated *hell*, there's a side-note suggesting *grave* as a close alternative. If we simply read it as *grave* every time we come across it then we would be right. The Bible doesn't support the idea of a fiery hell into which the wicked are cast. It simply says the fate of the wicked is an eternal grave.

An eternal grave is equated in the Bible with complete annihilation. Sometimes it's expressed metaphorically as a fiery end, because burning is something final. In fact, the Bible says that *'death and hell'* are themselves to be one day cast into a *'lake of fire'* (Revelation 20:14), which means the eventual and complete end of death and the grave. Put plainly death is the complete cessation of the life of the unrighteous. When they die they go into *sheol,* meaning the grave or the pit.

You may have noticed I said, 'the complete cessation of the life of the **unrighteous** when they die.' And you may be wondering what happens to the righteous when they die. Don't they also go into a grave, the same as the wicked? Yes, they do. But, as we've already touched on, they don't stay there forever. The saints are always spoken of as sleeping rather than dead, because they are going to be roused one day. But we'll follow up on this later. We've taken enough of a diversion for now and ought to get back to the main point of this book. In fact this chapter has been more diversion than anything else, and we haven't left ourselves room to talk properly about the verse from the Psalm. So let's do that in a fresh chapter. And we will at some point return to the subject of what the Bible has to say about the destiny of righteous people.

24 Depart and Pursue

'Depart from evil, and do good; seek peace, and pursue it.' (Psalm 34:14)

Join me on the beach for a moment. If you write the word 'righteous' in the sand and draw a wide circle around it so that everything inside the circle is righteous and everything outside the circle is unrighteous or, in other words, evil – that would be a good way to depict what the Bible means by evil. Everything that isn't righteous is evil. There are no half measures with God. No grey areas. And although there are obviously levels or degrees of evil from mere meanness right up to mass murder, all of them come under the heading of evil. Everything we do is either righteous or evil.

We might think this kind of zero tolerance of evil is bad news, but in a very important way it's really the best of news. It means that God's grace, the allowance which He extends to believers, has to work in the context of there being only righteousness or evil with nothing in between. Grace can never be partial, leaving us a little less bad, or making us only a little better in God's eyes. His grace, His allowance for us, will always be **complete** when we receive it: it will always leave us fully righteous. Because if there is only righteousness and evil, then if grace doesn't take us all the way to righteousness then it leaves us evil, and grace will have failed us. A grace that leaves us still evil in God's sight is no grace at all. So it has to be complete. But more of this a couple of chapters further on.

I mention all this because we need to be aware that when David says *'evil'* in this verse he's not talking exclusively about appalling crimes against humanity, atrocities that make the headlines and the history books. That's how we generally think of evil. Evil is the sort of thing that criminal masterminds who want to blow up the world do in the pages of spy thrillers. Our everyday misdemeanours aren't what we'd call evil. But in a biblical context they are. Everything that falls outside the circle of righteousness is classified as evil. There's no act that is good**ish** or a **little** bad in God's view. There's a clear divide. Every thought or act is either a righteous one or an evil one.

Get away

Departing from evil and doing good doesn't mean fending off the devil. We've established that. We are not fighting a supernatural being; we are fighting a very natural human being: ourselves. And this is rarely easy because we are struggling against our base-line nature. Being righteous doesn't come naturally to us. And sometimes it seems the harder we try the more we fail.

David makes it sound so easy when he says, *'Depart from evil.'* It seems like all we have to do is just walk away, like leaving home for the office. If only it were that simple. The problem is inside us, so when we walk away it tends to go with us. By using the word *'depart',* David confirms that evil is the place where we generally are, and from where we need to move away. We need to get away from that side of ourselves – from what we naturally are.

Under new management

But wherever we go, we are never going to escape our essential nature. It just isn't possible for us. And that's not what David is suggesting we do. That's not what God is asking of us. Departing from evil means getting away from it as **a way of life**. Stop taking the line of least resistance and staying stuck with who you are. We can't eradicate evil from our lives but we can stop ourselves being **governed** by it. That much we can do.

In a letter to the believers in Rome, Paul said we can either be servants of sin or servants of righteousness. There's no middle ground, we notice. What David is telling us is not to change our very nature, because we can't, but to change the 'organisation' we work for. Don't carry on serving sin, as we all naturally and unthinkingly do, but assert yourself and go and work for a better employer. Be a servant of righteousness. The pay is better and the conditions are much better.

Keeping the analogy of employment going, Paul said, *'the wages of sin is death; but the gift of God is eternal life through Jesus Christ our Lord.'* (Romans 6:23)

But how are we going to hand in our resignation, tell sin we're not working under it anymore, and move on to this new position, under righteousness? It's the best possible move in our spiritual career, so we don't want to miss out on it. David said the thing to do is *'depart from evil'*. Which is easy enough to say – and I can say it just as easily as he could – but how do we go about it?

David explained what we need to do when he said *'Depart from evil,* **and do good**.*'* The secret to departing from evil is found in that phrase *'and do good'*. To depart from evil and do good doesn't mean doing two separate things; it means doing one thing to accomplish another. Because to do good **is** to depart from evil. This is among the best bits of advice you'll get anywhere. And this is why…

The Expulsive Power of a New Affection

There's some very sound psychology in this fourteenth verse. The rather wordy heading over this paragraph is the title of a book by a Scotsman named Thomas Chalmers. He lived 1780–1847 and was a maths lecturer and preacher of some renown. Back in the days when live entertainment and learning was the only kind available, he could captivate an audience even as a sixteen year old. He wrote a number of books, and *The Expulsive Power of a New Affection* is certainly the oldest self-help book I've come across. His book explains something that psychologists have picked up on: that the most effective way to get rid of a bad habit is to cultivate a new one in its place.

Simply stopping an old habit leaves a vacuum that will soon be filled by either the return of the old habit or something equally unhelpful. Instead we should start a new habit that will oust the old one. Chalmers' book was Bible based, and tells us exactly what David is telling us to do: depart from evil by doing good. Start new habits of mind, or new affections, as Chalmers calls them, and let them do the work, or provide the expulsive power, of ridding you of your old unwanted habits. New affections initially divert us from the old ones and in the long run will replace them if we persevere.

Edinburgh

On a personal note, it was of great interest to me to discover that Thomas Chalmers had written this and other self-help books of a religious nature. In 2016 I visited Scotland and stayed in an apartment in Edinburgh opposite the Scottish National Portrait Gallery. While there, I went to the Gallery to have a look at the portrait of Chalmers to see if there was any family likeness. My mother was a Chalmers of Scottish descent, and it would have been nice to have found a connection between us. But much as I studied the picture it was hard to see any resemblance. I know I could always do some delving into the Chalmers' family history to see if there's a link. But I'm not keen to do that because I probably won't find one, and I'd rather continue enjoying the idea that there might be one!

But to get back to it, we have this psychologically and spiritually sound idea that the most effective way to get rid of old habits we don't want is to cultivate new ones we do want. In order to depart from doing evil we should concentrate on doing good. This is another of those occasions when the psychologists have got it right by tapping into something higher.

In 2017 a study of how best to introduce new habits was carried out at Stockholm University. Professor Per Carlbring, the lead author on the project, concluded, 'You cannot erase a behaviour, but you can replace it with something else.' It's better to take up a new habit to distract you from the old one than try to meet it head on. Resolutions on their own tend to fail, as many people know by about mid-January every year.

The study found something that works that's been in the Bible for centuries. In this case David said it around three thousand years ago. Doing good takes us away from our less good side and encourages our better side. It doesn't make us entirely good, but it can take us far enough in the right direction for grace to carry us the rest of the way.

Though as we'll find, grace doesn't only come to meet us when we're trying our hardest, when we're doing the best we can. That's not how it works. It's never absent from our lives when we're believers. All the while we place our trust in God and Jesus, we are considered righteous in God's sight through grace.

As I've said, and will say again, this categorising of everyone not righteous as evil doesn't mean there's no good in humanity. The Bible doesn't say that at all. There's a lot of good in a lot of people. We are capable of many good and great things. But because of our human nature we always fall short of righteousness whatever we do. In the strictest sense, without grace we are all evil, because there are no half measures, and we fall into one camp or the other. But there is still good in people. And Christians are meant to look for the good in others not the bad. For that to happen it must follow that there has to be some good to find! So it's definitely there. And where many people are concerned it's not at all hard to find.

Even as believers, all the while we have human nature we'll never depart entirely from evil. God's grace is needed to bridge the gap that sits between ourselves and righteousness. But by homing in on what's good we can shift our centre, so to speak, so that we operate more around an axis of righteousness than of evil. And that's going to bring God's grace in our direction to make us truly righteous.

Departing from evil and doing good, imperfectly as we'll do that, is one of the elements of God's Secret. When believed and practiced along with the other elements, it will lead to God considering us among those righteous people who know His Secret. As we said earlier, and it may make more sense now: we don't become God-fearing and righteous so that we can then learn God's Secret, we become God-fearing and righteous in the process of learning about the Secret and taking it on board.

'Seek peace, and pursue it'

Moving on, let's take a look at the other half of this verse of the Psalm. At first glance the two halves don't appear to rhyme in meaning as a verse of Hebrew poetry would, but in fact they do. *'Depart from evil, and do good'* and *'seek peace, and pursue it'* are two sides of the same coin. When we depart from evil, the place we are headed for is called peace.

When we talked earlier about the use of the tongue, we said that using it for evil is disruptive and damaging to relationships. Well that's true for all kinds of evil. The bad things we do have harmful effects on others, and on relationships. We may shrug off what we do sometimes as only harming ourselves and hurting no-one else, but that's rarely the case if we're honest. So when we greatly reduce the evil that we are responsible for, we do far less harm generally and we improve our relationships. And following David's advice, we don't only stop doing harm, leaving a vacuum in which we do nothing, we do good. And doing good is great for relationships, too. Our world becomes a markedly more peaceful and harmonious place when we depart from evil by heading off to find peace.

Shalom

The word 'peace' in this Psalm is a translation of the Hebrew word *shalom*, as is almost every other appearance of 'peace' in the Bible. It's a beautiful word in both sound and meaning. And it can refer to either inner or outer peace. *Shalom* is the absence of conflict internal and external. It can also mean or imply harmony, wholeness, welfare, tranquillity and even prosperity. And as you'll know if you've ever spent time in Israel or among Jewish people anywhere, the word is also used as both a greeting and a farewell. It's a great way of wishing someone peace and prosperity. Our English words farewell and goodbye have similar connotations. The one expressing the hope that the person leaving **fares well**; the other wishing that **God** may **be with** them. *Shalom*, though, is far richer in meaning than both.

Do good and you will depart from evil and find the tranquillity and harmony of *shalom*. And to identify what things qualify as good we need to go back to the beach and look at that circle on the sand. Good is everything inside the circle of righteousness. Good is everything David has been recommending so far in his Psalm. Good is one of the active ingredients in God's Secret. We don't need a list of all the good things we can do. How we need to act in this world becomes increasingly apparent as we familiarise ourselves with God's Secret.

The peace prize

In Matthew's Gospel Jesus is reported as saying, *'Blessed are the peacemakers.'* (Matthew 5:9) He wasn't talking about people like Barack Obama or Henry Kissinger who negotiate peace deals globally and are rewarded with a Nobel Peace Prize for their efforts. Because, although such people can broker peace on a grand scale, and surely do God's work on the world's stage in the process, they may not be so good at promoting peace at the level of their everyday relationships. That's what Jesus was talking about – things closer to home. We might wonder whether in the opinion of his family, friends and co-workers someone like Henry Kissinger would deserve a peace prize for his efforts towards the smooth running of family, business and social life. Such strong personalities can often be confrontational and so focussed on their objectives that they fail to be tolerant of those about them.

It's for our efforts at promoting and maintaining peace at this seemingly more mundane level, at the level of family and friends and associates, that a far greater peace prize than the Nobel Prize is offered. Those who make it into the class of people Jesus describes as *'the peacemakers'* are promised that *'they shall be called the children of God.'* A Nobel Prize and the sizeable cheque that goes with it are never going to come anywhere near this blessing. Nothing compares. And we are given the opportunity to receive this remarkable prize by seeking in our everyday lives to promote and maintain peace wherever we can with as many people as we can. The product of departing from evil by doing good.

Enquire and pursue

'…seek peace, and pursue it' – at first glance that reads like repetition. What's the difference between seeking peace and pursuing it here? This sort of question is always worth asking when it comes to making proper sense of Bible verses. A moment's thought will confirm there is a difference between seeking and pursuing. That same difference is found in the original Hebrew words in the verse. **Seeking** is used in the sense of looking for or enquiring into something, while **pursuing** is used in the sense of chasing after something with the intention of catching it. David says to use both when we want peace. Enquire and pursue. First find out the things that make for peace in any given situation, and then go after them and get a hold of them.

If we do that, we'll be using the 'new affection' of peace-making to expel the old habit of just being ourselves and going along with, or even fuelling, whatever discord there may be around us.

25 SURVEILLANCE

'The eyes of the LORD are upon the righteous, and his ears are open unto their cry.' (Psalm 34:15)

These days we are used to being watched. Like it or not, we live in a surveillance society. There are cameras almost everywhere in towns and cities. We're used to having eyes on us. We are assured that the reason for them is our safety, but we are still inclined to feel our lives a little snooped on sometimes. Equally we might wonder whether having the eyes of God on us all the time is really such a good thing. David certainly presents it in a positive light in this next verse of his Psalm. He's not expecting an outcry from anyone who might feel that their privacy is being invaded. Though according to David it's only the righteous who need to worry about it. And they are far from worried.

God's surveillance is selective. And whatever your opinion on the forest of cameras trained on us nowadays, there was no doubt in the mind of David that God's eyes on him were for his safety. And that's exactly the right way to think of it. When you have children in your care you keep an eye on them. Our Heavenly Father feels the same way. And although a parent will watch in case their child is getting up to mischief, the parent's overriding concern is that the child is safe. God's eyes are not on us to catch us doing something wrong. They most likely will, of course, but that's not the principal reason for them being on us.

His eyes in this context would be His angels' eyes. The angels are busy looking out for the righteous, covertly steering them along safe paths through life. Though the One who cares so much about this world will surely take a first-hand interest, too, and not leave **everything** to His angels. God who is the epitome of love is hardly going to keep remote from the objects of His love and take little or no interest in them. When the company I worked for was repairing

God's Secret

the extensive fire damage at Windsor Castle some years ago, every now and then our workers would sense someone looking over their shoulders. They'd turn around to find HRH the Duke of Edinburgh leaning over them to see how the work was going. He couldn't resist taking a personal interest. I wonder if the angels sometimes have a similar experience of finding God, in a sense, looking over their shoulders to see how things are going.

Is it fair?

We get a remarkable peep behind the curtain of everyday life in 2 Chronicles 16:9: *'For the eyes of the LORD run to and fro throughout the whole earth, to shew himself strong in the behalf of them whose heart is perfect toward him.'* God's eyes are absolutely everywhere. Through the angels He is constantly monitoring every square kilometre of the planet. **Scanning** the earth would be a good definition of eyes running to and fro over it.

God is constantly scanning the whole earth chiefly on behalf of a particular set of people: those whose hearts are perfect (or mature) towards God. They are a small minority, and He's interested in them above the vast majority. And that might not seem fair, but that's the way it is, and the way it has always been. It isn't God's fault that the numbers are so few, it's ours. God is watching to intervene if necessary on behalf of the God-fearing righteous people of the world. Not so much on behalf of anyone else.

It's not that God has no interest in everyone else. Far from it. God would rather have everyone saved and involved in His plans for the world. Most people, though, would rather go their own way, with all the attendant problems and cares of doing that. That's not what God wants for them, but He gives everyone the freedom to choose. He cares about the fate of everyone including the wicked. He hasn't written off the bulk of humanity. We are all His creations and He cares about us all. He is a God of love, and He shows it towards everyone. As Jesus said, God makes *'his sun to rise on the evil and on the good, and sendeth rain on the just and on the unjust.'* (Matthew 5:45) So if you ever hear someone use the expression 'The sun shines on the righteous' you can point out that actually it shines on the evil, too. God doesn't limit His kindness to the righteous. And when we consider that *'The face of the* LORD *is against them that do evil'* (which we'll come to in the next chapter), God is a model of restraint. Jesus made his point about God's kindness towards everyone in order to show believers that, as God's children, they should also be kindly disposed to all people, including the wicked. Like Father, like son and daughter.

Is it elitist?

It might be argued that God lavishing His special attention on a comparatively minor set of people down the centuries is elitist. It might look that way, but it isn't, certainly not in the sense we normally think of elitism. Elitism entails the distribution of, or entitlement to, favours without merit for a select few, usually through birth, connections or wealth. It's true that no-one merits God's special attention. Which might give it a passing resemblance to elitism. God's favour is bestowed freely on those who acknowledge His existence and respond to His call. No one can say they deserve God's attention and favour. It's His free gift to believers for believing. But this is far from the kind of elitism that operates sometimes in our societies.

For one thing, the privileged position of the righteous is never automatic, and never completely unwarranted. And for another, it's open to anyone who responds to God's call to become God-fearing and righteous. That's all that's required to bring the attention and favour of God upon us. There's an open invitation to become a saint. There's no open invitation to join **society's** elite. I certainly haven't received mine yet. And I'm guessing you haven't either. But that shouldn't bother us. Set against the invitation to be a saint, with all the blessings that brings, an invitation to join society's elite is not a great prize. One is a temporary and very mixed blessing, the other has the potential to be an eternal and unrivalled blessing.

God's Secret

But what about God's chosen people?
God's selection of saints is not elitist in the way that society operates. Saints aren't automatically born to other saints, or granted sainthood simply because they know other saints, or are in a position to help other saints. It doesn't work like that. But, having said that, what are we to make of God's 'chosen people'? They are historically the people of Israel, the Jews. We might ask: If they were chosen as a nation hasn't each generation been born into a favoured situation with God? In a way, yes.

God chose Israel as the nation through whom He would tell the rest of the world about Himself. They were to be God's ambassadors to the world, a shining beacon the world could look to, and from whom they could learn God's ways – His Secret. And God would so richly bless Israel that everyone would want to know their God.

This is why the Old Testament was given to us through Israel. The Old Testament is the Jewish Bible. And in its books we have the sad history of Israel's collective failure to rise to the occasion. Things turned out differently. But God hasn't forgotten them, and they are still central to God's future plans for the world (Appendix 1 at the back of this book has a few things to say about that). Jesus was born a Jew, we remember. The world has a Jewish Saviour.

No free pass
It all started for Israel when God chose a man called Abraham to be their founding father. The Bible says he was chosen because God considered him righteous, or potentially righteous. But as Abraham's family flourished and became the chosen nation of Israel, each individual Israelite wasn't, as a matter of course, favoured by God, regardless of how they behaved. There was no elitism in that way at all. Jesus' second cousin, John the Baptist, pointed this out to the Jews of his day. He told the Jewish religious leaders (those who were apt to think in rather elitist terms about their relationship with God), *'Bring forth therefore fruits meet for repentance: and think not to say within yourselves, We have*

Abraham to our father.' (Matthew 3:8-9) John told them that's not how it works. To be a child of Abraham in the truest sense, you need to be **like** him not just related to him. Being born into God's chosen people was not a free pass to favour.

If you look through the Bible, you'll see that God has a history of choosing people and giving them His special attention: Noah, Abraham, Gideon, David, Peter, Paul. These are some of the big names that come to mind because their stories are in the Bible. God saw potential in them, called them, and they responded. But God's special attention has always been on many smaller names too. It's on every saint. The situation may look elitist, because there is a favoured minority who know God's Secret, but because the Secret is open and available to anyone and everyone to live and learn, it can't properly be considered elitist.

Defending a lion

When it comes right down to it, though, whatever **we** might think of God's selection and preferential treatment of a comparatively small number of the world's population, it is after all **His** Creation and **His** prerogative. It's up to Him. We can't say how He should do things. For one thing, that attitude would be hugely lacking in the fear of the Lord. And for another, we'd be making the mistake, both serious and laughable, of judging the actions of the all-knowing, all-wise God with our limited and deficient understanding.

I must say it feels wrong and inappropriate to be writing in defence of God. As if He needs to be defended by the likes of any of us! Charles Spurgeon, the nineteenth century preacher, wrote this about defending the Bible: 'Defend the Bible! I would as soon defend a lion! Turn it loose and it will defend itself.' How right that sounds. But believers still defend the Bible, and we still try to explain the way God works among us. We do it because God has tasked His children with holding fast to His Secret and communicating its message in a world of ignorance, apathy and resistance. Added to which, God-fearing righteous people are so delighted to know God's Secret that they usually want to share it with those who don't have it. They'd like everyone to benefit from it.

Unbelief seems rational. In its own way it feels like freedom for those who choose it – freedom from the oppression of religion. But unbelief is by definition negative. It's the lack of something. It replaces something with nothing. And the choice of unbelief is so often based on misperceptions about religion, for which sadly, religionists are often responsible. What the unbeliever doesn't believe is so often something that true believers shouldn't believe either.

Does God break the rules?
Those looking for reasons to hang onto their unbelief will claim that God is unfair and doesn't operate by His own rules. For instance in the Bible God tells us not to kill people, and yet He kills or causes the deaths of many people Himself. To contend that God must Himself be bound by every rule that He makes for us is quite bizarre. It's like saying that the rules and restrictions that parents place on their children must also be binding on the parents. (I can just imagine parents everywhere looking for someone to hold their hand when they want to cross the road.)

Critics seem to lose sight of the fact that God and people are very different. In the final analysis morality is whatever God decides it will be. But God is love and God is righteous so His morality will be consistent with His love and righteousness. The morality that God imposes on us, and expects of us, cannot be of the same order as the morality that works within the Divine Mind. His righteousness is unimpeachable because He sees the entire picture. He can weigh every possible outcome of every action that He makes and we make.

What we see and know by comparison is like one single frame of an entire movie. What could you conclude about a film from having a glimpse of only one frame? A little perhaps, but hardly enough to tell the producer and director where they went wrong.

Whenever something in the Bible seems not to fit with what we might expect of a loving God, or whenever something in the world about us seems not to fit with what we might expect – that's when we need to acknowledge that it's only one frame that we're looking at. God sees the big picture, from beginning to end, or He wouldn't be God. Everything that God does or allows falls within the ambit of His love and righteousness. Even the evil that is permitted in this world is working for ultimate good (see the next chapter). God owes us no explanation or justification for anything He says or does. Though He lets us in on as much as we need to know, or, more likely, as much as we can handle.

Eyes and ears

To date, our surveillance society has entailed only cameras watching us. I wonder how people would react to having sensitive microphones everywhere, picking up what they say as they wander the shopping mall or sit on the bus. It's my guess that people wouldn't be too pleased. But for believers, something like that is already happening. Not only does God see what they're doing, He also hears what they're saying. But they're not displeased or offended by it – they couldn't be more pleased – because they don't think of it as an invasion of their privacy.

David tells us in this fifteenth verse of his Psalm that God's ears are open to the cries of the righteous. This is rhymed in the manner of Hebrew poetry with the meaning of the first part of the verse. And this sets the matter beyond question as to why God is watching us. It's certainly not to catch us misbehaving. It's to make sure we're okay. That comes out more clearly in the rhymed second half. God's ears are open, not in case we say something wrong and He can punish us, they are open in case we call out to Him. If we have a problem He wants to be there for us.

An open mind

Our call, or our prayer, doesn't have to be said aloud. It can happen in our minds and God will still hear it. For anyone concerned about surveillance this would probably be their worst nightmare – for someone to be able to eavesdrop not only on what they're saying, but on what they're thinking! But it could be where surveillance technology is heading. Already implants are being developed that can pick up electrical impulses in our brains, read them, and translate them. In this way mental commands can be given to computers. Biometrics is in its infancy, but things progress at an alarming rate these days. By the time you read this, the things I'm describing may already be in general use.

Leading tech companies openly say they want to develop human/digital hybrids. Some see this as the future of our species. One day they hope to be able to download our brains' 'software' into some technological hardware. Though even to envisage such a thing implies a simplistic and mechanistic view of what constitutes a human brain, the organ described recently in *New Scientist* as 'the most complex object in the known universe'. It requires the dehumanising of humans in a way that perhaps the development of evolutionary theory has been inadvertently paving the way for. Because it's hard to believe a culture which acknowledged God as its Creator, would go down the road of hybrid techno-humans.

Some maintain that with the level of dependency on technology we already have we are a long way down the road towards becoming hybrids. How far it will be allowed to progress we don't know.

Later in the book... I say that rather a lot, I know, or words like it. But everything about God's Secret is so interconnected that I'm often in danger of trespassing too far on subjects I have to talk about later. As I don't want to completely pre-empt what lies ahead, I need regularly to hold back fuller explanations. I suggest again that you re-read the entire book when you've finished and

Surveillance

have more of an overview. In addition to helping you understand the Secret, it will help explain my repetition of 'as we'll see later...'

As I was saying: later in the book we'll talk about how near God is to intervening in human affairs. This makes it likely that progress on the human/digital hybrid will not get too far. The nightmarish scenario, in which we directly interface with computers and our thoughts are just data that can be hacked, harvested or corrupted, when the 'web of things' becomes the 'web of minds', will most likely be shut down by the mind's original Creator.

'There is no new thing under the sun', said Solomon in Ecclesiastes. God has been listening in on our thoughts since He first created us. He knows what we're thinking. Not that He takes much notice of the unimaginable babble of thoughts that must be emanating from this planet at all times. What a cacophony that must be! He is selective in His surveillance and pays attention specifically to those whose hearts are towards Him. So again it doesn't have to bother most people that God is watching and listening, and it certainly doesn't bother those to whom it applies. They are pleased to know that when they are in trouble they can call out, or mentally let their distress be known, and God will hear them.

God probably won't spring instantly to their aid, as if they'd rubbed a magic lamp. Though it's not entirely out of the question. After all, if a situation is life-threatening they may not have time to wait for an answer. Daniel's three friends who were about to be thrown into the furnace weren't looking for an answer some time soon, they needed one right now. What more commonly happens though, is that God will work through normal rather than miraculous channels to bring about a deliverance from trouble. The miraculous will be disguised as the normal. Though if we have any spiritual savvy we will realise what's going on. Or we'll realise it afterwards when we look back at how things worked out so well after all.

God's Secret

And when we have the unconditional trust, which is an essential part of God's Secret, we can stop worrying. We'll know that our situation is in God's hands. We can 'let go and let God', just as King Hezekiah did when his city was surrounded by armies. We can remember David who said he'd been delivered from all his troubles, even though he was still being hunted by a powerful homicidal king. We can also remember the power of the imagination to bring peace of mind. Turn our thoughts towards a positive outcome and stop imagining the worst. And if you think that's impossible for you in your particularly bad situation, then remember Daniel when he spent a night with hungry lions padding around him, or his three friends who were thrown alive into a furnace. They would probably all have traded your situation for theirs, whatever your problem.

This isn't to minimise your problem – if you have one right now, or whenever you have one – or suggest you should pull yourself together, have more faith, and deal with it. Far from any of that. It's to say along with David that *'The eyes of the LORD are upon the righteous, and his ears are open to their cry.'* God is not asking us to be heroes, towers of strength, or stoically detached from our emotions – He's saying cry to me in your distress and I will see you and hear you and help you.

The only preconditions are that you are God-fearing and righteous – that God's Secret is with you. You are one of those people God's eyes and ears are trained on – a saint, in fact. And as we're going to see in the chapters on God's grace, being a saint is simpler than you might think. God's Secret, and the Gospel that it dovetails with, is simplicity itself once you begin to join the dots, as we are slowly doing. And while we're thankful to the theologians for the support and insights that they sometimes give us, we don't need them in order to understand the essential beauty and truth of God's communication to us.

26 THE GOOD, THE BAD, AND... NO-ONE ELSE.

'The face of the LORD is against them that do evil, to cut off the remembrance of them from the earth.' (Psalm 34:16)

Not far from where I live there are some lagoons that have been created from disused quarries. Now they make a beautiful conservation area that is home to a variety of creatures and plants, and is visited regularly by herons, cormorants, and geese among other birds. The area is also visited by people like me who like to take a stroll there occasionally. Along the shoreline of one of the lakes there is a line of waterfront properties that are as easy on the eye as the surrounding countryside.

The entire area is man-made, houses and landscape alike. I have only to look at it to know that there is a lot of good in people. It was a commercial venture, true, but it shows a lot of people working together to create something beautiful and worthwhile. I know because I was one of those people, and I feel good at having played a small part in it. Whenever I pause to talk to anyone who lives there, I know I'm talking to someone who feels blessed in their situation. This development is a typical example of the capacity that is within us to create good things.

The evidence for good in us is everywhere: in art, music, literature, friendships, family, love, medicine, engineering, sport – the list goes on. We humans are aspirational creatures, there's no doubt about that. But alongside all the goodness, we know there's badness, too. And as we found from our thoughts on the devil, our badness is self-generated. It's inside us. Innate badness resides there along with our aspirations of goodness. And the badness very easily gets the upper hand. We all know this for a fact from our own experience. It's no good pretending to ourselves that we always do the right thing from the best of motives. This bad world is our own creation not God's.

What exactly is evil?

We get daily reminders from the news media of the evil in the world. Some of what we hear is horrific beyond belief. It's incomprehensible how appalling some people can be in their treatment of others. It might seem, looking at the world, that the devil is more able to prove his existence than God. The evidence for a devil looks overwhelming. But we know better. What is overwhelming is the evidence for the human propensity for evil.

Evil is the only word for the level of inhumanity we sometimes encounter. Thankfully usually not first-hand. But what about lesser crimes: what about the more commonplace felonies that fill the daily news, and which, it has to be said, bring pain and misery to far more people than the occasional dreadful acts? Statistically speaking these lesser crimes are more likely to impact you and me, or someone we know. We probably don't think of them as evil, though. Until they get closer to home, or affect us personally, that is. Then we know they are. We know because of the gut-wrenching reaction we have to being burgled or scammed or threatened. These crimes are also evil.

But what about the very low-level crime that goes on around us, which hardly reaches even the local news, and which most people probably think doesn't matter much? I'm thinking of petty crimes against individuals or businesses or corporations or 'the system', where the view is often: 'nobody gets hurt, so why worry about it?' Probably no-one will classify these last misdemeanours as evil. Bumping up an insurance claim. Fibbing on a form. Overcharging. Petty theft from an employer. What's the problem? No-one gets hurt. Businesses can afford it. Why worry about it?

I've over-simplified things, I know, by positing three levels of evil. Really there are no properly defined levels. It's nowhere near that clear-cut. If we start from incomprehensible evils and move down through the more commonplace to the petty crimes that we may not even think of as crimes, let alone evil, there are innumerable degrees in between. And, apart from the pure evil at the top of the scale, we might find it difficult or impossible to say how far up or down the scale any other evil sits.

Not what we think
But in truth, it really doesn't matter how **we** classify something, or someone, as evil. What matters is how God thinks of them. David says, *'The face of the LORD is against them that do evil.'* These individuals that God has set His face against are evil by His definition. That may differ from ours, but the decider is of course whoever God chooses to call evil. Whatever we might think, these are the evil ones. This being so, and if we don't want to be among them, it's a good idea for us to be clear about exactly who they are. Worryingly, most people aren't clear about it at all. In fact, most people are likely to be **wrong** about it. So where do we start? One thing we know for certain about evil people is that they are not the righteous.

Back on the beach
Let's go back down to the beach. The sea hasn't washed away our circle with 'righteous' written inside it, so let's add a word to make it say 'the righteous'. Now the righteous are in the circle and everyone else is outside of it – the unrighteous, or the evil occupy the rest of the beach. That's how God sees it. No half-measures. As it is with righteous and evil deeds, so it is with righteous and evil people. In God's view we're either one kind of person or the other, and there's nowhere in between for anyone to sit.

That shouldn't surprise us. It follows on from what we've learned about righteous and evil deeds. But the idea that everybody is either good or bad might be hard to accept, because it's not how we're used to seeing the world. We're used to thinking of people as more of a mixture of good and bad. Some lean more heavily one way, some the other way. To divide everyone rigidly into good and bad is alien to us. It might even seem unchristian. Especially when, by the criteria God shows us, most people are going to finish up in the bad camp. Surely we should be more generous in our appraisal of others? Well, yes, **we** should. Definitely. **We** shouldn't be dismissing the bulk of humanity as evil. So why are most people going to be on the outside of that circle we drew in the sand, filling the rest of the beach? The reason is because what we drew on the sand illustrates God's view not ours.

We need to understand this from God's viewpoint, which is clear-cut and absolute. But we also have to see it from our own human viewpoint. This is one of those rare occasions when it's right for us to see things differently from God. It sounds a bit of a conundrum, but if we follow God's will on this we will see things differently from Him. This is not how it usually works. Usually following God's will means seeing things the way He sees them. But not this time. You'll see why as this unfolds.

Who are the evil?
We looked at the ways in which we can use the tongue for evil in a previous chapter, and now we need to look at evil in the wider sense. And, because it's God's view of evil we want to establish first, let's start with some Bible definitions.

We can hardly do better than start with a definition Jesus gave. When we were talking about good and bad speech, we quoted what Jesus said about a good man bringing forth good things out of the good treasure of his heart, and the bad man bringing out bad things. Well, here is Jesus in that same place being more specific about the bad things he had in mind: *'For it is from within, out of a person's heart, that evil thoughts come – sexual immorality, theft, murder, adultery, greed, malice, deceit, lewdness, envy, slander, arrogance and folly. All these evils come from inside and defile a person.'* (Mark 7:21-23 NIV) I picked a more modern translation this time because in the Authorised Version some of the old words for the evils Jesus listed are redundant even though the evils themselves aren't.

Some of the things on Jesus' list we'd all agree should be there. They are definitely evil. No question. But stealing and envying, arrogance and folly, up there with murder and adultery? What's going on there? We find this sort of list, where serious and not-so-serious evils are lumped together, a number of times in the Bible. The Apostle Paul lists drunkenness and anger alongside murder and adultery in one of his New Testament letters. He calls these and the other things on his list *'works of the flesh'*, because the flesh is his way of referring to our nature. He means evil works. And Paul concludes his list by saying: *'they which do such things shall not inherit the kingdom of God.'* (Galatians 5:21) It doesn't get more serious than that.

In that last line Paul is saying exactly the same thing that David is saying in Psalm 34. For someone not to *'inherit the kingdom of God'* is another way of saying that God is *'to cut off the remembrance of them from the earth.'* In other words, when God's Kingdom arrives and extends across the whole earth, they will be excluded from it. Evil people won't be allowed to ruin the world any more.

It's about outcome

So is stealing on a par with murder? Is anger on a par with the worst forms of sexual immorality? Is that what Jesus, Paul and David are telling us? No, it isn't. Of course not. What they are saying is not that these things are all equally bad, but that the **outcome** of continuing in them will be the same. I think of it as working in the same way that, on a more mundane level, you can be thrown out of a restaurant for brawling with customers and staff and smashing up the furniture, or, if the place has a strict dress code, you might be asked to leave for not wearing a tie, or for wearing shorts. The two reasons are vastly different in scale, but the outcome is the same.

Being an arrogant, prideful person is patently not as bad as being a murderer. But both can exclude us from God's plans to make this world a hugely better place for everyone. It can't really work any other way. God has promised a world free from evil of **every** kind. And unless that happens His kingdom will be essentially not a lot better than what we have now, and there will be hardly any point to it. He wants to turn this earth into a world free from murderers and brawlers, from the immoral and the adulterous, from the arrogant and the malicious; from the thieves and the greedy and deceitful people; and free from the fools who have no regard for anyone, not even themselves. Different levels of evil, yes, but none of which God wants in His Kingdom when it comes. He plans to give us something far better than that.

So it's one thing or the other. In God's view there's nothing in between. We are either righteous or evil. Most people on the planet are evil in God's view. In fact we are **all** evil but for grace, which we'll talk about in the next chapters. *'There is none righteous, no, not one,'* as the Apostle Paul said in Romans 3:10. That assessment of humanity is inevitable when judged by the absolute standards of a perfect Being. Anything less than God is imperfect. Which leaves none of us out. But He loves us, with all our faults, and so He has done much to remove the barriers between His perfect expectations of us and our inability to deliver on them.

Seeing things differently

Our view of humanity is different from God's. It has to be. We don't view other people from a place of perfection. We can't look at the rest of humanity and see them as evil. That would be inappropriate because we're a part of humanity ourselves. Even when God deems us to be righteous by making allowance for us through grace, we can't condemn the unrighteous as evil. Only God can do that. We are commanded not to judge others because we are in no position to do it. It's only by God's grace that we are not considered evil along with everyone else. We are told to be loving towards all people, seeing the good in them, or the potential for it. So this is how that conundrum works that we mentioned earlier. It's God's will that we see things **differently** from Him on this. He can see the bulk of humanity as evil, and condemn them for it. But we can't do that. In fact we need to be careful not to do it. Jesus once told an exaggerated story about a person presuming to remove a speck of sawdust from someone else's eye while they themselves have an entire plank of wood in their own eye. What the plank represents is our presumption to put someone else right. The plank represents an assumed superiority. We need to understand that only God is superior.

An angry face

Back to David's Psalm. It's an unusual way of saying that God is against certain people to say that *'the face of the LORD is against them'*. It's not an expression we'd ever use to describe anger, but we get the gist of what's being said. And the face is certainly the place where anger is best shown. Even when other indications may be ambiguous – demeanour, voice, or silence – there's no mistaking an angry look. And this is how God looks at *'them that do evil'*. At the moment they can't see that angry face and they're not aware of it. But it's there alright. We're told that *'God is angry with the wicked every day.'* (Psalm 7:11) There's not a day goes by when the angry face of God isn't turned towards the wicked. But He holds back from venting that anger.

Not the end of the world

God let's things carry on as they are because He's patient, even with the mass of humanity that He considers evil, and He won't intervene to deal with them wholesale until the time is right. He won't hold back forever. David says in this sixteenth verse of his Psalm that God intends to *'cut off the remembrance of them from the earth.'* One day they will all be gone and forgotten. When will that be? Do we have any idea when it will happen? It's very much tied up with what happens when Jesus returns and God's promised global Kingdom replaces the divided and struggling world we have now. The signs of serious unrest in the world about us indicate that it will happen soon. You'll find my reasons for saying this is at the back of the book in Appendix 1.

So what is God waiting for? Why doesn't He bring His plans for the betterment of the world to fruition right away? As we said, He is patient. And something He is patiently waiting for is the last of the saints to be called to Him. He doesn't want to bring the curtain down, as it were, before everyone who **can** be called **has** been called. He won't make a move until He knows that all who can be saved by responding to His call have been given the opportunity. That will be the right time to deal once and for all with the world's evil.

And how will He know when there aren't any more left to call? We could say, 'Well, He's God, so He'll know', which is true. But it's not a satisfactory answer. And we don't have to sidestep the question like this, because there's an answer which isn't evasive, and which makes good practical sense.

God will know for certain when to intervene in human affairs because a time will come when if He **doesn't** step in, humanity will annihilate themselves and probably destroy the planet too. At that point there will be no more righteous people left to call because humanity's tenure of the planet will be drawing to a quick and calamitous close. Unless God steps in there will be no more people and probably no more planet either. It will be Armageddon.

People get the wrong idea about Armageddon. Catastrophic though it will be, it's not the end of the world. It's God's intervention to stop that happening, when God will *'destroy them which* [would] *destroy the earth'.* (Revelation 11:18)

A new world begins with Armageddon
Armageddon doesn't so much signal the end of this present world but the start of a new and vastly improved one. Even though it will be a time of global upheaval like never before, it's something that believers look forward to rather than fear, because they know what's on the other side of it. It's the end of the world as we know it, because this is a world in which evil holds sway, but what follows

will be the better place that God has been promising ever since we humans first took a wrong turn.

You'll have gathered by now that the Kingdom of God is going to be on Earth and not in heaven. It has never been God's intention for us to live in heaven. We were promised a heavenly Kingdom, or a Kingdom **of** or **from** heaven, yes, but never a kingdom **in** heaven. Heaven is God's domain, not ours. When Jesus spoke of going to heaven himself, he said *'Whither I go, ye cannot come...'* As we've already seen, we don't go to heaven or hell at death, we go into the grave. It won't hurt to reinforce that truth here with some words from Psalm 115:

> *'The heaven, even the heavens, are the LORD'S: but the earth hath he given to the children of men. The dead praise not the LORD, neither any that go down into silence. But we will bless the LORD from this time forth and for evermore. Praise the LORD.'* (Ps 115: 16–18)

Clearly heaven is God's dwelling place, not ours. He gave us planet Earth. With the exception of Jesus, who ascended to heaven after his resurrection, no-one has gone there after they have died. The dead are not experiencing eternal bliss praising God for eternity; they are in the silence of the grave. The psalmist could hardly put it more clearly here. But then, speaking on behalf of all God-fearing righteous people everywhere, the psalmist goes on to say that **we** will live and bless God for evermore. He's adamant that he and those like him will not be **left** in the silence of the grave.

It's a fact of life that everyone goes to the grave. And sadly those whom God considers evil because they are not *'in Christ'* and still *'in Adam'* will stay there and experience nothing more forever. No heaven, no hell, no resurrection. Just silence. The dead who are *'in Christ'*, however, will be raised to life again when Jesus returns to build God's Kingdom on Earth. That's an essential part of the

God's Secret

good news of the Bible, and of God's Secret, as you probably realise by now.

Journey into space?

Purely as an aside here, it will be interesting, in view of the fact that humankind has been given planet Earth for its home, to see what becomes of America's national and corporate plans to colonise Mars. Will the endeavour be beset with angelic interference, technical glitches and setbacks that will divinely thwart it? That seems extremely likely. Though, perhaps the space programme will be made to progress so slowly that the major events in the divine programme that we've been talking about will overtake it. I have a strong feeling that people's dreams of colonising other worlds will come to nothing. We've been given the Earth, and nothing beyond it.

Good judgement

Something we haven't covered so far is judgement. It sounds rather ominous, but it isn't really. Armageddon and Christ's return are often associated in people's minds with a so-called last judgement. And rightly so. There is to be such a thing, because the evil have to identified and removed before the righteous can enjoy the new world. And this is the ideal place to talk about that event.

Some words from the Apostle Paul will help us here. He said: *'Because he* [God] *hath appointed a day, in the which he will judge the world in righteousness by that man whom he hath ordained; whereof he hath given assurance unto all men, in that he hath raised him from the dead.'* (Acts 17:31) The day God has appointed to judge the world is the day that He sends Jesus back to judge it on His behalf. Jesus has been given the authority and ability to decide who enters into the Kingdom of God and who doesn't. He will be its king.

And we can be thankful that someone of such faultless character and infallible insight has been appointed to the task. We are assured that he will judge righteously and mercifully. And, although sinless himself, he will judge us as someone who understands perfectly what it is to be human (Hebrews 2:17–18). So his judgement won't be harsh, it will be fair and full of grace.

Who will be judged?

So, according to God's communication to us, there is certainly a judgement to come and Jesus is the one who has been chosen to carry it out. It's only fitting that he should be the one to decide who will populate the Kingdom that he is to reign over as King. He will certainly want to root out all the evil people who would spoil his Kingdom for everyone else. But, and perhaps surprisingly, the judgement won't start with them. Their judgement must come, of course. But all in good time. Because there's a judgement that precedes theirs.

The Apostle Paul referred to Jesus as *'The Lord Jesus Christ, who shall judge the living and the dead at His appearing and His kingdom.'* (2 Timothy 4:1) When he comes, Jesus' first thoughts will be for those *'in Christ'* who've been waiting so long for him. The *'living and the dead'* whom he judges straightway at his appearance are two sets of people both *'in Christ'* – those who are already alive when he comes, and those he has resurrected.

So, first he's going to judge all those who are *'in Christ'*: the living ones, together with all the believers who've lived and died throughout previous generations.

Why them first? Because he wants them out of harm's way. The judgement will be happening at a time of trouble in the world like never before, as we've said. It's what people think of as the Apocalypse. Jesus will take all those *'in Christ'* to a place away from the turmoil to judge them. 'Judge' sounds rather ominous, and I'd much rather say he's going to be rewarding them all, but regrettably even some of those *'in Christ'* will not be considered suitable for the Kingdom. Because not all of those who become *'in Christ'* by belief and baptism will remain believers. For a number of reasons (outlined in Jesus' parable of the sower in Matthew 13) some will stop believing and go back to their old lives and ways. These will not be allowed to enter the Kingdom of God and spoil it for the God-fearing righteous who have kept their faith and who have been promised a better world.

A sad reality

But don't let all this talk of judgement worry you. It's not meant to. The sad reality is that Jesus has to make a decision on who can enter God's Kingdom and who can't. To let in all-comers would result in a world hardly any better than what we have now. Jesus must do it for the benefit of all those who have ever known and lived by God's Secret – for those he loves and who have responded to his love. Sad as it is that some people will be excluded for wasting the opportunity God has given them, it cannot be otherwise if His Kingdom is to be the place of peace, harmony and happiness that He has promised.

Judgement and grace

Another reason that believers, and would-be believers shouldn't be deterred by all this talk of judgement is **grace**. When I said just now that this is an ideal place to talk about judgement, I didn't mean this only because it fits in here with the sequence of events we're describing; I meant it also because the next two chapters are devoted to the subject of grace. As you'll see, God's grace takes the worry out of the judgement for believers. It makes His Kingdom attainable for even those who might consider themselves the most under-achieving of believers.

Grace makes the return to the grave of all those who turned their backs on their Saviour even more saddening. Especially if they walked away from him because they felt they couldn't live the life expected of them as believers – thought that the Christian life was too difficult for them to cope with. They will have completely misjudged the situation. They will have sorely underestimated the power of the sacrifice of Christ on their behalf, and will have failed to comprehend or believe in the true and full extent of grace. They could so easily have been welcomed into the Kingdom that they were called to inherit. Instead they are woken from what's referred to in the Bible as their 'sleep' of death only to be returned to a death that is permanent.

Those baptised into Christ who are alive when he comes back (probably many of this current generation) face a similar problem of rejection if they have stopped believing, or, even more sadly, if they have turned away because they felt that living the life of a believer was beyond them. In that they will have been greatly mistaken because of grace. Grace is the allowance God makes for our inability to be perfect. As I say, more of this in the next two chapters. Rest assured, grace will put this rather negative diversion into judgement in perspective. Before that, though, let's give a little thought to the matter of death as sleep which we have just referred to. In case you were wondering about it.

Dead or only sleeping?
Jesus often taught people by using the brief stories we call parables. We've mentioned some of them already. But sometimes Jesus didn't **tell** a story to illustrate a point, instead he acted something out. He performed an **acted parable**. I mention this because he performed one of these to teach us something about death.

While Jesus was teaching and healing one day, a man came to him imploring him to go and heal his daughter. But his daughter wasn't just unwell, she was dead. Jesus was so impressed with the man's confidence in him to bring his daughter back to life that he agreed to go back to the man's house. When he arrived there he told the mourners to be quiet *'for the maid is not dead, but sleepeth. And they laughed him to scorn.'* They knew death when they saw it. And she was dead. So they continued to wail and cry in the manner of mourners.

But Jesus had the mourners silenced and removed from the house. He then went in, took the girl by the hand, and she got up

God's Secret

(Matthew 9:18-26). What that illustrates, apart from Jesus' power to raise the dead, is that if Jesus comes to bring you back to life, then as far as he's concerned, you are not really dead, you are only sleeping. This distinction is made a number of times in the Bible. The saints, those *'in Christ'* and not *'in Adam'* any longer, are only sleeping in their graves because Jesus intends to send his angels to wake them up when he returns.

And here's something to ponder. If the saints from all previous generations are sleeping, and if they've all gone to heaven, as many think, must we assume they are all asleep up there?

No, they are all asleep down here.

The unfortunate people who have died never having associated themselves with the new Adam aren't sleeping, they really are dead. Or as David puts it in his Psalm: the remembrance of them is cut off from the face of the earth. They no longer have any part in what happens. They won't be raised when Christ comes. They never believed in God or His plans. They never wanted to have anything to do with Him or them, so, in a tragic sense, they got what they wanted. Or, equally tragically, because of the folly of their ancient ancestors (the probable scenario we spoke of earlier in this book), they grew up in parts of the world where the truths of God's communication were never taken, or were lost sight of, when the descendants of Noah spread across the globe after the great flood. Which has left them also, in the main, without hope of the resurrection. And apart from Christ and the grace that he has obtained for us, that would be the future for us all – the perpetual silence of the grave.

I think we may be seriously in need of cheering up after all this talk of death. So this is the perfect place for us to exit this chapter and head for the good news of the chapters on grace that follow.

27 THE GRACE ESCAPE (PART 1)

'The righteous cry, and the LORD heareth, and delivereth them out of all their troubles.' (Psalm 34:17)

There's a story about C. S. Lewis I'd like to tell. I've come across it a number of times and have no reason to doubt its authenticity. Though even if it's not true, the point it makes is both true and relevant, so it's well worth telling again. Apparently, during a British conference on comparative religions, theologians from around the world began earnestly debating whether anything about Christianity was unique. Because so much of it can be found in other religions.

Certainly the 'Golden Rule' of treating others as we like to be treated ourselves is common to all mainstream faiths. But the assembled religious experts were at their wits' ends to come up with anything that couldn't be found elsewhere. As the debate heated up, with each new suggestion being rejected, C. S. Lewis wandered into the hall and asked 'What's the rumpus about?' When he was told they couldn't come up with anything about Christianity that was unique to it, Lewis responded in his usual forthright manner, 'Oh, that's easy. It's grace.'

They thought about what he said for moment, and then they all had to agree that he was right. Grace isn't in any other religion. Only Christianity dares to take such a radical, counter-intuitive step. Only the God of love revealed in the Bible **would have** taken such a step.

Grace is what we want to talk about in this chapter and the next. But before we do that, we need to know a little more about the verse we've reached in Psalm 34. Because we haven't just randomly decided to talk about grace: it's the subject of this verse.

God's Secret

That's not immediately apparent but it becomes clear when we look closer.

More trouble

The verse mentions trouble. We talked about trouble back in chapter sixteen when we looked at verse six of David's Psalm. In fact that verse says very much the same thing as the verse we've just reached. For comparison, here's verse six again: *'This poor man cried, and the LORD heard him, and saved him out of all his troubles.'* Cast your eyes up to the verse under the chapter heading and you'll see this is almost identical. The only real difference between the two verses is that one talks from the standpoint of the poor, or God-fearing, man, and the other talks from the standpoint of the righteous.

Different worlds

That makes perfect sense, knowing as we do that the first half of the Psalm instructs us on being God-fearing, and the second half on being righteous. Verse six speaks from the perspective of being God fearing, and verse seventeen from the perspective of being righteous. These are the two complementary sides of a Godly character. God's Secret is with those who fear Him and those who are righteous, we remember. And there's a good reason why these two things are brought together in God's Secret and in the Godly character. It's because we live in two worlds. We each have an inner and an outer world – one full of things that go on 'out there', in events and circumstances, and one full of things that go on 'in here', inside our heads.

God saves us from all our troubles 'out there', and from all our troubles 'in here'. He truly gives us the best of both worlds. What follows is how this works.

Pivotal verses

It's well worth taking account of the fact that verse six is precisely at the centre of the eleven verses of the first half of the Psalm and verse seventeen is precisely at the centre of the second half.

The grace escape (Part 1)

These verses are both central. That has to be by design, so it's worth being aware of it. Everything about being God-fearing centres on verse six. And everything about being righteous centres on verse seventeen. Both verses are about us relying on God for our deliverance from all our troubles.

God-fearing people (verse six) are awed and humbled by seeing and appreciating God's power and goodness all around them, especially when His power and goodness touches their own lives, as they had touched David's when he wrote this Psalm. He felt so blessed at being delivered from all his external problems.

The righteous (verse seventeen) pursue righteousness (*'hunger and thirst after righteousness'* as Jesus put it) because they want to be right with God. But they struggle with righteousness. It eludes them. They cry out in exasperation at how spiritually inept they are. Again, God hears and delivers them from all their troubles – their internal troubles this time: the frustrations and anxieties that are related to trying to be righteous.

This is how these two central verses (six and seventeen) concern all our external troubles and all our internal troubles. Both of our worlds.

If you glance through the Psalm you'll see that the first half is about external problems and solutions: such as not lacking the things we need, not going hungry, being delivered from our enemies etc. And the second half is about internal problems and their solutions: such as giving more thought to who we **are**, what we say, and more thought to what we do.

Double deliverance

We know from previous chapters that God keeps an eye on believers. His angels camp around the God fearing to help keep them safe in the midst of external evils. God hears their cries and brings His subtle, and sometimes not-so-subtle, influences to bear on their situations. How He delivers us from external trouble is easy enough to understand. God's angels are on hand, keeping track of us. But how does God intervene in the internal world of the righteous to deliver them from all the evil inside them? That's not quite so easy to fathom. We can rule out mind control. It's not about God erasing or suppressing our anxieties. God doesn't interfere in that way. He doesn't interfere with **who we are**. So how does He manage to soothe away all the fears and frustrations of those who aspire to be righteous? You're probably already nodding to yourself that you know.

The answer is... and in my head there's a mental drum roll leading up to this word...

Grace.

It's such a little word – just one syllable and only five letters – but it's a word which means such a great deal. 'Amazing Grace', as it's called in the hymn, is so eminently appropriate. Because truly it is amazing.

Saving grace

We need to devote some space and time to grace. As we've been promising to do. It'll be time well spent and space well allotted. We've given it two chapters in the book for good reason. Grace ranks high – supreme, perhaps – among the concepts of the Bible. Certainly nothing else in Christianity works without it. Without grace there's no righteousness. Not for anyone. We'd all be permanently estranged from God. Jesus' sacrifice would save no-one.

Thankfully, it would not have been possible for that last thing to happen, because Jesus' sacrifice triggered grace. The introduction of grace was, still is, and always will be integral to the saving work of Jesus. They cannot be prised apart and must always be seen and appreciated together. Grace is at the very heart of Christ's saving work. When Christ became the new Adam and gave us the opportunity to relate to him rather than the old

The grace escape (Part 1)

Adam who failed us, as part of the package, we might say, came the grace by which God accepts us. God counts those *'in Christ'* righteous by the mechanism of grace. Through Jesus, and by grace, we escape our fatal association with the old Adam.

So, although it's not obvious at first glance, grace is what verse seventeen of David's Psalm is all about.

Grace is how God delivers the righteous from all their inner troubles. From their ongoing battles with themselves as they keep trying and failing to be righteous. No amount of willpower will do it. No list of resolutions will work. No amount of good intentions is ever going to pull it off. Righteousness will remain forever on our to-do list if it's down to us. It's a losing battle. And the harder we try the harder it gets. It will dispirit us and make us want to give up. It will make the message of Christianity seem not good news at all. Unless…

Freedom

Unless we do one of two things. We can imagine ourselves acceptable to God because of all the resolutions we make, the good things we do, and our anxious prayers for forgiveness as we continually fall short of the perfection we're striving for. Or we can take hold of the grace that is freely available to us through the sacrifice of Christ. One of those won't work; the other one will. One of them will leave us spiritually exhausted playing catch-up all the while; and the other will leave us spiritually emancipated. As Jesus said so well: *'the truth will set you free.'* (John 8:32) Grace is a huge part of the truth that sets us free.

How it works, or the mechanism of grace, as we called it just now, rather clumsily for something so sublime, is what we want to look at now. And as the best exponent of grace in the Bible was Paul, who became known as the Apostle of Grace, let's start with him.

God's Secret

Paul's problem

The Apostle Paul had a problem. Something or someone was giving him grief and getting him down. We might have called it a pain in the neck; he called it a *'thorn in the flesh'*. (2 Corinthians 12:7) There's been a lot of speculation down the years over what he meant. The front runners have been problems with his eyesight, which are hinted at in his letters, and problems with difficult people in the early churches, which are expressly mentioned in his letters.

His reference to it as a thorn in the flesh has to be metaphorical. If it were real he could simply have removed it, or asked Doctor Luke, or one of the other apostles, to remove it for him. Three times he prayed to God about it. Most of us will probably go well beyond three prayers trying to get a problem resolved. But Paul stopped at three because God came back with a clear answer: No.

The answer in full was *'My grace is sufficient for thee.'* (2 Corinthians 12:9) Now we have more speculation over what this might mean. But really we don't need the specifics for any of this or we would have been given them. So ruminating over them or arguing about them is not worth the effort. Let's just work with what we have.

It was a thorn. It was in his flesh. A thorn means a problem, as any hiker or gardener will bear out. Though what Paul really meant was more of a sharp stake of the sort you'd find in a defensive palisade of the time, a sharpened pole. It wasn't a little thorn at all. So not a small problem either. We might assume that because it was in his flesh it was in his body: an injury or illness of some kind. But Paul uses the term flesh elsewhere to describe his lower natural way of thinking as opposed to his higher spiritual thinking. So it's not likely that he means something different here. And that's confirmed by God telling Paul that His grace was sufficient for him. That points to the problem being in his mind.

The grace escape (Part 1)

It makes no sense to apply God's grace to a physical problem. Grace is intended to cover our spiritual deficiencies not our physical ones. We don't need God's grace to allow for a broken leg, for instance, because a broken leg is not a spiritual problem. It's not a sin. But we would need grace to cover a bad attitude towards having a broken leg. Paul's problem with his eyesight or with other people was not the thorn that required grace. The reason he needed God's grace would have been his attitude towards the problem, not the problem itself.

Practice what you preach
Had Paul's attitude been better, the problem wouldn't have bothered him so much. He would simply have trusted in God. As it was, it was getting to him and he was going to continue complaining to God about it unless God stopped him. Which He did. What God in effect said to Paul was: Yes I know you find this hard to handle, but I'm not going to hold that against you. The true thorn was the wrong attitude Paul found impossible to deal with. That's what he was asking for help with, not the underlying problem itself.

Of course, the removal of the underlying problem would have helped. But that wouldn't have helped Paul face an inconsistency in his thinking. Paul was a preacher of grace. Now he was going to have to apply his preaching to himself. He taught that by grace we are saved, not by our own performance as Christians, which is always going to be flawed. Now Paul had to apply that knowledge to his own situation. He had to acknowledge to himself that his standing before God was not marred by his bad attitude to his problem. Through grace, God accepted Paul as he was, warts and all. Which is exactly what God does for every believer. That's what makes the good news (gospel) **such** good news. No need for despair, our standing before God is not all down to us, it's mostly down to grace.

When Jesus said *'Come unto me, all ye that labour, and are heavy laden, and I will give you rest'* he wasn't talking about giving us a hand with physical labours and burdens. Though if we'd been around in Galilee in the 1st century and needed help with something, I'm pretty sure he'd have stepped up promptly and with a friendly smile. But when he said that, he had easing the burdens of our inner world in mind.

Ramping up the grace?
But if God is going to make ample allowance for us and consider us righteous when we become *'in Christ'*, why should we then bother too much about what we do, and how we live? After all, our righteousness isn't down to us. If grace saves us then why should we make all the effort to do good things and be good people? In fact the more we stray from the path, the more grace God will send our way – and more grace has to be a good thing surely?

Er… no.

That may be logical but it isn't spiritual.

Paul followed that line of reasoning to the same unspiritual conclusion: *'What shall we say, then? Shall we continue in sin, that grace may abound? God forbid.'* (Romans 6:1-2) No-one, having arrived at the point of becoming *'in Christ'*, with the spiritual, mental and emotional understanding that it takes to bring us to that point, is going to take that bad attitude. It's in the very nature of grace to motivate us to want to appreciate and enjoy it, not abuse it. It's like a present, something we've always wanted and could never afford to buy ourselves. When we're given something like that we are elated.

Grace is intrinsically motivational. So are we going to turn up our noses at it and not show any gratitude towards the giver? Not if we have any idea of what we've been given. If you know of a better present than the removal of all that stands between you and eternal life in an ideal world, I'd love to hear about it.

The grace escape (Part 1)

The problem is that many Christians don't know what they have. So they continue to agonise over their standing with God. They go on fearing that they are 'no good' as Christians. And it's **that** kind of thinking that's going to make people give up trying to live the Christian life, not grace. Grace gives us every reason to carry on. Because it drives home the truth that our Christianity is never down to our performance. It's down to what Christ has already done, and to the grace that God has made available to us as a consequence.

It's a shame that believers can sometimes be nervous around grace. It's been called a dangerous doctrine. People think it will promote spiritual idleness and bring Christianity into disrepute. If we're not sufficiently motivated to be righteous and do good things because grace will make up for our not bothering, then won't that make us careless and uncommitted to our Christianity? You might think so. But remarkably that's not what happens. God knows far more about human psychology that we do. Well, He made it after all.

Pulling the rug out

So, instead of God saying He'll consider us righteous if we keep our thoughts on a tight rein and work very hard doing lots of good things, and try really hard never to put a foot wrong – instead of that, God says that, *'in Christ'*, He'll consider us righteous right now, it's His gift to us, so go and enjoy being *'in Christ'*. How are we going to react to that? That's a more powerful motivator for doing good than struggling against our human nature in an ongoing cycle of resolve and failure.

Our nature has had the rug pulled out from under its feet. When that little voice inside says: 'You're useless; you've failed again; why do you bother; you're never going to get yourself right?' we can say: 'But I'm *'in Christ'*, so I'll just carry on *'in Christ'*. We can say: I am [or have] the righteousness of God *'in Christ'* [see 2 Corinthians 5:21], and though my sins occasionally shame and frustrate me, they will never get in the way of the righteousness that has been imputed to me through grace. And as long as I believe and appreciate that, my wayward nature can't take it away from me.

Grace against the grain

It's strange that believers are prone to undermine their faith by resisting the gift of grace, or by being reluctant to yield to it fully. Getting it so easily seems to go against the grain for us. We have a tendency to feel we aren't good enough unless we do enough. Which is fine when it comes to giving good value for our monthly pay cheque. By all mean let's do our best to be worth what they're paying us. But let's not mistakenly carry over that same conscientiousness into our spiritual life. Because it doesn't transfer successfully. We can't earn the perfection God is looking for however hard we try. And we don't have to. Christ has already paid dearly for it. This is not to say we can sit back and do nothing because Christ has saved us, end of story. It's to say that we won't want to do that. Because grace is such a powerful motivator when we understand and appreciate it.

Paul mentioned how much he'd been motivated by grace: *'But by the grace of God I am what I am, and His grace toward me was not in vain; but I laboured more abundantly than they all, yet not I, but the grace of God which was with me.'* (1 Corinthians 15:10 NKJV) Grace didn't make Paul take his foot off life's pedal and coast. His appreciation of grace made Paul work harder than anyone else! He was tireless in his work of expanding and maintaining the church in the 1st century.

He demonstrates the truth of the matter that good works are the natural outflow of an appreciation of grace. His appreciation was immense, because he'd been forgiven so much. He even referred to himself as the chief of sinners because of the dreadful way he'd persecuted the church in the past. Now he knew grace. So his enthusiasm was immense. He laboured more than anyone. If we show no appreciation, our grace is vain, or empty, not motivating us as it should. We really haven't grasped it if we don't respond positively to it.

Speaking of labouring…

Sorry if I seem to be labouring this, but it's so fundamental, and vital to take on board. Such a big part of God's Secret. The right, positive, healthy perspective is this: living a good life and doing good things is not about earning points towards a salvation that we might otherwise lose (that's fear-based faith). It's about showing appreciation for the salvation we've already been offered (that's love-based faith).

And here's another apology, because I'm about to labour it a little more. There are a few more points to make. But I'll move to a new chapter for that. So if you feel you've read enough on the subject of Grace for now (though I hope not) please jump to chapter twenty-nine. You'll pick up a little more on grace there, too, but as part of another subject.

28 THE GRACE ESCAPE (PART 2)

Grace versus works

The Apostle Paul had to contend with a lot of problems relating to grace and works in his day. They are usually referred to as problems of **faith** and works. But it's really grace that's meant. Faith is not a thing that can stand alone without reference to anything else. We can't just have faith. It has to be faith **in** something. There needs to be a reason for it. We don't as a rule have to say explicitly what the reason is, of course, because it's usually understood though unspoken. The word 'faith' in the expression 'faith versus works' is faith in grace. No other meaning makes sense.

Paul's problem back in the 1st century arose because the majority of believers in the early churches were from a Jewish background. Before becoming Christians they'd lived under a strict system of religious laws called the Law of Moses. This was God's Law given to His chosen people through Moses. You will have heard of The Ten Commandments. They were a part of this Law, but there were hundreds more. 613 is the number often cited. Sadly most of the people missed the point of much of the Law, which was to direct the nation towards a coming saviour, or Messiah, namely Jesus. Paul, who'd been an exemplary champion of the Law before accepting Christ, said *'the law was our schoolmaster to bring us unto Christ.'* (Galatians 3:24)

The Law demonstrated the impossibility of pleasing God by works. Not that God deliberately and unfairly put it beyond people; it's just that whatever God gives us to do will prove beyond us. Adam had only one commandment and he failed. The Law was good for the people. It certainly set them apart from the nations around them, whose systems of government were often arbitrary and sometimes brutal. But it was impossible to keep in its entirety. Human nature always got in the way. So salvation was still ultimately by grace – though it was grace linked to the future Jesus. A grace still to come, and be confirmed, when Jesus eventually triggered it. Even so, the faithful could take hold of it in prospect, even back then, if they comprehended what the Law was really telling them.

Something about a God who inhabits all of time and space is that He can experience future things as though they already exist. He's described as someone who *'calleth those thing which be not as though they were'*. (Romans 4:17) He could connect people with something that had yet to happen, because it was as real to Him before it happened as it was when it happened.

Looking at the Lamb

As an example of the Law pointing forward to the work of Jesus, there were plenty of sacrificial lambs to be offered under the Law which pointed forward to **the** Lamb of God. Someone wanting forgiveness from God would take an unblemished lamb to the priest as a sin offering. What happened then was that the priest would inspect the lamb and make sure it was unblemished. The point here was that the lamb represented and pointed forward to Christ. And, notably, the priest didn't inspect the man to make sure **he** was unblemished, he looked at the lamb.

We can see the significance of what was going on in such a ceremony. When we're *'in Christ'* and stand before God, He's not looking at us to see how perfect we are (or rather how perfect we're not), He's looking at the perfection of the offering that was made for us. In so many ways like this, the Law was a schoolmaster to teach the people about Christ. But once the real Christ had come along and been offered, all the legal and ceremonial things that pointed forward to him, by signifying his life and work, became redundant: its work was done and it ceased to apply as a legal code. The Law had to take a long step back. Now it's no longer needed as a unique system to regulate society and to guide people to their Saviour. But it still has much to tell us about the mind of God and the work of Jesus. That's why the Old Testament is still a big part of the Christian Bible today.

Paul's problem, and that of all the apostles guiding the early church, was the mindset of obedience to laws as the way to salvation that came with the Jewish converts. They hankered after laws. Rules were their comfort zone. They wanted to introduce aspects of the old Law into Christianity, and they wanted to press them on the non-Jewish members. So quite a bit of what we have in the New Testament letters concerns this confrontation between laws and grace. Which was not good at the time, but has worked out well for us, because it means we have a lot of sound reasoning on the value of grace over the works of the law. We're not so liable now to reduce Christianity to a treadmill of rules of conduct that we have to chase interminably.

But there are still those like the Jewish converts of old who get caught up in a 'salvation by works' mentality, believing it's what we do that saves us, not what Jesus has already done. They won't say it, perhaps, in quite that way, but that's what it will amount to when we analyse it.

Prove it!
Jesus' brother, James, had a lot to say about the grace and works dilemma. He got to the heart of the matter when he said: You show me your faith (in grace) **without** your works, and I'll show you my faith (in grace) **by** my works. (James 2:18) What he was driving at was: Where's the evidence for your faith if you do nothing about it? I can see no evidence that you properly understand or appreciate grace when it makes no appreciable difference to your life! This agrees with what Paul said about grace being vain or empty when we show no appreciation for it, or when we devalue it by working for our salvation regardless, as if grace didn't exist. The works don't save us, but they are evidence of our appreciation and understanding of the grace that does.

The grace escape (Part 2)

But here's a caution. Knowing that works are the barometer of our appreciation of grace, let's not go down the path of fearing that we're not showing **enough** appreciation to deserve the grace we've been given! That kind of thinking, which can be beguiling, is salvation by works creeping in through the back door. We didn't deserve the grace of God in the first place. Nothing is ever going to make us deserving of it. So it's foolish to start setting levels of acceptable appreciation for ourselves. There are no such levels.

Fear and trembling

But, having said all this about grace, there are still a few verses in the Bible that seem to be telling a different story. One in particular comes to mind. Writing to the believers at Philippi, Paul said: *'work out your own salvation with fear and trembling.'* (Philippians 2:12) On the face of it, that runs counter to everything the Bible says about salvation through grace. This has been one of the go-to verses for the kind of preachers who for centuries put all the emphasis on hellfire and damnation. And it's a verse that will feed our fears if we don't properly grasp grace. What Paul says is only a problem when we lose sight of the context in which he said it. Not to mention that it was said by the apostle of grace himself, so it can't be saying what it seems to be saying. So what's it all about?

If you read the whole of Paul's letter to the Philippians, you'll see that there was a lot of what he called *'strife and vainglory'* going on in that church. Believers are supposed to be equal in Christ, but that can come hard when people from all levels of society are brought together under one roof. Some were acting in a superior way, and it was causing a lot of arguments. So Paul wrote, *'Let nothing be done through strife or vainglory; but in lowliness of mind, let each esteem other better than themselves.'* And this is exactly what he meant when he told them to *'work out your own salvation with fear and trembling.'* He was counselling them to be respectful and humble towards one another.

Paul chose this same 'fear and trembling' approach for himself, towards the church at Corinth when he visited them, rather than exert his apostolic authority or his academic superiority over them. He told them, *'And I was with you in weakness, and in fear, and in much trembling.'* (1 Corinthians 2:3) He meant that he treated them with respect, not in a superior way that could have caused resentment and bickering.

The first thing to notice is that Paul says *'work out'* not **work for** your salvation. Next thing is that when Paul said *'your salvation'* we probably mistakenly take that personally. But it's not meant that way. In English the word 'your' can be singular or plural, but the Greek from which this word was translated is definitely plural.

Paul was addressing his remarks to the whole church at Philippi, telling them to get their act together. In realty the underlying message is very positive. There was no question mark over their salvation, just a question mark over the way they were going about it – or working it out among themselves.

The Grace Escape

There's another thing about grace we should mention while we're here. Back in chapter 16, which was about troubles and how God helps us through them, we quoted these words of the Apostle Paul:

> *'There hath no temptation taken you but such is common to man: but God is faithful, who will not suffer you to be tempted above that ye are able; but will with the temptation also make a way to escape, that ye may be able to bear it.'* (1 Corinthians 10:13)

We mentioned this verse when we were looking at verse six of David's Psalm – that matching pivotal verse in the first half of the Psalm to this seventeenth verse in the second half. We looked at this quotation because it can be applied to God helping us out in troubling situations. He provides what Paul refers to as *'a way of escape'*. God sometimes eases or eliminates our external problems when we can no longer cope. But while the verse can be applied that way, it applies even more to God rescuing us from our **internal** problems: those feelings of hopelessness we might have from fearing righteousness is beyond us.

The telling line of the verse is the last one: *'that ye may be able to bear it'*. Clearly God is not saying that He will always take our problems away, but He will help us cope. He can and does sometimes remove problems when they are difficult external situations. But that's not how it works with our internal problems. As we've said, God doesn't eliminate all our bad thoughts and inclinations in order to make us righteous. No, instead He gives us something that makes us able to cope with them, and to motivate us to move away from them insofar as we can. He provides us with His grace. The *'way of escape'* that makes us *'able to bear it'* is of course grace. Incidentally, the revised translation of *'a way to escape'* says, ***'the** way of escape'* (New King James Version). God had something specific in mind, not something general. Grace.

Paul knew first-hand what he was talking about because this is exactly the way it had worked for him. He was despondent over his inability to deal with his bad attitude to his *'thorn in the flesh'* problem. So God made a way of escape for him saying: *'My grace is sufficient for you.'* And that's the way it is for all believers: God's grace is sufficient for all of us. And that word 'sufficient' doesn't mean barely adequate, as when we feel we've done sufficient to get by in something. The word in the original Greek actually indicates **contentment**. It tells us that God is content with the grace He gives us. In which case I think we can be too.

Can we fall from grace?
In case you're wondering if it's possible for **believers** to miss out on grace, then, no, they can't. The clue is in the word **believer**. Grace works when you believe in its power for you. If you have faith in God providing it for you. A believer who turns his or her back on grace is likely to lose the benefit of it, and fall out of favour with God. And, as we've said, grace is at the very heart of Christ's saving work. Introducing it to the world was integral to the salvation

he accomplished for believers. So to doubt it is to doubt the full power of what he did.

We need to believe in the grace that God offers us for it to be effective for us. It is one of the most important features of God's communication to us, and of the Secret that He wants to share with us. It would be foolish to nullify it by sidelining it and working hard for our salvation in the belief that we have to **make ourselves** look good in the eyes of God. God already thinks we look good when we're *'in Christ'*. It's simple really, and easy. So believers needn't and shouldn't make living by God's Secret hard for themselves.

Falling from grace is an expression used to describe what happened to Adam and Eve when they were expelled from the Garden of Eden. And nowadays we might sometimes say that someone has fallen from grace when they've fallen out of favour with someone. But what does it really mean?

Whenever I hear the phrase 'fall from grace' used to describe what happened to Adam and Eve when they sinned in Eden I find myself wondering: how can that be right? Surely they didn't fall **from** grace, they fell **into** grace!

They could not have been living in a state of grace in the period before they sinned. How would that work? What would God have been making allowance for if they had not sinned at that time? But once they did sin, then they fell into a situation where they needed and received grace. Because they were spared from immediate death and shown the way of salvation for themselves and for all humankind to follow (Genesis 3).

It's the Law again
The true meaning of a fall from grace is given in Galatians 5:4. There Paul says that it's about returning to the Law, or relying on works, as a way of salvation. If we do that, we push grace out of the picture. No, we don't fall from grace every time we fail, every time we do something wrong in the normal way. That sort of

The grace escape (Part 2)

thinking is probably a carryover from the idea that Adam and Eve fell from grace when they sinned. Falling from grace whenever we fail would mean grace going absent at the very times we need it most. It would be rather like making the consequence of a trapeze artist's error the removal of the safety net.

So a return to law, or a reliance on works, is what is really meant by a fall from grace. Happily, though, that's something believers can pick themselves up from. That's the nature of grace. If we do fall from it, grace hasn't gone anywhere, **we** have. It's still there where it was. It's still there whenever a believer falls from it by thinking they must **earn** their salvation – or when they have the companion problem of fearing that they haven't **done** enough. Of **course** they haven't done enough, but Christ has.

A problem with explaining the 'mechanics' of grace is that it can make it sound a bit technical, and the spirit of it can be obscured or lost in the process. Hopefully that hasn't happened here. The essential thing to take from these two chapters is that grace is God's free gift of righteousness that is available to all those *'in Christ'*. God's Secret is with the righteous. And a big part of the Secret is that when we fear Him, believe Him, and trust Him unconditionally, our righteousness is something God presents to us, not something we present to Him.

29 GOD IS NEAR

'The LORD is nigh unto them that are of a broken heart; and saveth such as be of a contrite spirit. Many are the afflictions of the righteous: but the LORD delivereth him out of them all.' (Psalm 34:18–19)

The broken hearted that David talks about in verse 18 are not necessarily those who've suffered a serious loss, like a loved one, or whose romance has hit the rocks. The Hebrew poetic form tells us they are the equivalent of *'such as be of a contrite spirit'*.

Perhaps more than any other verse in the Psalm this one reflects the low state of mind David was in prior to writing it. He was broken hearted while in custody in Gath. It seemed certain his life would end there. Recognised as the man who'd slain Goliath of Gath, and many more Philistines in battle, what chance was there of the Philistines letting him go free? It seemed that everything God had said about David becoming a future great king of Israel after Saul was going to come to nothing. Perhaps God had changed His mind. Perhaps David hadn't come up to expectations. These kinds of thoughts must have been going through his mind as he awaited his fate. A broken heart, a contrite spirit – that was David alright. Such prospects he had. But it had all come to nothing.

Or had it?
David obviously rallied, because he became sufficiently motivated to escape by using a clever ploy. Either he mustered his old faith, trusted God to help him if he came up with a plan, or God sent an angel with a foolproof plan and helped him carry it through. Going by what David says in this verse the most likely development is that God made the first move, and then David rallied. David's broken heart and contrite spirit made him cry out to the Lord, as

God is near

we know from previous verses. He was extremely low, probably feeling abandoned by everyone, including God. But God wasn't far away. He heard and came close.

The good outcome of this dire situation was that David's trust in God rose to a new level. He'd been distressed and unsure of his future, but now he had not the slightest doubt that God was on his side. And he wanted everyone who aspires to righteousness to know for sure that God is never far away when they're in distress. So never give up on yourself or God. That's the message.

And another message from this situation is that although God is never far away, He'll show His hand only when the time is right, usually when we're not too proud to ask for it. When we stop thinking it's all down to us, then He will help. Many a time, though, He'll help anyway, even when we're excluding Him and getting in His way. But at some point in our lives as believers, if we haven't already done so, God will help us learn the humility and good sense to rely on Him. He doesn't hang back to see believers suffer; He does it to give them the opportunity to work out the best solution. One that involves Him.

God's closeness to the righteous is another essential part of His Secret. I know we've touched on it already because all the parts are related, but verse eighteen of the Psalm homes right in on it. Of course, in the strictest sense, a God who is everywhere cannot be anything but close to everyone. But this has to do with the closeness of God's affection and interest in us, not the omnipresence of His being.

We don't have to be standing right next to someone all the while to have a close relationship with them. Though with God it's actually very like that. God is never more than a prayer away. He's so close that He wants us to lean on Him. In the physical sense, you can't lean on someone who is nowhere near you; neither can you lean on someone in the spiritual sense who is distant and unconcerned about you. God knows us and empathises with us, so that we can lean on Him at all times, particularly in times of trouble. *'The LORD is nigh unto them that are of a broken heart; and saveth such as be of a contrite spirit.'*

Good and bad spirits

The word 'spirit' in this verse means **attitude** or **disposition**. It's quite often used that way in the Bible, and it can be misleading if we don't understand that. We can load the word with unnecessary connotations, thinking it means something beyond the natural. Spirit does sometimes indicate the power of God at work, but not by any means always. Often it's more mundane.

In the Book of Proverbs we can read of a 'haughty spirit', a 'faithful spirit', and even a 'hasty spirit'. The Apostle Paul wrote in his letters of a 'spirit of bondage', a 'spirit of slumber' and a 'spirit of meekness'. These all refer to states of mind we experience in the natural way, not states that come upon us unbidden in a supernatural way. (Knowing this helps towards explaining the phrase 'evil spirit', too, that we come across in the Bible.) A contrite spirit, such as David mentions in this eighteenth verse is a lowly state of mind.

A man of passion

This verse being in the righteousness half of the Psalm, tells us it concerns our inner world more than our outer. It speaks of our thoughts about situations more than the situations themselves. When David was broken hearted and in prison, his mental condition was in reality worse than his physical condition. His surroundings might have been dismal, but his thoughts were even more so. He needed saving from his internal situation as much if not more than he needed saving from his captors. He needed to come to his senses. At heart he knew better than to give up on God. But he'd sunk so low that he'd temporarily lost sight of the way out.

David was a man of passion, as we've said. His emotions could send him soaring high with elation, and could plunge him deep in misery. He wasn't the sort to jog comfortably along or just sit and watch the world go by. That much is obvious from the first time we meet him properly in the Bible narrative. At that time he was just a young shepherd sent by his father to take supplies to his brothers. They were with the Israelite army camped on one side of a valley staring belligerently across at the Philistine army camped on the other side. The stand-off had been going on for a while. To try and settle the matter, Goliath had stepped forward from the Philistine's camp and had offered to fight a champion from the Israelite army. Which seemed like a better solution than hundreds, maybe thousands on both sides dying in battle.

The only problem with this solution was that Goliath was literally a giant of a man, and all those in the Israelite camp tended to be staring at their sandals whenever he glared across at them. He repeated his offer daily, while the men of Israel hung back. Then David arrived looking for his brothers. And as soon as he heard Goliath bellowing his challenge to anyone who was man enough to face him, David's immediate reaction was: 'Are we letting this oaf get away with this? He's not only defying the armies of Israel, he's defying the God of Israel. Is no-one going over there to sort him out? Because if no-one else is, I'll go myself' – or words to that effect. And the rest is history.

David was passionate, confident and sometimes impulsive. He engaged fully with life. And not surprisingly it got him into trouble sometimes. David was who he was. The same is true of us all. We've touched on this before, but it's worth thinking about again. We each have an essential personality that remains constant through life, and which doesn't change when we become believers.

We are who we are
People aren't straightforward. I'm sure you've noticed that about them. Most likely you've noticed it about yourself, too. But it's tempting to simplify things for ourselves by taking the view that we're all basically the same, and that our differences are created

by the choices we make in life. In other words we've all chosen to be who we are. We all started out as the same 'factory standard' model and we've customised ourselves over time to become who we are.

Which tidies things up rather well. It makes everyone personally responsible for being the kind of person they are. Better still, it means that we can label other people as wrong simply because they're not like us. They've made different choices concerning who they want to be and have developed along different lines from us. And that would make them wrong in some ways. **Our** take on life must be right or we wouldn't have it, right?

But, as anyone who has brought up children will know, people are very much who they are, and who they are going to be, from day one. The personality comes with the child. And there is no standard model. You can't treat them all the same, because they are not all the same. We don't choose to be who we are. Personality happens to us, just as the shape and size of our body, and the kind of face we have happens to us. We might tweak things a little for whatever reason, but essentially we are, and remain, who we are.

This is not to ignore the nurture side of things. Upbringing obviously plays a part in who we become. The influence of parents and significant others in our lives clearly has a bearing on how we develop. But by far the greatest contributor to how a person turns out is the personality they were born with. Because even how we deal with the nurture we receive depends on our nature. Two kids growing up in the same environment will react differently to it, because they **are** different. A fundamental truth about all of us is that we are who we are.

On different paths
So the path of righteousness will differ for every righteous person. Not where it's leading, but in the baggage that we're each carrying with us along the path. We're all different. We each have a

different mix of personality traits to deal with. What tempts me may not be a problem for you, and you may struggle with something that doesn't bother me at all. This is another reason why we're not to judge others. To criticise another person for failing at something we find easy to handle is completely out of order. But we're likely to do that when we mistakenly assume that other people are working with the same mental, emotional and spiritual equipment that we have. That's rarely, in fact, never the case.

No-one has an identical mind to anyone else. We're all exceptions. I can't prove that, but I can confidently suggest that the likelihood of two personalities being identical is about the same as two sets of fingerprints matching whorl for whorl. I think it's safe to say we're all different.

Personality and character

I'm talking about **personality** here rather than **character**. There is a difference. Psychologists have their own names for these things, but we'll keep it simple by just using personality and character. The underlying sense of self which is the personality we are born with remains fairly constant throughout our lives. But character can develop. It can change, sometimes radically, in both good and bad ways. We can become good or bad, better or worse, but we are still essentially ourselves in the midst of all that.

Ask yourself this: when you decide to improve yourself in some way, who is doing the improving? – and who or what is being improved? That would be your personality, your essential self, making changes to your character. Or, in other words, the constant part of you making changes to the malleable part. Whether you go along with this reasoning is not vitally important, but surely you'll agree that we are all differently equipped when it comes to our mental, emotional, and spiritual abilities. We are who we are. Which means that, because the precepts and practices of righteousness are the same for everyone – God's Secret is the same for us all – that we will all tread a slightly different path of righteousness, or rather, experience the path in a slightly different way.

Grace the leveller
But our differences don't make it harder for some and easier for others to be **considered** righteous by God. Our differences simply mean that grace will help us with different things and in different ways. God will make allowances for me because of the things I find hard to cope with, and for you for the things that affect you. Always it will be appropriate for us.

In the construction industry they sometimes use something called levelling compound. Where there's an uneven surface and they need a nice flat one, they spread this fairly thick liquid substance over the ground or the floor and it sets into a smooth and level top surface. No two uneven surfaces are alike. The irregularities are always different. But the liquid compound always spreads and produces the same perfectly level result.

That's a mundane and poor analogy of how grace works, but it work for me. Death is sometimes referred to as 'a great leveller', but grace qualifies too – and in a far pleasanter way! We are who we are. We're all different, but grace makes all believers equal before God, whoever they are and whatever they bring with them to Him. And nobody is ever made more or less righteous than anyone else. No saint can feel either superior or inferior to their fellows. They are all raised to the same acceptable level by grace.

The evils of the righteous?
This is where we need to look at verse nineteen of David's Psalm. *'Many are the afflictions of the righteous: but the LORD delivereth him out of them all.'* One reason we brought these two verses together in this chapter is that verse nineteen reiterates much of what's been said in previous verses, so we don't have to give it a separate chapter. The other reason is that it makes a particular point that rounds off this set of verses about trouble and

deliverance through grace. And it rounds them off in quite an unexpected way. I don't think anyone would see this coming.

The word 'afflictions' that appears in verse nineteen is very rarely translated that way. Only six times does it appear as 'afflictions', compared with the four-hundred and forty times that it's translated as '**evil**'. In fact in the five other places where the word 'afflictions' is used, 'evil' would have been a valid translation, too. But we can fully understand why the translators have shied away from putting 'evil' in this verse, because it would then read: *'Many are the [evils] of the righteous: but the LORD delivereth him out of them all.'* They chose not to translate it that way, against overwhelming support for it, because it looks and feels so wrong. But it only looks wrong when we leave grace out of the picture.

On the evidence we've looked at, I would say that *'the [evils] of the righteous'* is exactly how the verse **ought** to be read. What we have here is powerful confirmation of how amazing grace truly is. Without the deliverance of grace the righteous are as evil as anyone else in God's sight. Regardless of their belief and trust, the righteous are still beset by many internal evils. So, although the translators backed away from it, the remarkable truth is that: *'Many are the [evils] of the righteous: but the LORD delivereth him* [and her, of course] *out of them all'.*

We could take that to mean that the righteous are beset by many evils **around them** from which God delivers them. That would be true after all. But this nineteenth verse of the Psalm is in the half that deals with the inner world of the righteous not the outer world of the God-fearing. It's about the righteous being troubled by natural evil tendencies within themselves, and being told that they need not feel dispirited and remote from God as a result. It's about them being delivered from all that by grace. The righteous can take heart from this aspect of God's Secret.

30 KEEPING BONES

'He keepeth all his bones: not one of them is broken.' (Psalm 34:20)

Broken bones were the bane of a soldier's life at one time. Not that they are such a good thing now, of course. But things are so much better now, what with modern field hospitals and medicines. Back in David's time, a broken bone could do far more than temporarily take a man off the battlefield. It could mean deformity or death. It could mean poverty from being unable to fight or work ever again. Life was more civilised in ancient Israel when the laws of God were observed and the people were encouraged to help one another more. But generally speaking, in those days, a broken bone was a serious issue. It would most likely have been the result of a blow from a heavy sword or cudgel, not from a fall or stumble. Healing would have been slow and imperfect, if it happened at all.

For the Lord to protect people from broken bones was a literal God-send. David said, and no doubt from experience, that God keeps all his bones – every one of them. For a clearer definition of 'keep', all we have to do is look at the first appearance of the word back in Genesis 2:15 where Adam was put into the Garden of Eden *'to dress it and to keep it'*. That meant he was to **look after** the garden, and that's what God does in a sense for all the bones of the righteous. He looks after them. Now I know what you're probably thinking. Does that mean believers never ever break a bone? And you're pretty sure you know one who has.

Bear in mind that we're reading a Psalm here, and that it's the Psalm of a soldier who was apt to use military allusions to express himself. As he did with angels encamping around those that fear God. What David was saying metaphorically is that God takes a really close interest in believers – He looks after them in their daily lives as attentively as He would have looked after David on the battlefield. God would have ensured that nothing happened to David in battle that would cause him to lose his promised destiny. How that translates for a believer is that they might still accidentally break a wrist or an arm. But nothing can happen to them that will affect their ultimate wellbeing – their destiny in God's unfolding plan of which they have become a part – so long as they maintain their faith and trust in Him.

But there's far more going on in this verse.

Who do we think David was talking about when he said *'his bones'* in verse twenty? Was he still talking about the righteous ones he mentioned in the previous verse? His band of followers, that is, and by extension, all believers? Or was David referring to himself in the third person, as writers sometimes do? Then again, both could be true because Bible verses quite often work on more than one level. In truth, this one's working on another level entirely! I was going to say a deeper level, but it would be more appropriate to call it a far higher level. From something we're told in one of the gospel records, we know that David had in mind neither himself nor his followers – nor even the righteous in general. When he said *'his bones'*, he had a particular **person** in mind. Remarkably he was thinking of someone who wouldn't be born for another thousand years!

Predictive text

If you're acquainted with the account of Jesus' crucifixion, this mention of bones not being broken may have a familiar ring to it. When the Roman soldiers came to break Jesus' legs as he hung on the cross they saw that he was already dead and so they didn't bother. The legs of those being crucified were sometimes broken in order to speed up their deaths. It was thought to be an act of mercy so they didn't suffer too long. But in the case of Jesus and the two men crucified along with him, it was ordered by the authorities because the religious festival of Passover was about to start and the authorities didn't want the bodies on view and defiling the festival. Here's what the Bible narrative says:

> *'Then came the soldiers, and brake the legs of the first, and of the other which was crucified with him. But when they came to Jesus, and saw that he was dead already, they brake not his legs... these things were done, that the scripture should be fulfilled, A bone of him shall not be broken.'* (John 19:32,33,36)

The Apostle John here made an unmistakeable reference back to the Psalm of David. There's no other similar place in the Bible that it could refer to. So we're not guessing there's probably a link, we're told there is. And this brings a whole new dimension to the Psalm. I said in an earlier chapter that David knew Jesus would come and that he wrote about him. Well, this is one of the places he did that. Psalm 34 is what's known as a Messianic Psalm because it predicts things about the coming Messiah, or the second Adam as we also know him.

Back when it was written, this Psalm was a glimpse into the future. It was written a thousand years before Christ. And there are many Psalms like this one which mention Jesus in advance. In fact it's probably true to say that there are allusions to Jesus in all 150 of them. David definitely knew Jesus was coming.

Future proof

God gave the writers of the Old Testament insights like this in order to help them, and us, to understand more about the one who was coming. They were also given these insights to provide proofs, when the time came, that Jesus was truly the one everyone in Israel was watching and waiting for. He fulfilled the predictions about a coming Messiah to the letter. And he didn't, as some critics have suggested, contrive events in his life to line up with the prophecies in order to give himself credibility with the people of Israel who were familiar with them. He had no control over many of the prophecies he fulfilled, such as where he was born. And he was certainly in no position to <u>contrive</u> his legs not being broken as he hung upon the cross.

Promises

Some years after writing Psalm 34, David was to learn that the Messiah would be one of his own descendants. At the same time he was to learn something even more incredible than that. Not only would Jesus be David's great-great-great – and so on grandson, but he would also be the **son of God**. This is what God told him:

> 'And when thy days be fulfilled, and thou shalt sleep with thy fathers, I will set up thy seed after thee, which shall proceed out of thy bowels, and I will establish his kingdom. He shall build an house for my name, and I will stablish the throne of his kingdom forever. I will be his father, and he shall be my son.' (2 Samuel 7:12-16)

What prompted God to reveal this to David at this particular time in his life was that David had expressed a wish to build a house, or temple, for the worship of God. Israel's centre of worship was still the Tabernacle, a mobile tented structure that the Israelites had carried around with them for forty years, following their escape from slavery in Egypt. David felt God required and deserved something a lot better now, something more permanent, a house of God. But God turned it around and said, no, I will build **you** a house.

This is one of those rare occasions, when a pun works both in the original language and in translation. God gave **house** its other meaning, that of a family line. We use the term house to refer to a royal or aristocratic family, as when we call the British Royal Family the House of Windsor.

God promised David that after his death (which is referred to as 'sleep' we notice: a state from which he'll one day wake up) one of his descendants would reign over an **everlasting** kingdom. As Israel's king, David could expect that his descendants would sit on his throne and rule after him. But clearly God had a lot more than that in mind.

God's Secret

One day a special king of the Royal House of David would live and reign forever. He was told that this special descendant would be God's son as well as the son of one of David's progeny – a young woman named Mary, as it turned out. That Jesus' mother Mary was a descendant of David is demonstrated in the family tree provided in the third chapter of Luke's Gospel. Another family tree in Matthew's record tells us that Joseph was also of the House of David. Though that's not quite so relevant as Mary's lineage, because Joseph wasn't Jesus' true father.

David was very aware that Jesus would come. And he was given many insights into Jesus' character and his work that he wove into his divinely inspired Psalms. David would also have been aware of many aspects of the Law of Moses that pointed to Jesus. That Law was in place when David lived, and, as we mentioned before, it was a 'schoolmaster' to bring people to Christ. Well, David was a star pupil. And something he was sure to have noticed in the books of the Law is a connection between something the Law said about bones not being broken and his own inspired reference to the same thing.

An angel of death

We mentioned in Part One of this book that the sacrifice of Christ was in the mind of God even before He began the work of Creation. It's so essential to His recovery plan for the world that God refers to it and drops hints about it, both strong and subtle, all the way through His communication. What we're going to look at now is one of the less subtle ones.

One of the milestone events in the founding of the nation of Israel was the night of the Passover, when God rescued His people from slavery in Egypt. The night they left Egypt they were told to eat a special meal. They were told to kill an unblemished lamb. But before cooking it, they were to smear some of the lamb's blood on the doorposts and lintels of their front doors. A powerful angel was going to speed through the night slaying every firstborn in Egypt. But he would pass over the houses where he saw the lamb's blood

Keeping bones

around the door frames. One of the instructions concerning the preparation of the lamb was *'neither shall ye break a bone thereof.'* (Exodus 12:46)

It pointed forward to Jesus. He was to be the unblemished (signifying sinless) Lamb of God whose blood would one day be spilt to save God's people everywhere. Do we really think that the powerful angel God sent on this mission would have blundered through the night killing all the wrong people if there had been no blood daubed on the door frames to alert him? That's unlikely. He'd have known which houses to go to alright. The blood wasn't so much for the angel's benefit as it was for the people's benefit who'd put it there.

God was planting a message that salvation would one day come through the blood of His own Lamb. All those who put their trust in Jesus' blood would be saved. The Israelites had to put their trust in the lamb's blood. Anyone who saw no point in it, and didn't bother to take advantage of the protection the blood provided, would get a very unwelcome visit from the angel.

So the spilling of the lamb's blood pointed forward to the spilling of Jesus' blood. And around 2,000 years after that first Passover night, just as the annual observance of the Passover was about to commence in Jerusalem, Jesus was being killed, his blood was being shed (by the same Roman soldier sent to break his legs but who instead thrust a sword into his side to make sure he was dead) – and not a bone of his body was broken.

The man Jesus

The point is graphically made that we are saved by the blood of Christ. His death has seriously hampered the machinery of sin and death that Adam set in motion, and will one day bring it to a standstill. As mentioned in an earlier chapter, because of Adam's failure everyone born from him was born to sin and die like him. That was his legacy to us. But then came Jesus who, although he was born into Adam's doomed line through Mary, was more like his Heavenly Father than his earthly mother. He resisted every temptation to sin. God said of him, *'This is my beloved Son, in whom I am well pleased.'* (Matthew 3:17)

In the normal way, we might notice that when someone takes after their mother or father, it's not always about looks. They share characteristics, ways of thinking and talking and doing things. We can readily appreciate how Jesus, having grown up steadily acquiring a deep understanding and a strong awareness of his Heavenly Father, would more likely 'take after' Him. Even by the age of twelve Jesus was *'about* [his] *Father's business'.* (Luke 2:49)

He was the Son of God, but he never lost sight of the fact that he was 'the son of man', and he often referred to himself in that way. He felt the pull of his humanity, the inclination to think and do wrongly, as keenly as anyone else does. More so, in fact, because such a lot rested on his shoulders and he knew it. He knew he had to be sinless, without blemish, when the time came for his sacrifice.

We all know from experience, that when it's extremely important that we don't mess up, that's when we're most likely to do exactly that. The pressure is on and we wobble. Just watch a world class tennis player as he or she keeps trying and failing to put away the shot that will clinch the match, and you'll know what I mean. The greater the pressure the more likely the failure. So any advantage we might think Jesus had from his divine parentage would have been more than offset by the huge responsibility resting on him. Yet he did it. He achieved an extraordinary and total victory. Through an immense and unprecedented love and respect for his Father, Jesus coped with and overcame his sin-prone nature.

The death of the devil

When we thought about the devil, a few chapters ago, you'll recall we found that it isn't a malevolent creature, the stuff of nightmares, after all. It's a negative part of the nature of each one of us. Some additional and strong support for this comes from what we're told happened when Jesus died. There's a remarkably clear statement in the New Testament letter to the Hebrews that settles the matter for us. *'Forasmuch then as the children are partakers of flesh and blood, he* [Jesus] *also himself likewise took part of the same; that through death he might destroy him that had the power of death, that is, the devil.'* (Hebrews 2:14)

'He also himself likewise' – that's pretty emphatic. That's really hammering home the point that Jesus **was** flesh and blood like other people. And the reason for hammering it home is to tell us that when he died he **destroyed** the devil. His human nature and the devil were one and the same thing. And after he was brought back to life he was given a new nature that had no devilish content.

Should anyone ever tell you that the devil is an evil being, simply refer them to this Bible verse, because, if what they're saying is true, then Jesus destroyed that creature long ago when he died. We should no longer be tempted, and we all know that's not the case. We're all still pretty devilish. This only makes sense in light of what we know about the devil being Jesus' sin-prone nature, which died along with him on the cross. And over which he emerged victorious three days later. We are still tempted, and we sin, because for us the devilish side of our nature is still alive and well and living inside us.

God with a devil?
While we're thinking about the humanity of Jesus, there are ramifications for the idea of the Trinity that shouldn't be ignored. He experienced the devil in him as we all do. Which doesn't seem like something a divine being would do. Jesus had human nature. He had a Heavenly Father, yes, but he was still flawed in his nature because he was related to Adam through Mary.

Much is made in the Bible of Jesus' humanity and how it means that he can understand what we humans are all going through because he has been through it himself. And without human nature he could never have qualified as a second Adam. He needed to be someone who could be tempted as Adam was in order to replicate the situation. Jesus may have had more Godly inclinations than the rest of us because of who his Father was, but that didn't make him incapable of sin, neither did it make him God.

And had Jesus been God, an immortal part of a divine Trinity, then his 'death' on the cross would surely have been a sham. The agonies of mind he went through in the Garden of Gethsemane prior to his death would also have been pretence. And I don't believe for one moment that was the case.

By allowing himself to be killed, Jesus created an anomaly in the established order of cause and effect where death occurs as the result of sin. He died never having done anything wrong. God **had** to intervene and raise him. Or there would be no justice in the world. Punishment for sin would have been meted out to someone who'd not sinned. So now there's a new Adam. One who didn't fail. And God will consider differently the destiny of anyone who lines up behind the new Adam. *'In Adam all die, even so in Christ shall all be made alive.'*

When we're *'in Christ'* we're rather like those Israelites of old who sat in their houses on that very first Passover night with their meal of sacrificed lamb before them, which had no bones broken. They were trusting in its blood to save them from the angel of death as he scoured the land like a grim reaper. In Christ, we don't have to fear death any more. In a sense it's going to pass right over the righteous. They're related to the new Adam, not the old one.

You'll recognise much of the above as the divine symmetry of the two Adams that we spoke of in Part One. It's such an integral part of God's Secret. So it's no surprise that David brings it up poetically in his Psalm by his reference to Jesus' bones being kept and not being broken.

31 Outcomes

'Evil shall slay the wicked: and they that hate the righteous shall be desolate.' (Psalm 34:21)

'Better is the end of a thing than the beginning thereof' says Solomon in Ecclesiastes 7:8. To which we might say, well, that depends on how it turns out. But what he means is that it's not until the end of a project or phase that we know how it went, and whether it was worthwhile or not. The end is better because then we have the results. The end may be better, too, because the work is done and we can relax and enjoy the fruits of our labours. Reaping a good harvest is better than sowing in the hope of one. In many ways it's better to be at the results end of things.

And that's where our thoughts are going to be in these final two chapters. We know how things are going to work out for this world – without doubt there is to be a better ending than beginning. We know that. But more importantly, from a personal perspective, we can also know how things will turn out for us. Our futures are decided by the decisions we make now.

The last two verses of David's Psalm distil the message of God's Secret into two simple sentences. These verses tell us what it all comes down to. They tell us of two different kinds of people who have very different destinies. One set of people is bound for desolation, and the other set is going to **avoid** desolation. It makes me a little uncomfortable to say these things because I know I may sound a little like a fear preacher here. That's definitely not the intention. There's no mileage in fearing God in the wrong way. But this verse and the next one taken together bring the Psalm to something of a dramatic close.

You'll see what I mean about the two very different outcomes when you put verse twenty-one, shown at the head of the chapter, alongside verse twenty-two, shown here: *'The Lord redeemeth the soul of his servants: and none of them that trust in him shall be desolate.'* We'll look at this verse properly in the next chapter. I put it here only to show how the two concluding verses work together to bring the Psalm to a climax. They reveal the only two possible outcomes for everyone who now lives, or who has ever lived on the planet. We're either going nowhere or somewhere. There's desolation ahead for the evil. There's the avoidance of desolation for those who trust God.

There's desolation or the avoidance of it.

It all sounds a little scary. Not a good way to finish a Psalm – or a book, for that matter. I'm sure the upbeat David didn't intend his conclusion to come across in a negative way, especially when it's the end of such a positive Psalm. He's been verbally punching the air with gratitude to God for most of it. He would have meant for it to end positively. And in fact it does. He'd been rescued from what looked like certain death, and had a lot to be happy about. So now he turns his attention to the bigger picture where everyone can be rescued from death.

He knows it's not just about him and his little personal rescue. He's looking forward to the ultimate and permanent rescue, redemption or salvation (any of these words will do) of **all** those who are righteous. At the same time, he's looking forward to the eventual permanent removal of all those who are evil, because these are two aspects of the same thing. They will and they must happen together. We can't have one without the other. And both of them are positive in their way. Certainly the combined effect of them is positive.

We can't have one without the other

God can't fulfil His promise – He can't make good on His declared purpose to provide a peaceful, secure, harmonious world for His saints to live in, not without the removal of everything that would ruin it. That includes removing the kind of people who would ruin it. They're the kind of people who generally ruin everything. We touched on this when we looked at verse sixteen: *'The face of the Lord is against them that do evil, to cut off the remembrance of them from the earth.'* Incorrigibly evil people have no place in the realisation of God's plans for the world. And we know, too, that such people aren't just the ones we think of as the very worst among us. By God's definition they are everyone not righteous. That means everyone who has not responded to the call to be a saint, and who is not a believer. In short it means everyone not *'in Christ'*. Again, let me say, this is not meant as fear-mongering. I'm just setting out the logic behind what God has to do to achieve the world He has promised us.

You've probably heard the saying *'the meek shall inherit the earth.'* Jesus said it in his Sermon on the Mount found in Matthew's Gospel. You might have wondered, as many have on hearing it, how the meek could possibly take over the world. It's run by the strong, the ambitious, and the powerful, who are never going to step aside and hand everything over to the humble, God-fearing righteous. But they won't have any choice in the matter. God's plan is for the meek to take possession of the world, and they'll do that because all other kinds of people will face the desolation of being removed from it. It gives me no pleasure to write such things, but sadly it is the only way.

Desolation means extreme sorrow and emptiness. The opposite and alternative is extreme happiness and fulfilment. When Jesus spoke of the meek inheriting everything he was quoting another Psalm of David. The whole verse of the Psalm reads like this: *'But the meek shall inherit the earth; and shall delight themselves in the abundance of peace.'* (Psalm 37:11) The effect of expunging evil from the world is to bring about an *'abundance of peace'* – a peace more pervasive and profound than anything the world has known since Adam and Eve were evicted from the Garden of Eden. There will be no wars or threats of wars, no aggression or oppression of any kind; no murders or muggings; anger or abuse; no stealing or cheating or lying. People will *'delight themselves in*

God's Secret

the abundance of peace'. And no one will ever be able to take it away from them.

Too good to be true?
But don't misunderstand this to mean that the world is to experience another form of oppression. It won't be a Kingdom of fear where no one dares to step out of line or they'll be removed. The global Kingdom will be populated to a great extent by those who have longed for it to come. They will all be delighted not fearful. The prophet Isaiah saw it and described it like this: *'Behold, a king shall reign in righteousness, and princess shall rule in judgement.'* (Isaiah 32:1)

This reassures us that everything pertaining to the administration of the Kingdom will be fair and just. Knowing that Jesus himself is the one destined to be king, this is exactly how we would expect it to be. It will be a Kingdom and a world in which love holds sway and blessings abound. All the necessities of life will be in superabundance, so no-one need fear or squabble over not having enough. (Psalm 72 describes some of these things). It will be a time to relax and enjoy the world made new.

It may all seem too good to be true, as things so often are in this present world where high expectations are seldom met because their achievement depends on unreliable human factors. But the Kingdom of God will not disappoint. It will be everything that at heart most of us have always wanted, and which has always eluded us because of our flawed human nature. And it **will** come because God has planned it, and promised it in His communication to us. Without it, His plans for this world from the very beginning will come to nothing – which He won't let happen.

It's not a fairy tale kingdom that believers are deluding themselves about because it helps them cope with this present world to think that something better is coming. It is an essential and very real component of God's Secret. A little further on in Psalm 37 (where we read about the meek inheriting the earth), there are some more words appropriate to what we're talking about here. And this will make perfect sense now that we've pieced together so much of God's Secret. In fact, I think that by now you could pause at every phrase in these three verses and recognise something from God's Secret.

> *'Depart from evil, and do good; and dwell for evermore. For the Lord loveth judgement* [righteous judgement], *and forsaketh not his saints; they are preserved for ever; but the seed of the wicked shall be cut off. The righteous shall inherit the land, and dwell therein forever.'* (Psalm 37:27-29)

Have a good apocalypse

In passing we notice that the meek are not lined up for places in heaven. Right doctrine is reinforced here. Heaven is not where God's promised Kingdom will be. Nowhere are the saints told to expect places there. They don't re-locate to heaven at death. They are all *'preserved for ever'*, as the Psalm says. They await resurrection from the sleep of death to join the saints who are alive when Jesus comes to establish God's Kingdom.

The Book of Revelation, the last book of the Bible, which has so much to say about the momentous happenings at Jesus' return, tells us that when the Kingdom of God is about to be set up, in the wake of all the earth-shattering events that will lead up to it, an angel will be despatched, *'having the everlasting gospel to preach unto them that dwell on the earth, and to every nation, and kindred, and tongue, and people.'* (Revelation 14:6) A final plea will go out to all the peoples of the earth who have survived the apocalyptic events of these final days of mankind's rule. Anyone who still chooses to ignore God's offer of righteousness *'in Christ'*, anyone incorrigibly stubborn enough or just plain foolish enough, will be removed.

That word 'removed' reads suspiciously like a euphemism for 'ended'. And there's no getting away from it, that's what it comes down to. Their lives will be over. Having generously been given the opportunity to share in the world-wide paradise of God's Kingdom, they say, no, they'd prefer to remain their old evil selves and go their own way. But there is nowhere for them to go. The entire world is about to turn righteous. Their decision can only mean the end of them. Truly, as David said, *'Evil shall slay the wicked.'* Their attachment to it will exclude them from the new world.

The apocalypse, because that's what we're talking about here, is only bad news for those who are bad. For believers the experience will turn out to be entirely positive. But anyone who wants to persist in the unrighteousness that has spoiled the world up until then, will not have a place in this world anymore. How can it be otherwise? Because they'd only ruin it for everyone else.

FOMO

As I say, the intention here is not to generate the wrong kind of fear of God in anyone. Far from it. Because the dread of punishment is not the right and proper foundation for love and faith. What I hope I'm doing here, instead of instilling a dread of our **loving** God, is instilling more of a fear of missing out, or a FOMO, as it sometimes appears in acronym. (Apologies if this acronym has slipped out of use now. It's hard to keep pace with these things.)

Now that you know something of God's Secret – the panoramic spiritual vistas it opens to us and the unrivalled opportunities it sets before us – I hope your reaction is not to get anxious over what is happening in the world, and what is going to happen, but to have a healthy FOMO. It's entirely positive. Wherever you are in life, it hits you with a positive message: the avoidance of desolation and rescue from an eternal death.

Discovering that you're on the road to desolation is extremely helpful if it wakes you up to where you could be heading. It means you don't keep motoring on, enjoying the view, relaxing to the sounds, thinking how pleasant the ride seems, thinking about all the things you might do… until your engine stalls, and you run out of fuel in the middle of nowhere. You hadn't spotted the sign miles back that said **Desolation This Way** ▶ Instead of that happening, you can turn back. You know how sometimes when you're cruising along and you miss the sign to where you want to go, there are often one or two more turn-offs just up ahead that lead to the same destination. Like that, you're never permanently stuck on the road to nowhere if you don't want to be. You can always pull off and get on the **Desolation Bypass** and motor happily on to somewhere better.

Maybe you just touched the brakes to slow down your life for a moment because you're approaching an exit sign right now.

Not helping ourselves

Sad to say most of us don't help ourselves. The awful truth is that so many people are orchestrating their own permanent demise by ignoring the offer of righteousness in Christ. But it's everyone's free choice. And although God is someone *'Who will have all men to be saved, and to come unto the knowledge of the truth,'* (1 Timothy 2:4), He will not force it on us. The bigger truth, though, is that His love can only operate in a climate of freewill. He is only able truly to love us because He is free not to; and we are only able truly to love Him because we are free not to. It's the only way love can exist. It can't be forced on anyone or programmed into them. If many choose not to love, that's their freewill decision, and God will not condemn them to eternal torments in hell – which is a sleight on the character of God – but He will leave them undisturbed in the unknowingness of death.

And **He** doesn't destroy the wicked, as David points out in this verse in Psalm 34, *'Evil shall slay the wicked.'* Their own evil destroys them. Their folly keeps them on the road heading away from all the good things God plans for the world. He won't give the wicked what they freely choose to reject. He'd rather we all knew and lived by the truth, His Secret, but for love to be love, He can't impose that on anyone.

Do yourself a favour

Again we remind ourselves that the wicked are not only the arch-villains of this world. The wicked certainly includes them, but by God's definition, it also includes all those who want no part in His plans for the world and who are not prepared to take up His invitation to be a part of them. For whatever reason – be it scepticism, atheism, agnosticism, scientism, hedonism, whatever – the wicked chose to go their own way.

I'm reminded again of something Solomon wrote: *'There is a way that appears to be right, but in the end it leads to death.'* (Proverbs 14:12 NIV) Among the different ancient Hebrew words for *'way'* the one in this verse means 'a trodden path', a place where many people have gone before and continue to go. It's where the grass is rubbed out. So it looks like the right way. But although it **looks** right, **feels** right, **seems** right, it's the wrong way, and it leads nowhere.

Something else Solomon wrote also comes to mind here: *'He that getteth wisdom loveth his own soul.'* (Proverbs 19:8) This is the direct opposite of killing ourselves by persistently hanging onto evil. We know that the soul Solomon talks of in this verse is nothing other than ourselves. Getting the wisdom of God's Secret is the very best thing we can do for ourselves. If we have any real regard for ourselves, **and we should**, then we should get this wisdom, this counsel, from God that also goes by the name of God's Secret.

Solomon also expressed it negatively when he wrote: *'He that refuseth instruction despiseth his own soul.'* (Proverbs 15:32) That's another way of saying what David says in Psalm 34: *'Evil shall slay the wicked...'* We do ourselves so much harm when we refuse what God offers. To turn away from righteousness is not only to reject God, it's also to despise ourselves, to seriously undervalue ourselves, and limit our lives. Because to refuse God's instruction, or counsel, is to live what Solomon called fleeting and meaningless lives, and to squander the opportunity of a great future. It's the worst possible thing we can do for ourselves.

God doesn't want any of us to do that. We might mistakenly believe that religion is all about what God wants for Himself but in truth He wants what's best for us. *'God is love'* remember. His message to us is not delivered in the bullying, threatening tone of: Do this or else! His tone is: Please do this because I made you and I love you, and this is the very best thing you can do for yourself and for me. I want to give you the world. But it's your choice to make.

Lifestyle choices – a health warning

Lifestyle is the sum of our attitudes and habits. David in effect says in Psalm 34 that so many people are killing themselves by an unhealthy lifestyle. It's not that they don't eat right or go to the gym regularly, but because they're not living from right attitudes and habits. As Paul once put it, *'Bodily exercise profiteth little: but godliness is profitable unto all things, having promise of the life that now is, and of that which is to come.'* (1 Timothy 4:8) Physical fitness is temporary, but godliness is good for us now, and for a life to come. An evil lifestyle is counter-productive because it will lead to an eternal grave. Nothing could be more counter-productive than that! And evil is not just big evil, it's all of it. It's all detrimental to us. Unrighteousness carries a health warning from God Himself.

Being among the evil means we'll miss out on the perfect peace that accompanies righteousness. The stress we get from unrighteous living can help to undermine our immune system and slowly kill us. That's bad enough to contemplate. The bigger picture, however, is that while the immediate effects of the stress of unrighteous living will shorten our lives, the long-term effects will be devastating. Desolating even.

Hating the righteous
The evil *'hate the righteous'* says David. They've no time for those who want to believe in a saviour and to do the right thing. The righteous will probably be pleasant to them and want to help them, too, which won't always go down well. They see the righteous as weak and misguided – fools, even – because they need the crutch of religion. Actually it's a crutch we all need. The imagined strength of the evil is a weakness. And the weakness of the righteous is a strength, because their reliance is on God.

The wicked compound their problems by hating the righteous people that God loves. It's rarely a good idea to act badly towards those with powerful connections! They distance themselves even further from God. They suffer from the **reverse** of something I think of as 'the Hiram effect'. Let me explain.

The Hiram Effect
When David became king of Israel, he developed a friendly alliance with Hiram, the king of Tyre. It started when, on hearing David had become king, Hiram sent timber, carpenters and masons to build David a house. The friendship continued with David's son Solomon. Hiram was delighted to supply timber and craftsmen to help build the Lord's temple at Jerusalem. *'There was peace between Hiram and Solomon; and they two made a league together.'* (1 Kings 5:12) Hiram prospered through his friendship with Israel, and with David and Solomon in particular.

And this reflects something that God promised many years before to Abraham, a founding father of Israel: *'I will bless them that bless thee, and curse him that curseth thee.'* (Genesis 12:3) 'The Hiram effect' is how I describe the goodness God shows towards those who are good to the righteous. It's the outworking of a promise God made to Abraham. And those who hate the righteous will most likely experience the reverse of 'the Hiram effect'. God will curse them, as the promise to Abraham says.

Outcomes

The promise originally applied to Abraham and his family who became the people of Israel, but, as Paul says: *'they which be of faith are blessed with faithful Abraham'* and *'if ye be Christ's, then are ye Abraham's seed, and heirs according to the promise.'* (Galatians 3:9,29) As we had occasion to say in an earlier chapter, those God counts as the true children of Abraham, and heirs to the promises made to him, are not necessarily those born into his family, Israel, but those who believe as Abraham did. Which means 'the Hiram effect' works for those around believers, too.

Promises to Abraham: The hope of Israel

God made a number of promises to Abraham, all of them relevant to believers. And now we've looked at a part of one, we shouldn't miss the opportunity to look at the rest of it. In full God said to him: *'I will make of thee a great nation, and I will bless thee, and make thy name great; and thou shalt be a blessing: and I will bless them that bless thee, and curse him that curseth thee: and in thee shall all families of the earth be blessed.'* (Genesis 12:2-3)

Israel has had a chequered history because of its relationship with God as His chosen people. But the nation remains central to God's plans for the world. He made them promises He intends to keep, like this one to Abraham. All families of the earth will be blessed through Israel. That's already been set in motion by what Christ, the Jewish Messiah, has accomplished. *'In Christ'*, all people of the earth will one day be blessed. Abraham was also told, as was David, that the saviour would be born as one of his descendants. We should never lose sight of the Jewish roots of Christianity. Paul called Christianity *'The hope of Israel'* (Acts 28:20), and it still is. We can't escape this conclusion when we read the New Testament.

If you're wondering why something as big as the Jewishness of God's Secret isn't mentioned in David's Psalm, a moment's thought will clear that up. David had no need to mention the Jewish nature of God's Secret. It's self-evident in Psalm 34. It's a Jewish song, written in Hebrew, and structured as an acrostic on the

God's Secret

Hebrew alphabet, by an Israelite soon to be king in Jerusalem, containing a reference to the Messiah, Jesus, on the cross. In the light of all that, I doubt that it would ever have occurred to David to point out that the Secret is Hebrew in nature. He assumes we'll know.

Now there is just one verse left in David's Psalm for us to look at.

32 REDEEMING FEATURES

'The LORD redeemeth the soul of his servants: and none of them that trust in him shall be desolate.' (Psalm 34:22)

Conspiracy theorists have rumbled on for years about a coming New World Order which they tell us is being contrived behind the scenes by those they say are really in power. It's something they've long been trying to resist and expose. Surprisingly (even for them, perhaps), in a sense they've been right all along. Though not in the way they think. There is certainly a New World Order on the way. But they've been very wrong about the nature of it and about who has been manoeuvring it into place behind the scenes.

What's coming is not a sinister dystopia where the many are enslaved by the few. What's coming is the new world promised by God in His communication. He refers to it as *'a new heaven and a new earth'*, meaning a complete change. He's been working behind the scenes through His angels and His Son, moving nations into position like pieces on a chess board, watching and waiting for the right moment to call 'checkmate'. That's the moment when the cry goes up that *'the kingdoms of this world are become the kingdoms of our Lord, and of his Christ; and he shall reign for ever and ever.'* (Revelation 11:15)

Even if the conspiracy theorists are right about there being an elite group of powerful individuals working secretly towards world domination (and, who knows, they could be? It's a very human thing for people to be doing), no-one need worry about it. Because any such group will be swept aside, along with the rest of the current world order, when God's global Kingdom is established under the kingship of Christ. *'A king shall reign in righteousness'* God promises in Isaiah's prophesy (32:1).

Freedom!

No-one who puts their trust in God will finish up desolate. In the final verse of Psalm 34 we're told that *The LORD redeemeth the soul of his servants...'* The word for 'redeem' there means sets free. It links with what David experienced when he was imprisoned and facing death at the hands of Achish. That's how David saw the outcome for all God's servants – knowing God's Secret sets them free. They can experience the true freedom of living a life without fear. They are freed from all the anxieties that plague the bulk of humanity. They know what's really happening in the world, and that they are a part of it. They might get a little troubled from time to time, as David obviously did, but they have the way of escape, the key to freedom.

As Jesus said: *'If ye continue in my word, then are ye my disciples indeed; and ye shall know the truth, and the truth shall make you free.'* (John 8:32) What Jesus had in mind when he said *'the truth shall make you free'* would have encompassed most if not all of God's Secret. Jesus knew it and taught it. Continuing in Jesus' word is keeping his teachings in our hearts and minds and living by them. They are *'the truth'* that sets us free from all uncertainty and worry, even concerning death and the future of the planet.

Servants

The term *'servants'* needs some re-evaluation when applied to a believer's relationship with God. And while we're about it, it needs to be reconciled with us being sons and daughters of our Heavenly Father. We don't think of ourselves as our parents' servants unless there is something seriously wrong in our family. We need to ask how it is that we are God's *'servants'*.

The meaning of the word in Psalm 34 has to be different from our usual understanding of it. Think about it. Why would God need servants? Especially, why would He need **human** servants when He has countless powerful and dutiful angels at His beck and call? God isn't like a king or queen or a landed aristocrat who needs a staff of people to help them deal with all the things that need to be done to run their affairs. God needs absolutely no-one when we get right down to it. He can do all things, and better than anyone else could do them for Him.

So why servants? And why angels, for that matter? God is surely capable of inhabiting and enjoying eternity and infinity all by Himself without help from anyone else, and it would run flawlessly. In fact the addition of others seems more likely to have a negative effect on the running of the universe. Clearly God **chooses** to involve others in what He does. *'God is love'* and the involvement of others is the ideal way of expressing that love, and of expanding it by having it reciprocated. Involving others brings the opportunity to generate more love. The angels take delight in working for God. And they take delight in working for us, too, because that's what God wants them to do. They couldn't be any happier. They serve God not as lowly, co-opted underlings just doing a job, but because they want to be involved, and have a part in the love that's going round.

This is where believers as the servants of God comes in. We are not servants in the sense of being hired hands with jobs to do or consequences to be faced. That's how fear-based religion works, and being *'in Christ'* is not about being in fear. The way in which we serve God is not by doing what He cannot, or rather would not, do for Himself, which is how it generally works between masters and servants – we serve Him by doing whatever He asks of us, and which is always chiefly for our own benefit, not His. Doing what He asks is our opportunity to return His love.

Living by His counsel, by His Secret, is our opportunity to show how much we appreciate Him for giving us this life and the prospect of a better one; to show how in awe of Him we truly are, and how highly we regard all that He says and does. Our compliance is proof that we comprehend God, insofar as we are capable, and that we appreciate, trust and love Him.

God's Secret

Only when we understand this does it make perfect sense for Jesus to say: *'If ye love me, keep my commandments.'* (John 14:15) In our regular relationships it wouldn't be at all appropriate to say 'If you love me you'll do as I say.' That would put our backs up because it wouldn't be a loving thing for anyone to say. But once we see where Jesus is coming from with this, we know it makes perfect sense. His gift to us of guidance is among the best things he can give us, second only to his gift of salvation. And to respond by doing what he asks is the best thing we can do for ourselves.

To this we should add John's words: *'For this is the love of God, that we keep his commandments: and his commandments are not grievous.'* (1 John 5:3) God hasn't made it grievous, or a struggle, for us. I hope I've got that point across in this book. It's important that we don't mistake the gospel, or good news, for bad news – something we will never live up to. That was how it was under the Old Testament Law of Moses. Swimming against a tide of commandments and making no headway. Now we are carried along by the gentle currents of the grace of the New Testament.

Being God's servants doesn't mean we are working for our salvation, as if to earn it. Jesus tells us that however much we do, we will always remain *'unprofitable servants'*. (Luke 17:10) We can never do enough for God. If we think we can do enough to earn eternal life in a perfect world, then we've either set the value of paradise ridiculously low, or put our own abilities ridiculously high. It isn't going to happen. Redemption will always be a gift through the grace of God to those *'in Christ'*. It's a free gift. We can't work for it. But we can work to show our appreciation for it.

Grammarians and free gifts

Grammarians and pedants are fond of telling us that phrases like 'free gift' are tautological. If it's a gift then it's free, so we don't need to call it a **free** gift. It's just a gift. I'd agree with that, being a bit of a nit-picker myself sometimes. But the phrase comes from the Bible, Romans 5:16; so are we nit-pickers saying that God has got this wrong? Well, that's something I for one wouldn't want to say. There are no redundant words in the Bible. Sometimes something called an intensive plural is used in the original language to emphasise a word. That's not quite what 'free gift' is, but it may be the kind of thing that's going on here. When we look at the original language the tautology disappears and becomes a straightforward repetition. In the Greek it's a *charisma charisma*. *Charisma* means gift, so literally it's a **gift** gift. Which leaves us asking what is a **gift** gift, as opposed to just a gift?

When Paul wrote about a **gift** gift in his letter to the believers in Rome, he was making a distinction between the 'gift' that Adam gave us as a result of what he did and the one that Jesus gives. *'The gift of God is not like the result of the one man's* [Adam's] *sin…'* (Romans 5:16 NIV) Adam gifted us with death. Not a gift we're all especially excited about. Not really a **gift** at all, but he gave it to us, so a gift is what it is. In contrast, though, through Jesus, God gave us a **gift** gift, or a gift that truly is a gift. He gave us a gift that could **truly** be defined as a gift. He gave us the gift above all gifts, as we might call it.

The other half of the secret

When we reached verse 11 of Psalm 34 we reviewed what we'd covered in the first half. Now we've arrived at the end of the second half, we'll do the same and look back over what we've been thinking about. It's been quite a journey. And a profitable one, I hope. This will serve as a handy reminder of some of the places we've visited along the way.

1 A good long life

At the outset of this second half we are told that the righteous enjoy a good and long life. They are blessed to be able properly to enjoy life's journey because they have no fear of where it's taking them. Not just to death and extinction. They may have a little natural trepidation, perhaps, because death is not a nice thing to contemplate for anyone. But generally speaking they don't **fear** it, because they can look beyond it to what God has promised for the God-fearing righteous. And it'll be a good, long life whatever the duration of this present mortal phase, because immortality awaits them. The verses that follow in David's Psalm are our guide to how to live if we want God to consider us righteous.

2 Watch what you say

The first thing we learn about becoming righteous is that we need to watch what we say. This is vital because what we say and how we say it is a sure guide to what's going on inside us. And the second half of the Psalm is more about our inner world. We are what we say. So our speech matters a lot. We can do so much good or harm depending on the way we use our tongue. Implicit in dealing with what we say is dealing with **who we are**.

Jesus said that out of a good heart come good things and out of a bad heart come bad things. It's elementary really. But the simplest of things can be overlooked, and often are. And we can't afford to overlook this if we want to be considered righteous. The Apostle James said, *'If any man offend not in word, the same is a perfect man, and able also to bridle the whole body.'* (James 3:2) In other words, if we have our tongues under control, we pretty much have ourselves under control. The two are very much connected.

3 Act as if

It seems as if David put things in the wrong order when telling us to deal with our speech before dealing with ourselves, as he does in the next verse. If we are what we say, then surely it makes more sense to work on who we are first, and then let that positively affect how we talk. That will certainly work. But David is giving us the valuable insight that if we keep a check on what we say it will have a good effect on who we are. So, if you want to be a righteous person, start acting like one! This is another of those occasions when the popular psychologists and self-help writers have inadvertently connected with some higher wisdom. If we want to be a certain way then it helps if we act as if we are already that way. Keep yourself from saying bad things and from being deceitful, and you are practicing righteousness. Your heart may not be there yet, but you can help it along the way to where it ought to be by acting as if it's already there.

4 Find perfect peace
God's secret reveals that the way to perfect peace is to use our imagination positively. Instead of worrying endlessly that things will never get better, or distressing ourselves by catastrophising over all that might possibly go wrong, we can use our imaginations in a positive way to picture how well things will turn out, because we trust that God is in our lives and helping us.

5 Being a bit of a devil
The devil is not a supernatural being that we have to contend with. It's a part of our own human nature. Whenever we feel prompted to think the wrong thoughts and do the wrong things, we are experiencing our own natural inclination. Satan is not a supernatural being either. A satan is simply an adversary, something or someone that opposes us, so the word applies to other people, or to organisations who are opposing us in some way. This is how it's meant to be understood in the Bible.

6 Good and bad
The uncompromising truth about life is that we're all either good or bad in God's view. There is no middle ground. We're either believers and considered righteous, or we're not and we're considered evil. It seems a severe over-simplification, but the reality is that, viewed through the divine lens of perfection, we are **all** evil. But God sees the righteous differently when He cloaks them in the perfection of His Son – when they become *'in Christ'*.

7 Grace
Grace really is amazing. And the concept is unique to the God of the Bible. No other religion has it. Yet grace has troubled and confused believers, it seems, ever since there have been believers. Because it looks like we don't have to do anything to earn our salvation. And… well, yes, that's exactly what it does

God's Secret

mean. Straightening up our lives as much as we can by aligning them with God's righteousness is how we **show our appreciation** for God's free gift, **not how we earn it**. And, importantly, for grace to be effective we must be believers who **believe**.

For every part of God's Secret I've wanted to say, '**this is the most important part**', because they all look that way. But if ever there's one that seems to nudge slightly ahead of the rest, it's grace. But as soon as I say that I see how indispensable Jesus is to grace, and how indispensable belief is to grace, and… In truth, grace and all the other parts of the Secret all depend on **Jesus**: everything centres on him, he doesn't 'nudge slightly ahead' of the other elements of God's Secret, he stands a long way out in front. The Apostle Paul made this abundantly clear when he wrote: '*For all the promises of God in Him* [Jesus] *are Yes, and in Him* [Jesus] *Amen…*' (2 Corinthians 1:20 NKJV)

8 Nearness
Believers are under benign divine surveillance. God keeps an eye on them. He wants them to know that He's close by. Even though He is immeasurably greater than us, He is not aloof and distant. He knows everything about every one of us, right down to the number of hairs on our heads (Matthew 10:30). He even knows our thoughts. But none of this is cause for alarm. The very opposite. Believers don't ever think of it as intrusive. It means they can relax in the knowledge that God cares enough to keep an eye on them, and that they are always in safe hands.

9 The indispensable Jesus
Jesus has been central to God's plan and message from the very beginning. The whole thing revolves around him, as we reminded ourselves only a few moments ago. Though it never hurts to remind ourselves of it. Without him, and the plan of salvation that God envisaged and carried out through him, there would be no Creation. No you, no me, no anyone. God's message to us is essentially about getting back on track to where we were headed

before Adam derailed us. So the subject of Jesus, the second Adam, is everywhere we turn in the Bible.

10 Outcome bad

Just as there are ultimately only two kinds of people, there are only two possible outcomes for everyone. We're told the evil will be desolate: they'll be removed from the earth to make way for the kind of people God made the world for in the first place. This is not meant as a threat. It's a promise. The removal of all those who would spoil it is the only way the world will ever be enjoyed by the meek who are to inherit it. There can be no *'abundance of peace'* in the earth, as promised, if evil people are left to carry on with 'business as usual'. The world is the birthright of all righteous believers because they are welcomed into the family of God who owns it.

11 Outcome good.

Which brings us to the outcome for the righteous. *'For God so loved the world, that he gave his only begotten Son, that whosoever believeth in him should not perish, but have everlasting life.'* (John 3:16) Or as David said it a thousand years earlier than John, *'none of them that trust in him* [Yahweh] *shall be desolate.'* They will be redeemed.

Not a formula

Listing the aspects we've covered like this is meant only as an aid to memory. I find this kind of thing handy, so maybe you will. But a list like this can trivialise the aspects if we're not careful. It can make them seem like the twenty-odd things you must know and do for a successful life. We have to keep in mind that we're talking about the mind and message of God here, which cannot be reduced to a mere formula for living. It's more than that.

When we add the above aspects to the ones we found in the first half of the Psalm, we have a good guide to what God's Secret is. The two sides of the Secret meld together perfectly. This list isn't exhaustive, and this book certainly isn't, but we wanted to keep the book to a manageable size. There's certainly enough here to provide a good grounding in the counsel of God that He gave us in His communication, the Bible. Most of the rest of it comes from living it and becoming more thoroughly acquainted with it along the way. And from rubbing shoulders and comparing notes with other saints on the same journey.

No commandments

Interestingly, and significantly, David's Psalm about God's Secret has nothing directly to say about God's commandments. The nearest things we get to a 'Thou shalt' or a 'Thou shalt not' are the more generalised mentions of watching our tongues and avoiding evil. God's Secret isn't about commandments. It's about who we **are**, and what we **believe**, not so much what we do. Because when we sort out who we are, what we do will take care of itself. Paraphrasing what Jesus said: Out of the good treasure of our good hearts we will bring forth good things. Or to paraphrase his brother James: when we have control of our tongues it's because we are in control of what's going on inside us.

Being God-fearing and righteous are both things of the mind and heart. Even though being God-fearing is about our outer world, our circumstances, it's still very much about our attitude and approach to our circumstances, our acceptance of God in whatever happens to us. Who we are is ultimately of more concern than what we do. As I said earlier in this book, the idea of it is not to change your life but to change you, because your life will follow where you go. God's Secret is about changing you and letting what you do take care of itself. As it will.

If only…

Often cited as the two most depressing words in the language are 'if only…' They tell of missed opportunity, of what might have been, of wrong choices… It's starting to depress me just writing about them. We've all used those two little words at some time in our lives. Even God has used them… though not about His own decisions, of course. God uses the phrase about the people who

Redeeming features

ignore His generosity. And His lament is uttered more in sadness than anger. *'If only you had paid attention to my commands, your peace would have been like a river, your well-being like the waves of the sea...'* (Isaiah 48:18 NIV)

Like a river

Sit yourself on a riverbank for a while and let yourself be mesmerised by the little swirls and eddies in the water. Watch the occasional leaf float by and the fish idling in the slow current. There's a tree shading you from the sun and a soft breeze cooling you. You're taking time to rest and to enjoy just being. The big questions of life have all been settled for you and you have no existential anxieties. All you're daily needs are being met without undue effort. You know that you are a loved and valued person. You are a part of the grand scheme of things. You have loving friends. You have not a real care in the world, only superficial ones. You can sit and enjoy the peace of the river mirrored in your soul, in yourself. Peace like a river.

Like the waves

Now transfer yourself to a beach, or to a grassy cliff top, where you're watching the sea. You're stretched out on your stomach with your elbows bent and propping your chin on the palms of your hands. You watch the waves continue to roll in one after another, never ending. As one wave spills over onto the beach and its flattened undertow ebbs back into the sea, so the next wave rolls in over it. Another is gathering momentum behind that, and another... Your well-being, your **righteousness** (same word in the original Hebrew language of the Old Testament) would be *'like the waves of the sea'*, continuous, unstoppable, and endless, if only you'd taken notice of the commands (counsel) that God was so eager for you to have.

Where do we stand?

Finally, well almost, a word from one of God's prophets and teachers, Jeremiah: *'For who hath stood in the counsel of the Lord,*

God's Secret

and hath perceived and understood his word? Who hath marked his word and heard it?' (Jeremiah 23:18)

In other words: Who among you knows God's Secret? Who has seen it and understood it from His communication to us? Who has taken sufficient note of it and let it sink in?

You? Me? I certainly hope so.

We know that our search for God's wisdom is likened in the Bible to a treasure hunt. Proverbs 2:4–5: *If thou seekest her as silver, and searchest for her as for hid treasures; then shalt thou understand the fear of the* L<small>ORD</small>*, and find the knowledge of God.'* How fascinating it is, in the light of all we've been saying, to find that the word translated *'treasures'* in that verse, is a less common word for treasure that actually means 'hidden or secret thing'!

Notice, too, that the verse says *'then **shalt** thou'*, not 'then **might** thou' find the hidden secret things of God. With the right approach you **will** find these treasures. And, ancient though it is, this wisdom doesn't date because God doesn't date. His wisdom is as timeless as He is. It's as fresh as tomorrow morning's dew. I wish you well in your search for it. You've already uncovered much of it in your progress through this book, certainly some of the most precious gems in God's communication. I hope you'll store them up as good treasure in your heart and want to add more.

APPENDIX 1: THE LAST DAYS

You will have read much about a coming Kingdom of God in this book. But I've saved the news of how soon it will here for this appendix.

I can't give you an exact date for when the *'kingdoms of this world will become the kingdoms of our Lord'* because no-one can fix it precisely. Even Jesus couldn't: *'Of that day and hour knoweth no man, no, not the angels of heaven, but my Father only.'* (Matthew 24:36) So, anyone telling you that 'the end is nigh' and you should head without delay for your survival shelter if you have one (I don't) is almost certainly mistaken.

But we're not left in the dark. We're told to watch for certain signs to alert us when the Kingdom of God is not far off. The state of the world will be a pointer to its coming. There's a period leading up to the establishment of the Kingdom which is called *'the time of the end'*, or *'the last days'*. I prefer to think of it as 'the time of the beginning' because it heralds a new and better era for the world. You'll know this already from what you've read, but what you won't know is **when, or how much longer we must wait.**

So, here is the news: we are in the last days.

In this 21st century the world is becoming increasingly unstable, politically, economically and socially. The veneer of civilisation is wearing thin at an alarming rate. World leaders are trusted less and less. Nations are becoming increasingly ungovernable. And each new advance in technology, ostensibly created for our convenience, enjoyment, or safety, seems to add to the general instability, as everything about life, including vital services, is moved unthinkingly to an inherently unstable and vulnerable digital location. With gathering speed, the world is becoming more precarious. The Judeo-Christian religions that helped unify society

God's Secret

and steer progress for centuries over much of the world, have been marginalised. 'The Lost World' was once just the title of a book, but now it seems more like the name of our planet.

No, I'm not finishing this book on a negative note. This is going to end very positively. Because against the backdrop of the above cheerless observations, I want you to read the following extracts from God's communication. Allow them to build a picture in your mind. This is a glimpse behind the curtain at what's really happening in the world, what's developing behind the headlines, regardless of the aims and ambitions of world leaders and organisations.

- Jesus foresaw a time when Jerusalem would no longer belong to the Jewish people. That happened in 70 AD when the Romans, whom he referred to as Gentiles, forcibly ejected and dispersed the people of Israel. Then Jesus said that this situation would not be allowed to continue: *'Jerusalem shall be trodden down of the Gentiles, until the times of the Gentiles be fulfilled.'* (Luke 21:24) There was to be an end to non-Jewish occupation of Jerusalem and Israel generally. The people would return to their land. Then Jesus added the remarkable information that the generation which sees the Jewish people back in the land of Israel after their dispersion, will witness the end of this age and the commencement of a new age (Luke 21:32).

The Jews began returning to Israel after the land was officially declared a homeland for them in 1948. Also significant – because **'Jerusalem** *shall be trodden down until...'* – was the people's full possession of the city of Jerusalem after the Six Days' War in 1967. Which generation saw these things? We did. I speak as someone born close to 1948. For all of us living now, our time is unmistakeably what is described biblically as *'the last days'*. If that sounds apocalyptic to you, then you'd be absolutely right. But it's not bad news. It will be earth shaking, but the world is long overdue for a good shake up.

Appendix 1: The last days

- Jesus said: The period prior to his return is going to be very like the days leading up to the big flood in Noah's day. Those days were characterised by ever increasing evil. The world was filled with violence, and most people carried on as if God didn't exist.

  The Apostle Peter made this comment: *'There shall come in the last days scoffers, walking after their own lusts, and saying, Where is the promise of* [Jesus'] *coming? For since the fathers fell asleep, all things continue as they were from the beginning of creation.'* (2 Peter 3:3–4) He went on to say that's how it was in Noah's day before the flood came. They all ignored Noah, heaping scorn on his insistence that an unprecedented deluge was soon to come from God.

  That's how people in 'the last days' will view Jesus' return. They'll say, 'That's rubbish. Nothing like that's ever going to happen. You surely don't believe that?!" Peter said that a general attitude of debunking would be another sure sign that we were in the last days. It's certainly moving that way. And as a believer, Peter, saw it positively, saying, *'Nevertheless we, according to his* [God's] *promise, look for new heavens and a new earth, wherein dwelleth righteousness.'* (2 Peter 3: 13) Believers will see the state of the world as a sure sign that, at last, God's promise is about to be fulfilled: these evil times are drawing to a close, and a world *'wherein dwelleth righteousness'* is about to begin.

- Here's something from Paul's description of society in the last days. It's a long quote but very descriptive. And you'll probably notice more than a few similarities with the state of society today, or where it's heading: *'This know also, that in the last days perilous times shall come. For men shall be lovers of their own selves, covetous, boasters, proud, blasphemers, disobedient to parents, unthankful, unholy, without natural affection, trucebreakers, false accusers, incontinent, fierce, despisers of those that are good, traitors, heady, highminded, lovers of pleasures more than lovers of God; having a form of godliness, but denying the power thereof...',* to which he adds, *'Ever learning, and never able to come to the knowledge of the truth.'* (2 Timothy 3:1-7) It's almost as if Paul could see the negative effects of social media on the world, amplifying the baser aspects of human nature.

- Speaking of digital communication, the prophet Daniel said that during *'the time of the end: many shall run to and fro, and knowledge shall be increased.'* (Daniel 12:4) It's cryptic, but some see it as a reference to the internet which has brought an explosion of information across the world. The word 'many' can also mean 'much'. So the **much** running to and fro could refer to the increased traffic of knowledge. It's not certain, of course, but I wouldn't rule it out as a reference to the global impact of technology in the last days. I'm no technophobe, but we can't turn a blind eye to the cumulative negative impact of technology, which appears to be far outstripping its benefits.

- While we're on the subject of Daniel and his God-given ability to see the future, we should mention that he foresaw four major world empires. Starting from Babylon, where he lived, only three more world-wide Empires would follow. After that (following the collapse of the Roman Empire) the world would break up into an unstable mix of strong and weak nations. This is where we still are. It's worth taking time to read Daniel Chapter two where he describes how he came to learn this by interpreting a dream for King Nebuchadnezzar. For our purpose here, though, we want to draw attention to the information that in the days of these strong and weak nations God will intervene dramatically: *'And in the days of these kings* [or world leaders] *shall the God of heaven set up a kingdom, which shall never be destroyed: and the kingdom shall not be left to other people, but it shall break in pieces and consume all these kingdoms, and it shall stand for ever.'* (Daniel 2:44)

Appendix 1: The last days

- Daniel described the final period of the last days as *'a time of trouble, such as never was since there was a nation even to that same time...'* (Daniel 12:1) It doesn't get any worse than that. But at the same time, for many it could hardly get any better, because he adds that *'many of them that sleep in the dust of the earth shall awake.'* The saints who've been sleeping will awake because the promised Kingdom is about to happen. Jesus is back! There are two sides to Armageddon. It's a bad time for the wicked and a good time for the righteous.

- Jesus described the final period as a time of *'distress of nations with perplexity'.* (Luke 21:25) There will be such distress across the world that people everywhere will be utterly perplexed over how awful things have become, and probably at how quickly things have plunged into such a fearful state. He goes on to say, *'Men's hearts failing them for fear, and for looking after those things which are coming on the earth...'* The world will be in complete turmoil. Having experienced the effects of a pandemic, we know that unrest and fear can become as contagious as the virus that spawned them, and how easily instant digital communication can now create and fuel global unrest.

- Thankfully God will intervene before mankind brings the world to a violent and permanent end. Jesus assures us, *'And except those days should be shortened, there should no flesh be saved: but for the elect's sake those days shall be shortened.'* (Matthew 24:22) For the saints' sakes, for the God-fearing righteous – for **their** sakes, God will step in. He has promised this world to them, so He is not going to allow the evil to annihilate it.

- Among the closing words of Jesus' prophecy of the last days, he offers some much-needed reassurance for those *'in Christ'*:

'And when these things begin to come to pass, then look up, and lift up your heads; for your redemption draweth nigh.'

(Luke 21: 28) When the world is in such a time of trouble, from which no escape seems possible, believers should not despair along with everyone else, they should take heart. It's a sign of the nearness of Christ.

Very soon they'll see what the whole world is going to see: *'And then shall they see the Son of man coming in a cloud with power and great glory.'* 'Son of man' is a name by which Jesus sometimes referred to himself. He'll put down all unrest and put a halt to the madness of self-destruction that is the path we're currently on. We're told that God will *'...destroy them which destroy the earth...'* (Revelation 11:18) Peace activists, ecologists, eco-warriors and the like mean well, I'm sure, but they've not seen the bigger picture. God will never allow us to destroy our planet by neglect, pollution, war, or any other means.

Mock me if you will for believing such things about the events coming at this time of the end. It'll make me feel a bit like Noah. But I hope that by now you've read enough in this book and seen enough of what's already going on in this world to realise that there is something in what the Bible is telling us. Seen from the point of view of those who have God's Secret and who are therefore *'in Christ'*, the impending upheaval is not a threat, it's a promise of better things.

The whole Jesus

Being a Christian isn't just about taking some of Jesus' sayings, a selection of the ones that appeal to us, and trying to copy his loving approach to people. Following him means the whole package. Some of the things he said turned people away from him back in his day when they heard them. They were *'hard sayings'*. But being a believer means following the whole Jesus, not just the parts that suit us. There's no integrity in that. That's not really Jesus. It's our own version of him.

Appendix 1: The last days

The only Christ to be 'in' is the real one, the one who lived and breathed God's Secret, and who taught the whole counsel of God. What a pleasure and an honour it will be to meet such a man. He is the saviour that the world needs desperately and soon. In truth, we all need him personally now. Don't leave it till things deteriorate.

To make another comparison with Noah's day, you don't want to be outside the ark when the rain starts falling. At present, the door is still wide open.

And looking at the world around us you can surely see the dark clouds gathering, just as I can.

No, I don't want to scare anyone into coming aboard. As you'll realise by now, that's not the best of motives for joining those already safely aboard. The best motives are outlined in this book and fully explained in God's communication. This is all about promoting an awareness of, and an interest in – a passion for! – what's really happening in the world, and the One behind it all. And encouraging a healthy fear of missing out.

APPENDIX 2: ACROSTIC

This second appendix is purely an add-on. You don't need this for God's Secret. But it's an interesting and rewarding diversion if you ever have the time and inclination to look into it. At the time of writing, it's still on my to-do list, as is following up the thought that all the acrostics in the Bible are interrelated, lending meaning to one another.

I mentioned in Chapter 10 that Psalm 34 is an acrostic based on the 22 letters of the biblical Hebrew alphabet. Each line begins with the next letter of the alphabet making the Psalm a kind of A–Z of God's Secret. Each of the letters has a meaning derived from the original pictogram from which it has evolved, so it's likely that God has used the acrostic to provide additional shades of meaning to the verses. For example *beth*, the second letter of the alphabet, has come from a pictogram of a tent and so signifies a dwelling or house. In fact, *beth* is the Hebrew word for house (*beth-lehem*, means house of bread).

The Hebrew letters as they are written today don't always bear much resemblance to the pictograms from which they originated, so don't go cross-eyed trying to see the likenesses. I'll make no comment on the table below, which is the generally accepted version. But I will comment on the deliberate blip in the sequence which omits one of the letters and duplicates another. It's an A–Z with a twist.

The meanings given are based on *Hebrew Word Pictures* by Dr. Frank T. Seekins. Writers sometimes differ on the meanings, as they do on the English renderings of the letters themselves, but not drastically.

Appendix 2: Acrostic

Letter	Name	Attributed origin and meaning	Verse in Psalm 34
א	Aleph	**Ox** strength	1
ב	Beth	**House** home, family	2
ג	Gimel	**Camel** lift up, pride	3
ד	Daleth	**Door** pathway, enter	4
ה	He	**Window** to reveal	5
ו	Vav	**Nail** add, connection	? 2nd line verse 5
ז	Zayin	**Weapon** cut, cut off	6
ח	Cheth	**Fence** private, separate	7
ט	Tet	**Snake** surround	8
י	Yod	**Closed hand** work, deed, make	9
כ	Kaph	**Open hand** cover, open, allow	10
ל	Lamed	**Ox-goad** control, authority	11
מ	Mem	**Water** liquid, chaos	12

God's Secret

נ	Num	**Fish** activity, life	13
ס	Samech	**Prop** support, turn slowly	14
ע	Ayin	**Eye** see, know experience	15
פ	Pe	**Mouth** speak, word, praise	16 & 22
צ	Tsade	**Fishhook** catch, desire, need	17
ק	Qoph	**Back of head** behind, last	18
ר	Resh	**Head** person, head, highest	19
ש	Sin	**Teeth** consume, destroy	20
ת	Tav	**Mark** sign, seal, guarantee	21

It's a little ironic that the sixth letter, which means connection, is missing, and creating a disconnection. But that's probably a kind of inverted appropriateness, drawing attention to a missing connection.

The removal of *vav* from the acrostic sequence leaves us a letter short at the end, which is made up for by the repetition of *pe*.

Appendix 2: Acrostic

So why remove *vav* and why duplicate *pe*? Or, to ask the real question: Why remove a 'connection' and add an extra 'mouth'?

In Hebrew *vav* is a conjunction used very like our word *and*. It's a connecting word. In fact it does appear in the sequence as the start of the second line of verse five (as shown in the table). So verse five could be said to contain both *he* and *vav*, and the sequence is unbroken. But whether omitted or squeezed into verse five, either way the reason for it appears to be to make way for the doubling of *mouth*, which has the associated meanings of 'speak', 'word' or 'praise'.

The reason for it all could be to make and highlight a connection between verses 16 and 22.

These are the two verses:

16. 'The face of the LORD is against them that do evil, to cut off the remembrance of them from the earth.'

22. 'The LORD redeemeth the soul of his servants: and none of them that trust in him shall be desolate.'

There's no doubt about a connection here. The verses cover two inseparable events: the removal from the earth of the evil and the establishment in the earth of the God-fearing righteous. These are the two events we described in Chapter 31 as 'the essential message of God's Secret'. As we also said, 'God can't fulfil His promise – He can't make good on His declared purpose to provide a peaceful, secure, harmonious world for His saints to live in – without the removal of everything that would ruin it. That includes removing the kind of people who would ruin it.'

These two events are brought together in the final two verses of the Psalm, and it looks as though they are emphasised in the slight tweaking of the acrostic structure.

God's Secret

We notice, too, that the word 'mouth', *pe,* also appears in the opening verse of Psalm 34 where it's connected with blessing and praise. '*I will bless the* LORD *at all times: his praises shall continually be in my mouth.*' So, by tweaking the acrostic the Psalm is made to begin and end with a reference to the mouth, or, by association, with blessing and praise. This happens overtly in verse one and covertly in verse 22. From that we might take it that blessing and praise is the overarching theme of the Psalm. And because the Psalm is our A–Z of God's Secret we might also take it as the overall theme of God's Secret. It wouldn't be surprising. The Secret starts and ends with blessing and praise.

Now I'll leave you to look, if you wish, into the extra shades of meaning the letters of the acrostic provide for the rest of the verses.

Afterword

I envied my children when they had only just learned to read and still had such a wealth of great reading ahead of them. Now I envy every reader of this book who may stand at the threshold of a life 'in Christ'. What I've covered in this book is plenty to be going on with, most of the essentials are here, but there's so much more that awaits you if you choose to follow through. God's Secret is bigger than can be squeezed into this or any book apart from the Bible itself.

I found this exploration of God's Secret fascinating. It has taken me to places within myself that I needed to go, and helped me to see and value the truths of the Scriptures more than I believed possible. It has been a life-enhancing experience for someone who thought he already knew God's Secret thoroughly. I hope you've caught some of that fascination along the way, and that the impact has been similar for you.

Feedback

As someone who almost never responds to those 'How did we do?' emails that follow many a transaction these days, I feel a little conflicted saying this. But if you feel this book could be improved, let me know via the Dawn Christadelphian Publications office. It may be that you feel some points could be made clearer, given more space, or less, or that there are points you feel should have been included, or maybe not have been. Bear in mind that I can't cover everything in a book this size, and this is more of a chat than a text book. I can't promise I'll agree with you, but I'd appreciate feedback all the same. Constructive suggestions may be helpful for reprints, should there be any.

Thanks, and grace and peace to you.

Colin Attridge

More books available from DCP

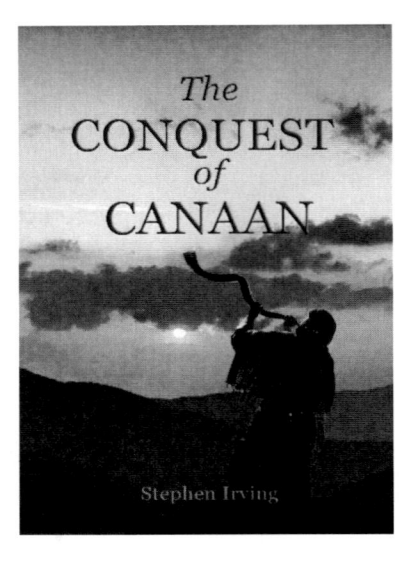

Think on These Things
whatever is true, honest, just, pure, lovely, of good report, virtuous, praiseworthy
COLIN ATTRIDGE

The Conquest of Canaan
Stephen Irving

A Challenge to Theistic Evolution
from Biblical and Scientific perspectives
SIMON PERFITT & LAURIE BROUGHTON

Peace with God
A study of the Atonement
GEOFFREY MITCHELL

A POSITIVE Faith

A Hundred Little Encouragers

COLIN ATTRIDGE

The Biblical role of Shechem

Maurice K Collishaw

So much better...

HEBREWS
An exposition of the letter to the Hebrews

Geoffrey Mitchell

The endurance of Job

Stephen Irving

Dawn Christadelphian Publications

5 Station Road,
Carlton,
Nottingham,
NG4 3AT,
U.K.

☎ +44 (0)115 961 2624

info@dawncp.co.uk
www.dawncp.co.uk